OXFORD THEOLOGICAL MONOGRAPHS

The
Fatherhood of God
from Origen to Athanasius

PETER WIDDICOMBE

CLARENDON PRESS · OXFORD

Oxford University Press, Walton Street, Oxford OX2 6DP
Oxford New York
Athens Auckland Bangkok Bombay
Calcutta Cape Town Dar es Salaam Delhi
Florence Hong Kong Istanbul Karachi
Kuala Lumpur Madras Madrid Melbourne
Mexico City Nairobi Paris Singapore
Taipei Tokyo Toronto
and associated companies in
Berlin Ibadan

Oxford is a trade mark of Oxford University Press

Published in the United States by
Oxford University Press Inc., New York

British Library Cataloguing in Publication Data
Data available

Library of Congress Cataloging in Publication Data
The fatherhood of God from Origen to Athanasius.
Peter Widdicombe.
(Oxford theological monographs)
Revision of thesis (doctoral)—University of Oxford.
Includes bibliographical references and indexes.
1. God—Fatherhood—History of doctrines—Early church, ca.30–600.
2. Origen. 3. Athanasius, Saint, Patriarch of Alexandria, d. 373.
4. Arianism.   I. Title.   II. Series.
BT153.F3W53   1993   231'.1'09015—dc20   93–16301
ISBN 0–19–826751–7

3 5 7 9 10 8 6 4 2

Printed in Great Britain on acid-free paper by
The Ipswich Book Co. Ltd., Suffolk

To
Karen

Acknowledgements

THIS book is a revised version of a thesis submitted to the University of Oxford for a doctorate in theology. I would like to express my thanks to Maurice Wiles for his careful and generous supervision of the thesis and for his help in the preparation of the manuscript for publication. I would also like to thank Rowan Williams for his assistance in the supervision of the thesis and for his comments on the manuscript. The thesis was examined by Kallistos Ware and Frances Young who made helpful suggestions about how it might be revised. Kallistos Ware kindly read the completed manuscript.

The Vicarage, Penn   *P.W.*
July 1992

Contents

References and Abbreviations

THE works of Origen are cited according to the text of the Berlin edition Die Griechische Christliche Schriftsteller der ersten drei Jahrhunderte, unless otherwise stated at first citation, and by book (where appropriate), chapter, and section.

C.Cel.	*Contra Celsum*
Com. Jn.	*Commentary on John*
DP	*De Principiis*

The works of the Arian controversy are cited according to the text of the edition of H.-G. Opitz, *Athanasius Werke*, iii. 1: *Urkunden zur Geschichte des arianischen Streites*, in the form *U.* followed by document, page, and line number.

The works of Athanasius are cited according to the edition of H.-G. Opitz, *Athanasius Werke*, ii. 1, where they are available, by title, chapter, or section, followed by 'Opitz' and page and line numbers. *De Incarnatione* and *Contra Gentes* are cited according to the edition of R. Thomson. The *Festal Letters* are cited according to the text in the *Library of Nicene and Post-Nicene Fathers*. Otherwise references are to the Benedictine edition printed in the edition of J. P. Migne, *Patrologia Graeca*, and are cited by volume and column number, except that references to *Contra Arianos*, which is all in *PG* 26, are cited by column number only.

CG	*Contra Gentes*
DI	*De Incarnatione*
CA	*Contra Arianos*

PERIODICALS AND SERIES

CAG	*Commentaria in Aristotelem Graeca*
GCS	Die Griechische Christliche Schriftsteller der ersten drei Jahrhunderte
JAC.E	*Jahrbuch für Antike und Christentum, Ergänzungsband*
JTS	*Journal of Theological Studies*
NAKG	*Nederlands archief voor kerkgeschiedenis*
NedThT	*Nederlands theologisch tijdschrift*
NPNF	Nicene and Post-Nicene Fathers

Introduction

THE concept of the fatherhood of God has had a central, if recently an increasingly controversial, place in Christian thinking about God and about salvation. But however self-evident its importance may appear, it was not always so. Although Christians seem to have referred to God as Father as a matter of course from the earliest days of the faith,[1] it was not until the fourth century with Athanasius that the fatherhood of God became an issue of sustained and systematic analysis. Athanasius laid the foundations for the development of a fundamental precept of later trinitarian thought—that the Father–Son relation is part of the definition of the word God. The parameters of his discussion of God as Father are broadly those within which subsequent orthodox writers—most immediately the Cappadocians—were to think about God as Father, Son, and Holy Spirit.

Little attention has been given to the history of the idea of the divine fatherhood in early Christian thought. The present study, it is hoped, goes some way to redressing this. It is the purpose of the study to examine the genesis of Athanasius' theology of God as Father and to analyse its structure against the background of the Alexandrian tradition. It is important to recognize that Athanasius was not the first Alexandrian to write about the divine fatherhood. He was writing within the context of an Alexandrian tradition of

---

[1] For a survey of the use of the word Father to refer to God in Greek and biblical literature, see G. Schrenk, πατήρ, A, C–D, and G. Quell, πατήρ, B, in G. Kittel (ed.), *Theological Dictionary of the New Testament*, ed. and trans. G. Bromiley, v (Grand Rapids, 1967). On the biblical usage, see also W. Marchel, *Abba, Père! La prière du Christ et des chrétiens* (Analecta Biblica 19: 2nd edn., Rome, 1971); Joachim Jeremias, *The Prayers of Jesus*, various translators (London, 1967); James Barr, 'Abba Isn't "Daddy"', *JTS* NS 39 (1988), 28–47, a searching critique of Jeremias' argument; and the study of the use of the phrase 'children of God' in the Bible by R. A. Culpepper, 'The Pivot of John's Gospel', *NTS* 27 (1980–1), 17–31. Reference to the fatherhood language of the second-century Apologists will be made when Origen's use of the phrase 'Father of all' (*Timaeus* 28C) is discussed below, pp. 78–9.

reflection on the fatherhood of God, a tradition in which the terms Father and Son were the determinative metaphors for theological discussion. This tradition had a deep influence on his formulation of the idea of the fatherhood of God. It is only when his idea of the divine fatherhood is seen in the light of this tradition, and of the Arian challenge to it, that its distinctive shape and complexity can be fully appreciated.

For this reason, the first two Parts of the book provide a survey of the Alexandrian background. Origen was the most important of Athanasius' Alexandrian predecessors, and it is to him that the first long section is devoted. While he did not make the fatherhood of God a topic of systematic analysis and seldom treats fatherhood as a distinct theme, the present study demonstrates that Origen believed that the affirmation that God is Father lay at the heart of the Christian faith. It is fundamental to his conception of the divine nature and of salvation: to know God fully and thus to be saved is to know God as Father; having been servants, we become sons by adoption through faith in the one who is Son by nature.

The three main tenets of Origen's argument for the eternity of God's fatherhood, that the words Father and Son are the given terms of Christian tradition, that Father and Son are correlatives, and that the generation of the Son is eternal, were taken up by subsequent Alexandrian writers, by Dionysius, perhaps by Theognostus, and by Alexander. At points, the arguments and, indeed, the actual phrases that Alexander uses resemble those of Origen, suggesting the possibility that he drew directly on Origen's writings. These three writers, along with Methodius of Olympus are discussed in Part II. Although he was not an Alexandrian, Methodius' writings are considered here, since his criticism of Origen set the stage for the early Arian debate. Part II also takes up the implications of early Arianism for a theology of the divine fatherhood.

It was Arius' explicit repudiation of two of Origen's tenets, the eternal generation of the Son and the argument from correlativity, that led Athanasius to make the fatherhood of God an issue of crucial theological concern. For Arius, to believe in the eternal generation of the Son was to deny the fundamental precept of Alexandrian theology that for God to be God there could be only one ingenerate first principle. The positing of another eternal principle alongside the Father was to curtail the freedom of God. For Athanasius, the description of God as Father identified the divine being as the loving and fruitful source of all existence. God's freedom was expressed in his being as a relation of Father and Son.

The discussion of Athanasius' approach focuses on the three *Orationes contra Arianos,* where he first set forth his conception of the divine fatherhood and which established the terms within which he was to deal with the subject in his later writings. The threat posed by Arius forced Athanasius to attempt self-consciously to determine what the Church's tradition of referring to God as Father meant for a coherent theology of the divine nature and of salvation. His thinking about the fatherhood of God was prompted largely by what he saw as Arius' denial of the divine status of the Son.

According to Athanasius, to deny that the Son was divine in the same sense as the Father was divine was tantamount to denying the eternity of God's fatherhood. He adopted the three tenets of Origen's argument for the eternity of the divine fatherhood and expanded them. This study makes plain that in places the structure of his arguments are similar to those of Origen. But the issues which he faced were far different from those which confronted Origen. In the course of his three *Orationes contra Arianos* Athanasius adapts Origen's tenets to refute the Arian teachings concerning the Son, making them the basis of a doctrine of God fundamentally at variance with Arius', a doctrine in which fatherhood is the determinative concept.

For Athanasius, the word Father signified that the divine nature was both inherently generative, giving life to the Son and through him to all other things, and inherently relational, a relation of Father and Son in which mutual love is eternally both given and received. His conception of God as Father is integral to his defence of the divinity of the Son, and to his doctrines of creation, salvation, and the church. Only if God is conceived to be eternally Father and so eternally Father of the Son is it possible to conceive of him as the eternal source of existence and as the God who meets us in our need through the incarnation, death, and resurrection of his Son. It is the relation of love between the Father and the Son which is the model for the life of the Christian community. While for Arius it would seem that it was logically possible to speak of God without referring to him as Father, this was not possible for Athanasius.

Two methodological points need to be borne in mind if we are to gain a clear sense of the place of the theme of divine fatherhood in the Alexandrian tradition. It is necessary to attend closely to the contexts in which Origen and Athanasius discuss fatherhood and the ideas they associate with it, since fatherhood is not dealt with as a formal theological topos. Because Origen makes the description of God as Father a subject of analysis only rarely, and even with Athanasius the occasions are few, a picture of these writers' sense of God as Father can only be built up through a detailed examination of their writings. Only in this way is it possible to avoid falling into anachronistic assumptions about what the use of the term Father for God must have meant to them. It is also necessary to consider the significance of fatherhood in the structure of each author's theology as a whole. Only thus is it possible to identify the common and the dissimilar elements in their thinking about the fatherhood of God and to assess whether and in what ways the common elements held the same meanings for them in their different theological contexts. These methodological considerations and the nature of the sources help explain the structure of this study. Both Origen and Athanasius wrote extensively, many of Origen's writings are exegetical rather than systematic, and Athanasius' analysis of fatherhood is deeply intertwined with his anti-Arian defence of the Son. This is reflected in the length of the sections given to each.

The study of the history of God as Father in Alexandrian thought from Origen to Athanasius has a direct bearing on the nature of the continuity inherent in Alexandrian reflection on the nature of God, whether it runs from Origen to Athanasius or from Origen to Arius. The implications of the present study are twofold: that the fatherhood of God is of fundamental importance to the theology of both Origen and Athanasius and seemingly not of commensurate importance to the theology of Arius; and that, with reference to this topic at least, continuity lies between Athanasius and Origen. This Alexandrian conception of God as Father was to become of central concern for the Fathers and subsequent Christian thinkers in both the Eastern and the Western trinitarian traditions. Following Athanasius, they understood the Father to be the 'fount of the godhead' and that it was this that distinguished his persona from that of the Son and the Holy Spirit. This study will help deepen our appreciation of how this dominant theme began and why it was so influential, and it will help in the determination of how coherent its development was. In the context of modern debates about divine fatherhood, the examination of Alexandrian thinking about the concept will help us to consider whether it is either desirable or possible to call God Father if we are to maintain an intelligible doctrine of God.

Part I

Origen: Father, Son, and Salvation

FOR Origen, the affirmation that God is Father lies at the heart of the Christian faith. It is fundamental to his conception of the divine nature, to his perception of the relation between God and the Son and its difference from the relation between God and the created order, and to his understanding of the process of redemption. The description of God as Father is a commonplace of his theological vocabulary. His writings are · replete with biblical quotations in which God is referred to as Father, many of which are from the Gospel of John; he also quotes *Timaeus* 28C where Plato refers to the 'Creator and Father of all', but relatively rarely.

Origen does not make God's fatherhood a topic of systematic analysis and often uses the title Father as a synonym for God. This makes it difficult to determine in many passages what particular significance, if any, he attributes to the description of God as Father, and what specifically the description tells us about the nature of God's being. But even if he seldom identifies fatherhood as a distinct theme, it has a perceptible prominence for him that it did not have for earlier Christian writers, and on occasion he does explicitly address the question of the theological significance of describing God as Father.

The main elements of Origen's portrayal of God's fatherhood are woven into the texture of his theological thinking. They appear, consistently and more or less fully developed, throughout his writings, early and late, exegetical and more systematic. Examined within the context of the whole of his theology, these elements can be seen to form a coherent pattern which corresponds to the larger patterns of his doctrines of God and the Trinity, revelation, the incarnation and salvation, and which is integral to them.

In order to be in a position to appreciate properly what Origen is actually doing with his conception of the fatherhood of God, it is necessary to consider it in relation to the overall shape of his theology. Most of his comments about the fatherhood of God are made in the course of his reflections on the relation between the Father and the Son, and on the way in which we are saved, but his statements about fatherhood in these contexts point to implicit assumptions about the place of the attribute of fatherhood in God's nature. To set the scene, therefore, we begin the study of Origen with a substantial discussion of his doctrines of God and of revelation (Chapters 1 and 2). We shall then be in a position to examine the Father–Son relation and the role that the idea of fatherhood plays in his thinking about the nature of God (Chapter 3) and to look at how he thinks that we come to a knowledge of God as Father and are adopted as sons (Chapter 4).

1

The Doctrine of God

ORIGEN draws on biblical and Middle Platonist ideas about God to develop a distinctively theological statement about God's nature. The philosophical doctrines he employs are bound up with his scriptural exegesis and serve soteriological ends. He does not discuss the nature of God as an abstract metaphysical topic. The passages in which he systematically analyses God's being are rare; they tend to be short and are almost always directly linked to questions of revelation, salvation, and exegesis. Saving knowledge for him is to be found in the Bible. Philosophical doctrines are the handmaiden to a proper reading of the inspired Scriptures. Whether or not Origen is successful in combining biblical and philosophical conceptions of God, his intention is theological, and the study of his doctrine of God and the place of fatherhood in it must be undertaken in recognition of this.

The principal descriptions which Origen ascribes to God and which will be discussed in this chapter are that God is incorporeal, mind, one and simple, the good, 'he who is' (ὁ ὤν), and that he transcends being and mind. The discussion will demonstrate the manner in which he links Middle Platonist and biblical ideas, and turns them to theological purposes. Origen's most lengthy, systematic, and philosophical treatment of the nature of God is found in *De Principiis*, and it is mainly to its structure and content that reference will be made, though others of his works will also be drawn on, especially the *Commentary on John* and *Contra Celsum*.

De Principiis is an example of a Middle Platonist genre of philosophical treatises on physics, concerned with describing and defining God and the world. The concerns of *De Principiis* parallel those of the writings of Albinus, Iamblichus, Alexander of Aphrodisias, and others.[1] The title περὶ ἀρχῶν, used in classical philoso-

[1] M. Harl, 'Structure et cohérence du Peri Archôn' in *Origeniana*, H. Crouzel,

phy to designate collections of the opinions of philosophers 'on the principles' of being, was a traditional designation for works devoted to God and the world, and it was used by Middle Platonist and Christian authors prior to Origen. Although Origen employs the title in the plural, Harl concludes that inasmuch as Origen believes in a single ἀρχή, a triune God, he has used the title in a formal, traditional manner.[2]

Under this title, in a genre of writing inherited from Greek philosophy, Origen has composed a Christian treatise in which the stress is placed on the necessity of establishing a coherent and encompassing science of God. Harl has identified a double intention in *De Principiis*: one is polemical, directed against deviant ideas, and the other is the deepening of the Christian faith.[3] Torjesen, in a recent reinterpretation of *De Principiis*, grants that Origen's philosophical concerns in the treatise are plain, but suggests that the predominant concern is soteriological.[4] The philosophical concern in *De Principiis* is intimately bound up with the formation of character and the soul. The characteristics that Origen uses to illuminate the nature of God become the elements out of which he constructs his soteriology.

Origen sets out his doctrine of God in the first chapter of *De Principiis*. But before turning to the content of the chapter, the question of its title needs to be addressed, a question which has a bearing on how Origen construes the nature of God and the relation of fatherhood to it. In Rufinus' version of the work, the words *De deo* appear as the title for the first chapter, *De Christo* for the second, and *De spiritu sancto* for the third.[5] However, several modern scholars in their editions of *De Principiis* have

G. Lomiento, and J. Ruis-Camps (eds.) (Quaderni di 'Vetera Christianorum' 12: Bari, 1975), 11–32, compares *De Principiis* with Albinus' *Epitome* and the *Corpus Hermeticum*; G. Dorival, 'Remarques sur la forme du Peri Archôn' in *Origeniana*, 33–45, with treatises of Iamblichus and Salustius; and R. Berchman, *From Philo to Origen: Middle Platonism in Transition* (Brown Judaic Studies 69: Chico, Calif., 1984), p. 228, with Alexander of Aphrodisias.

[2] Harl, 'Structure', pp. 21–2.
[3] Ibid. 14.
[4] Karen Torjesen, 'Hermeneutics and Soteriology in Origen's *Peri Archôn*', in E. A. Livingstone (ed.), *Studia Patristica* 21 (Leuven, 1989), p. 333.
[5] *DP* (GCS), pp. 16, 27, and 48.

adopted as chapter titles Photius' description of the topics covered in the book. Photius states in codex 8 of the *Bibliotheca* that 'I have read the first principles of Origen, in four books. The first is concerning the Father, the Son and the Holy Spirit (περὶ πατρὸς καὶ υἱοῦ καὶ ἁγίου πνεύματος)'. He makes a similar statement a few lines later: 'His first book is a collection of fables concerning the Father, and, as he says, concerning Christ, and concerning the Holy Spirit, and also, concerning the beings endowed with reason'. (Ἔστι δ' ὁ μὲν πρῶτος αὐτῷ λόγος μεμυθολογημένος περὶ πατρὸς καὶ (ὡς ἐκεῖνός φησι) περὶ Χριστοῦ καὶ περὶ ἁγίου πνεύματος, ἔτι καὶ περὶ λογικῶν φύσεων).[6] But it is notable that Origen does not discuss the attribute of fatherhood in the first chapter; that is reserved for the second. Nor does he use the word Father to refer to God, other than in biblical quotations, except once in section 1 and once in section 8, the penultimate section of the chapter.

Koetschau, in the GCS edition of *De Principiis*, places the words Περὶ πατρός at the head of the first chapter, with *De deo* underneath; Περὶ Χριστοῦ, with *De Christo*, at the head of the second; and Περὶ ἁγίου πνεύματος, with *De spiritu sancto*, at the head of the third.[7] Harl, in her edition of *De Principiis*, uses the phrase 'Sur le Père, le Fils, le Saint-Esprit' as the overall title for the first four chapters, and in her chart of the plan of the book 'Le Père', 'Le Fils', and 'Le Saint-Esprit' respectively as titles for each of the first three chapters.[8] She identifies the titles in the chart as Photius' titles. Her edition is a translation of Rufinus' version of the work —Greek texts are found in an appendix—and she gives French translations of Rufinus' chapter titles in the body of the edition.[9] In the appendix, where she includes a translation of Photius' description of the subjects treated in *De Principiis*, she explains her use of Photius' phrases by remarking that Photius lists the subjects treated in *De Principiis* with an almost perfect exactitude and concludes that the phrases from Photius 'nous semblent des titres authentiques'.[10]

[6] *Bibliothèque*, trans. R. Henry, I (Collection Byzantine: Paris, 1959), p. 9.
[7] *DP*, pp. 16, 27, and 48.
[8] *Traité des principes (Peri Archôn)*, trans. M. Harl, G. Dorval, and A. Le Boulluec (Paris, 1976), pp. 20–1.
[9] Ibid. 29, 37, and 48.
[10] Ibid. 298.

In the Sources Chrétiennes edition, Crouzel and Simonetti place a conflation of Photius' two phrases, Περὶ πατρὸς καὶ υἱοῦ (Χριστοῦ) καὶ ἁγίου πνεύματος, at the head of the Latin text of the first chapter as the title for the first four chapters of the book.[11] Their text is that of Rufinus with a facing page translation—Greek texts are included in the volumes of notes—and they use the Latin titles for the individual titles of the first three chapters.[12] They do not make it clear that their overall title is a conflation; indeed, they imply that the phrase is found, in the form in which they reproduce it, twice in the codex.[13] They give no explanation for their use of Photius' phrases.

In the edition *Vier Bücher von den Prinzipien*,[14] Görgemanns and Karpp place *De deo* at the head of Rufinus' Latin text of the first chapter and 'Von dem Vater' at the head of the facing page translation.[15] In a footnote to the title *De deo*, both of Photius' statements are cited, but the footnote to 'Von dem Vater' reads: 'Da dieses Kapitel den Gottesbegriff allgemein behandelt, in Hinsicht auf das Problem der Körperlichkeit, könnte man erwägen, ob nicht Rufins Überschrift zutreffender ist.'[16]

It remains an open question whether or not Origen actually used titles in *De Principiis*. But of the two possibilities, those of Rufinus and those of Photius, the titles of Rufinus are more probable. Photius' descriptions of Origen's subjects are paraphrases and there is no necessary reason for concluding that he understood them to be titles. He does not keep to the same wording; in his second summary of the contents of the first book of *De Principiis*, he makes the comment: 'as he [Origen] said, concerning Christ', whereas in the first he uses the word 'Son'. If Rufinus' title *De Christo* was Origen's title, it would appear that Photius was prepared to change Origen's words in order to bring them into

---

[11] *Traité des principes*, trans. H. Crouzel and M. Simonetti (SC 252, 253, 268, 269, and 312: Paris, 1978–84), I. 90.

[12] Ibid. I. 90, 110, and 142.

[13] Ibid. I. 91 n: 'Titre grec: Photius, *Bibl.* 8 (deux fois).'

[14] *Vier Bücher von den Prinzipien*, trans. Herwig Görgemanns and Heinrich Karpp (Texte zur Forschung 24: Darmstadt, 1976).

[15] Ibid. 98–9.

[16] Ibid.

harmony with classical trinitarian language. It is unlikely that Rufinus would have altered περὶ πατρός to the less clearly trinitarian *De deo*; it is more likely that Photius (or someone earlier in the manuscript tradition) would have altered *De deo* to περὶ πατρός. In the light of the formulations of Nicaea, such an alteration could have seemed so natural as to go unobserved; it might even have been made unwittingly.

The title *De deo* is appropriate to the substance of the chapter, which deals with the formal philosophical descriptions of God's being. It is in the second chapter that Origen turns his attention to the question of how to reconcile the idea of divine incorporeality with the ideas of God as Father and of the generation of the Son. He may have avoided referring to God as Father in the first chapter in order to make his book parallel as closely as possible the συγγράμματα of the Middle Platonists,[17] and he may have thought that it would be counter-productive to refer to God with the word Father in the course of an argument directed partly against a too literal reading of biblical anthropomorphisms.[18]

Modern scholars have failed to acknowledge the ambiguities in Photius' statements about *De Principiis* and, with the exception of the two German scholars, who then do not carry it over into their translation, they have failed to perceive the disjunction between Photius' description of the first chapter and its content. This uncritical acceptance of Photius as authoritative is not defensible. Rufinus' *De deo* has a greater claim to reliability.

The characteristic that Origen treats as most basic in his statement of the doctrine of God in the opening chapter of *De Principiis* is incorporeality,[19] and he returns to it throughout the work. Indeed, the idea of divine incorporeality and the closely related idea of the knowledge of the incorporeal—which for Origen is saving knowledge—together act as a framing issue for the treatise. This is illustrated in Harl's chart of the plan of *De Principiis*. The four parts of the work—the list of subjects

---

[17] This suggestion was made to the author by Robert Berchman.

[18] But this possibility must be set against the fact that Origen seems generally not to have been worried that the description of God as Father would be viewed in this way.

[19] Harl, *Traité des principes*, pp. 20–1.

announced in the preface; the general exposition in Books I. 1–II. 3; the treatment of particular questions in Books II. 4–IV. 3; and the recapitulation in IV. 4—all end with comment on incorporeality.[20] Origen finds the attribute of incorporeality attested in the Bible and thinks that the recognition of this attribute is the necessary precondition for the proper interpretation of the biblical descriptions of God. The other characteristics he assigns to God's nature are dependent on that of incorporeality. There are parallels to the *De Principiis* discussion of incorporeality in the *Commentary on John*[21] and *Contra Celsum*,[22] which confirm many of the details in the earlier and more systematic account.[23]

Origen announces in the Preface of *De Principiis* that he intends to clarify a number of the unsettled issues in apostolic teaching. One of these is whether or not that which the Greek philosophers call incorporeal, ἀσώματος, is to be found in the Scriptures, and whether or not it is a characteristic of God's nature (and the natures of the Son, the Holy Spirit, and the rational creatures). 'We must', he writes, 'also seek to discover how God himself is to be conceived, whether as corporeal and fashioned in some shape, or as being of a different nature from bodies, a point that is not clearly set forth in the teaching.'[24]

According to Origen, the issue is complicated by commonly held misapprehensions about the meaning of 'incorporeal'. These he is at pains to clear away in the Preface. He acknowledges that the word itself is largely unknown to Christians and that it does not appear in the Bible. Against those who would counter this claim with the example of the use of the word 'incorporeal' in *The Teaching of Peter*, he puts forward two arguments: the writing

---

[20] In his emphasis on incorporeality, Origen expresses common Middle Platonist stress on the transcendence of God. See G. Stroumsa, 'The Incorporeality of God: Context and Implications of Origen's Position', *Religion* 13 (1983), 345, for a summary of the Middle Platonist discussion of the theme.

[21] *Com. Jn.* XIII. 20–5.

[22] *C. Cel.* VI. 69–72.

[23] For an analysis of the reliability of Rufinus as a translator of Origen, see Henry Chadwick, 'Rufinus and the Tura Papyrus of Origen's Commentary on Romans', *JTS* NS 10 (1959), 10–42, and J. M. Rist, 'The Greek and Latin Texts of the Discussion on Free Will in De Principiis Book III', in *Origeniana*, 97–111.

[24] *DP* Pref. 9.

does not have the authority of Scripture, and, even if that point were to be waived, the meaning given to the word in *The Teaching of Peter* is not the meaning that the Greek philosophers assign to it. *The Teaching of Peter*, and the simple and uneducated, assume that what is ethereal is incorporeal, but this is an inadequate conception.[25]

Origen begins his argument for God's incorporeality in the first section of the first chapter of *De Principiis* with a study of the scriptural verses which, he says, were being used by some to prove that the Bible taught that God is a body. Such people take the phrases 'Our God is a consuming fire' (Deut. 4: 24) and 'God is spirit, and those who worship him must worship in spirit and truth' (Jn. 4: 24) to indicate that God is a body, because they believe that spirit and fire are body.

The doctrine that fire and spirit are corporeal is Stoic in origin, and although Origen does not name his opponents in *De Principiis* I. 1, it is likely that the argument was directed against Christians whose interpretation of biblical imagery had been influenced by Stoic philosophy. In Stoic metaphysics, existence is defined by body; there is no incorporeal reality. The word 'spirit' designates a bodily reality which is of the purest sort. Thus in the Stoic reading, the Christian Scriptures, inasmuch as they describe God as spirit, were interpreted to support a corporeal conception of God. So Celsus could charge that when the Christians 'say that God is spirit, there is no difference between [them] and the Stoics among the Greeks who affirm that God is spirit that has permeated all things and contains all things within himself'. Origen, well versed in Stoic thought, replies that while God's providential oversight permeates all things, it does not do so like the spirit of the Stoics, for whom the first principles are corporeal and the supreme God destructible.[26]

Origen may also have had in mind three other groups who failed to read the Bible in the correct way: the unsophisticated Christ-

---

[25] *DP* Pref. 8–9.

[26] *C. Cel.* VI. 71. J. M. Rist, 'Beyond Stoic and Platonist: A Sample of Origen's Treatment of Philosophy (*Contra Celsum* IV. 62–70)', in H. Blume and F. Mann (eds.), *Platonismus und Christentum: Festschrift für Heinrich Dörrie, JAC.* E 10 (1983), 238, remarks that Origen is a 'master of Platonic and Stoic lore'.

ians, the Marcionites, and the Gnostics. The less sophisticated Christians took biblical anthropomorphisms literally, a tendency which Origen thought was given theoretical support by the Stoic manner of reading the Bible. Instead, Scripture was to be interpreted allegorically in light of the idea that God is incorporeal.[27] In the *Commentary on John*, Origen remarks that when the terms 'light, fire and spirit' are used of God, they should be treated in a manner similar to such words as 'eyes' or 'hands' or 'wings' which are understood of God allegorically.[28] The Marcionite distinction between the God of the Old Testament and the God of the New Testament was supported by a literal reading of Old (and New) Testament descriptions of God's moral nature.[29] And in *De Principiis* I. 2 it becomes clear that Origen too is intent on dealing with the materialist implications of Gnosticism, a concern also found in his exegesis of John 4: 24 in the *Commentary on John*.

As a Platonist, Origen cannot conceive of a non-material body. For him, the attribution of corporeality to God entails also the unacceptable attribution of materiality, corruptibility, and divisibility. He writes in *On Prayer* that it is necessary

to remove a mean conception of God held by those who consider that he is locally 'in heaven', and to prevent anyone from saying that God is in a place after the manner of a body (from which it follows that he is a body) —a tenet which leads to the most impious opinions, namely, to suppose that he is divisible, material, corruptible. For every body is divisible, material, corruptible.[30]

In the *Commentary on John* XIII, he maintains that all material reality, including that which some refer to as the fifth element, is subject to alteration from without. If God were to be thought of as material, he necessarily would also be variable, changeable, transformable: ἀνάγκη καὶ τὸν θεὸν ὑλικὸν ὄντα τρεπτὸν εἶναι καὶ ἀλλοιωτὸν καὶ μεταβλητόν. However spiritual and ethereal a body is

---

[27] Stroumsa, 'The Incorporeality of God', argues that Origen develops his allegorical method of exegesis, which allows for the reconciling of the idea of God's incorporeality and the Biblical portrait of a personal God, in reaction to the implications for Christians of Stoic or Platonic conceptions of God.

[28] *Com. Jn.* XIII. 22. 131.

[29] Stroumsa, 'The Incorporeality of God', p. 348.

[30] 22. 3.

conceived to be, it is nevertheless destructible.[31] In *On Prayer*, he outlines the metaphysic that defines οὐσία as primary and corporeal, and implicitly denies its validity: ὀυσία is primary and incorporeal.[32]

Origen develops his reply to those who maintain that Deuteronomy 4: 24 and John 4: 24 testify to a bodily God on their own terms, a method of argumentation that he often employs.[33] By taking a scriptural phrase that is similar to the two cited by his opponents—'God is light, and in him is no darkness' (1 Jn. 1: 5) —he demonstrates the inadequacy of their interpretation of Scripture. He argues that this light is the light 'which lightens the whole understanding of those who are capable of receiving truth'. In support of this contention, he quotes Psalm 35: 10 (LXX) 'In thy light we shall see light', which he applies to the Son as Word and Wisdom revealing the Father.[34] Once he has established that light, properly understood, has to do with knowledge and truth, he concludes that it is inconceivable that the light of 1 John 1: 5 could be confused with the light of the sun, which is corporeal, on the grounds that it is an incontrovertible truth that that which is of a bodily nature cannot be the basis for the acquisition of knowledge.

The verse 'God is spirit' is to be read in the same way (as is 'God is a consuming fire'). It is customary in the Bible, Origen explains, for spirit and bodily reality to be contrasted. The example that he chooses to illustrate this is 2 Corinthians 3: 6 'the written code kills but the spirit gives life',[35] which he also uses in his discussion of John 4: 24 in the *Commentary on John*.[36] The verse is of importance for his approach to scriptural interpretation, as well as

---

[31] *Com. Jn.* XIII. 21. 127–8.
[32] 27. 8. Origen's rejection of this Stoic doctrine is one of the reasons why he entertains the possibility that God transcends being. See e.g. *C. Cel.* VI. 64, discussed below, pp. 35–6.
[33] Rist, 'Beyond Stoic and Platonist', demonstrates, in reference to the argument of *C. Cel.* IV. 62–70, that Origen 'sets Celsus right within the Platonist terms of [Celsus'] own school' (p. 229). Origen also follows this procedure in *C. Cel.* VII. 42–5, writing about *Timaeus* 28C. In both these instances, as in the opening sections of *De Principiis*, Origen puts his argument into a theological setting, rather than a metaphysical one.
[34] *DP* I. 1. 1.
[35] *DP* I. 1. 2.
[36] XIII. 23. 140 and 24. 146.

for his argument for the incorporeality of God. The word 'letter' means that which is corporeal and 'spirit' that which is intellectual. In the reading of Scripture, it is the spiritual or intellectual meaning for which one must aim. Only then will knowledge be revealed, a knowledge which is spiritual because it reveals God, the one who is truly spiritual. Commenting on 2 Corinthians 3: 15-17, and introducing the Holy Spirit into his argument for God's incorporeality, he remarks: 'But if we turn to the Lord, where also the Word of God is, and where the Holy Spirit reveals spiritual knowledge, the veil will be taken away, and we shall then with unveiled face behold in the holy Scriptures the glory of the Lord.'[37] It is as we turn to God who is incorporeal that we are given the intellectual perception necessary to be able to read the Scriptures properly for their spiritual meaning. Thus we are able to recognize that the biblical descriptions of God as spirit and fire testify not to a God who is corporeal, but to a God who is incorporeal. In Origen's Platonist philosophy, epistemology is dependent on ontology: the inspired Scriptures are the vehicle through which one comes to a knowledge of the highest realities, the Father, Son, and Holy Spirit.

Origen concludes his discussion of God's nature in the first chapter of *De Principiis* by returning to the problem that he introduced in the preface: whether or not the notion of God as incorporeal is present in the Bible, even if the word is not.[38] (He comments on it again in Book IV, the last book of the work.[39]) It is of fundamental importance for him that it should be, since both his metaphysic and his epistemology are rooted in Scripture and it is crucial that the key concept that supports his spiritual/allegorical method of exegesis should itself be a scriptural category. To prove that the idea is found in the Bible, he brings forward what he considers to be the critical text for understanding the nature of God and the relation of Father and Son, Colossians 1: 15, where Paul says of Christ that he 'is the image of the invisible God, the first born of all creation'. This verse, and John 1: 18 'No one has

[37] *DP* I. 1. 2.
[38] *DP* I. 1. 8.
[39] *DP* IV. 3. 15.

ever seen God', establish that God is invisible by nature, and to say that God is invisible, he claims, is tantamount to saying that God surpasses the nature of bodies.[40] In *De Principiis* IV[41] and in the *Commentary on John*,[42] he argues that the biblical term 'invisible', ἀόρατος, and the Greek philosophical term ἀσώματος are equivalent. Accordingly, the Bible proclaims that God is not a body, but that he is incorporeal. Origen uses both terms throughout his writings to describe God.

But incorporeality is an attribute which Origen ascribes not only to the Father. He makes it plain that it also characterizes each member of the Trinity. He extends his discussion of God's invisibility, and the biblical basis for the concept, to encompass the relationship between the Father and the Son. In the penultimate section of the first chapter of *De Principiis*, he argues that the Son does not *see* the Father, but rather *knows* the Father:

It is one thing to see, another to know. To see and to be seen is a property of bodies; to know and to be known is an attribute of intellectual existence. Whatever therefore is proper to bodies must not be believed either of the Father or of the Son; the relations between them are such as pertain to the nature of deity.[43]

In the *Commentary on John* XIII, he sums up his discussion of 'God is spirit' simply by asking the rhetorical question: who is more fitted than the Son to reveal God's nature? It is through the Son that we too may know the manner in which God is spirit.[44] In *De Principiis* I. 1. 3 he makes it clear that the Holy Spirit also shares in the incorporeality of the divine nature. And the Trinity as a whole is explicitly said to be incorporeal in a number of places in *De Principiis*.[45] In *De Principiis* IV. 3: 15, he writes: 'But the substance of the Trinity, which is the beginning and cause of all things, "of which are all things and through which are all things and in which are all things" [Rom. 11: 36], must not be believed

[40] *DP* I. 1. 8.
[41] *DP* IV. 3. 15.
[42] *Com. Jn.* XIII. 22. 132.
[43] *DP* I. 1. 8.
[44] *Com. Jn.* XIII. 24. 146.
[45] *DP* I. 6. 4; II. 2. 2; IV. 3. 15; and IV. 4. 8.

either to be a body or to exist in a body, but to be wholly incorporeal.'[46]

The affirmation of the incorporeality of God is not a formal metaphysical exercise for Origen. It has immediate soteriological importance. If ontology and epistemology are integrally related for him, he thinks of epistemology largely in soteriological terms. His presentation of the close connection between incorporeality and soteriology in *De Principiis* is a paradigm for the way in which he presents the whole of his doctrine of God and salvation. It is important background for understanding the way in which he thinks about the fatherhood of God and salvation. It will be useful to set this out in some detail before going on to consider the other principal attributes he assigns to the divine being.

Throughout his analysis of incorporeality in *De Principiis*, Origen relates the attribute to the process by which we come to know God and are saved. Torjesen has pointed out that in Origen's theology the process by which the soul comes to the saving knowledge of God takes place through a pattern of complementary movements in three stages. The threefold activity of the Trinity as Father, Son, and Holy Spirit is matched by a corresponding threefold response of the soul in its journey to the knowledge of God. This pattern of movements is present in *De Principiis* and runs as a *leitmotif* throughout his other writings. As we shall see, it forms the backdrop to his conception of how the

---

[46] The question of whether or not Origen thinks incorporeality is unique to the Trinity is disputed. D. Bostock, 'Quality and Corporeity in Origen', in *Origeniana Secunda*, H. Crouzel and A. Quacquarelli (eds.) (Quaderni di 'Vetera Christianorum' 15: Rome, 1980), p. 336, maintains that Origen 'does not distinguish between the Trinity and the rest of creation in terms of a distinction between incorporeal and corporeal nature, but in terms of a distinction of function, in that the Trinity alone is the source of goodness and holiness'. He regards *DP* I. 6. 4 and II. 2. 2 as having been doctored by Rufinus. However, G. Dorival, 'Origène et la résurrection de la chair', in *Origeniana Quarta*, L. Lies (ed.) (Innsbrucker theologische Studien 19: Innsbruck, 1987), p. 313, points out that Bostock fails to comment on *DP* IV. 3. 15 and 4. 8 and notes that neither Jerome nor Justinian gives an alternative redaction for *DP* IV. 3. 15. H. Crouzel, 'L'Apocatastase chez Origène', in *Origeniana Quarta*, p. 284, concludes, on the basis of *DP* I. 6. 4, II. 2. 2, and IV. 3. 15, that Origen thinks that the Trinity alone is incorporeal. It is possible that Origen considered the pre-existent souls also to be incorporeal, though as with several aspects of his thinking about their pre-existence, he does not make this clear.

Christian comes to a knowledge of God as Father. Commenting on Origen's discussion of the saving activity of the Trinity in *De Principiis* I. 3. 7–8, Torjesen observes:

The work of the Holy Spirit comes first; it is the work of purification because he is the principle of holiness. Through participation in the Holy Spirit the soul itself becomes holy; this is the preparatory stage which makes it possible for the soul at the next stage to receive the wisdom and knowledge of Christ. Since Christ, as Logos, is wisdom and knowledge the soul receives the gifts of wisdom and knowledge, through participation in Him. The final stage of this soteriological process is participation in God the Father.[47]

Elsewhere Origen describes a similar sequence within the knowledge of the divine which progresses from a knowledge of the incarnate Christ to the pre-existent Logos and finally to the knowledge of God.[48] The upward progression of the soul in the knowledge of God corresponds to a downward movement of revelation and accommodation on the part of the Trinity,[49] a downward movement which, as we shall see, is prefigured in Origen's doctrine of creation. Torjesen argues that this soteriological pattern informs Origen's general hermeneutical procedure in the exegesis of Scripture and that he applies the same procedure to the treatment of the philosophical questions in *De Principiis*.[50]

In the course of his exegesis of the scriptural passages that he uses to support the argument for the incorporeality of God in *De Principiis*, Origen delineates several elements of this conception of salvation. That God is light means that God is a spiritual power by which we are enabled to comprehend the truth which is God; the Son as light and word and wisdom draws us to that saving truth. Origen uses the first person plural in his quotation of Psalm 35: 10 'In thy light we shall see light' to weave the reader into the spiritual

---

[47] 'Hermeneutics and Soteriology', p. 338. See also her *Hermeneutical Procedure and Theological Method in Origen's Exegesis* (Patristische Texte und Studien 28: Berlin, 1986).

[48] e.g. *Com. Jn.* XIX. 6. 33–8, which will be discussed further below, pp. 41 and 81–2.

[49] Torjesen, 'Hermeneutics and Soteriology', p. 339.

[50] Ibid. 340–2.

teaching of the verse.[51] That God is fire means that he is able to purify us, which means that he and the Son will then be able to make their abode with us (Jn. 14: 23), a statement that goes beyond the purely metaphysical significance of the verse to point to its soteriological importance.

In the discussion of 'God is spirit' in the *Commentary on John*, the soteriological focus of Origen's thinking about God's incorporeality is delineated more sharply than in *De Principiis*. Paraphrasing John 14: 23, he writes that when the Spirit[52] 'finds a suitable dwelling place in the soul of a saint [who, for Origen, is one who has been purified] he gives himself up, if I might thus speak, to abiding in it'.[53] This he sees as the reason behind the verse 'I will make my dwelling among them and I will walk among them and I will be their God and they will be my people' (Lev. 26: 12; 2 Cor. 6: 6). The qualification 'if I might thus speak' suggests that he is aware that by using such a spatial image to describe the presence of God within the perfected soul he might be perceived to have introduced a contradiction into his argument. But the idea that God gives himself to the sanctified soul and stays with that soul is such an important part of the biblical imagery of salvation on which Origen relies in the development of his soteriology that he is willing to take the risk of seeming to undermine his argument.[54] It is a fundamental tenet of Origen's theology that God as Father, Son, and Holy Spirit is present with the saint. He can be present because of his nature as incorporeal spirit. There is nothing less at stake in the argument for the incorporeality of God than the possibility of our sharing in the eternal life of God, Son, and Holy Spirit.

Having established in the first four sections of *De Principiis* I. 1

---

[51] Torjesen, 'Hermeneutics and Soteriology', p. 344, points out that the incorporation of the hearer is an essential element of Origen's hermeneutical procedure. For a discussion of the four steps that Origen follows in the exegesis of a passage of Scripture, see below, p. 61.

[52] Here Origen is referring to God. There are times when it is unclear whether he is referring to God as spirit or to the Holy Spirit.

[53] *Com. Jn.* XIII. 24. 143.

[54] The theme of God coming to man and dwelling with him recurs in the *Commentary on John*, and it is of particular importance in the *Homilies on the Song of Songs*.

that the Bible does not teach the corporeality of God, Origen turns in *De Principiis* I. 1. 5 to the positive task of identifying what God is. He is mind, he is a One and a Unity, the necessary source of all things. In *De Principiis* I. 1. 6, he writes:

God therefore must not be thought to be any kind of body, nor to exist in a body, but to be a simple intellectual existence (*intellectualis natura simplex*), admitting no addition whatever, so that he cannot be believed to have in him a more or less, but Unity (μονάς), or if I may so say, Oneness (ἑνάς), throughout, and the mind (*mens*) and fount from which originates all intellectual existence or mind.

In this theological formulation of God as *intellectualis natura simplex*, above all created being and intellect, Origen brings together for the first time two previously separate strands in Middle Platonist thought: the Aristotelian definition of God as self-thinking thought and the Neo-Pythagorean idea of God as monad.[55] God is the simple and necessary first principle of all things.[56]

Mind, as Origen perceives it, is the ontological opposite of bodily nature, and thus particularly fitting as a description of God. He devotes a long passage in the first chapter of *De Principiis*, sections 5 to 7, to a discussion of the characteristics of mind that make it suitable as a description of God. The mind's lack of the physical properties of bodies, which, in terms similar to the *Phaedrus*, Origen lists as movement in physical space, size, shape, and colour, does not diminish its powers; rather, it enhances them. Not only is the mind able to move and to act in the absence of such properties, but its ability to effect its intentions is increased. For in a 'simple and wholly mental existence' there are no impediments to actions and its purposes are accomplished instantly.[57] Anything which limits the actions of another is an addition to it and makes it

[55] Berchman, *From Philo to Origen*, 117, and Anthony Meredith, 'Review of Robert Berchman, *From Philo to Origen*', *JTS* NS 37 (1986), 557–9.

[56] If God is 'one and simple', the Logos is 'multiple' (*Com. Jn.* I. 20. 119). Origen's conception of his two first principles, God and the Logos, reflects the Middle Platonist reading of the *Parmenides*. See E. Dodds, 'The Parmenides of Plato and the Origin of the Neoplatonic "One"', *Classical Quarterly* 22 (1928), 129–42, for a discussion of the influence of the *Parmenides* on Middle Platonism.

[57] *DP* I. 1. 6.

composite. That which is composite, pre-eminently corporeal substance, is divisible and subsequent to the things which make it up:

But God, who is the beginning of all things, must not be regarded as a composite being, lest perchance we find that the elements, out of which everything that is called composite has been composed, are prior to the first principle himself.[58]

By definition, the first principle in order to be first has to be simple and has to be incorporeal. Otherwise it would not be possible, according to Origen's logic, to avoid an infinite regress that would make it less than first.

Furthermore, although he does not explicitly say so, Origen is assuming that God's nature as mind is integral to the eternity of God. Time does not apply in the realm of being, but only in the realm of becoming.[59] The one in whose actions there is 'no delay or hesitation' is not subject to the strictures of time.[60]

The idea of God as mind is important to Origen's doctrine of universal providence and foreknowledge.[61] It allows him to portray God as a God who is actively involved in the world that he has created, while not being defined by the bodily character of that creation. Furthermore, the definition of the first principle as mind, untrammelled by material reality, and as eternal, plays an important part in Origen's explanation of the eternity of God's fatherhood and the generation of the Son.

As with the idea that God is incorporeal, soteriological concerns are also at the forefront of Origen's consideration of God as mind. Origen concludes his arguments for the simplicity of God, and his

---

[58] Ibid.

[59] *C. Cel.* VII. 46. For a discussion of Origen's conception of time and eternity, in relation to their place in the thought of Classical and Late Antiquity, see Richard Sorabji, *Time, Creation and the Continuum: Theories in Antiquity and the Early Middle Ages* (London, 1983), 122–3.

[60] *DP* I. 1. 6.

[61] Christopher Stead, 'The Concept of Mind and the Concept of God in the Christian Fathers', in B. Hebblethwaite and S. Sutherland (eds.), *The Philosophical Frontiers of Christian Theology: Essays presented to D. M. MacKinnon* (Cambridge, 1982), 39–54; repr. in his *Substance and Illusion in the Christian Fathers* (London, 1985), comments on various aspects of the Fathers' use of the concept of mind to describe God.

status as the source from which all intellectual existence originates, with a discussion of human knowing. As mind, God is the source of all intellectual existence, an idea which provides for a continuity of natures between God and man. He explains that there is a 'certain affinity between the human mind and God, of whom the mind is an intellectual image', which, when it is 'purified and separated from bodily matter', is able to acquire some perception of God.[62] In the closing section of the first chapter of *De Principiis*,[63] Origen demonstrates that his theory of the way in which one comes to a knowledge of God is established by the Bible. Applying the principles of the spiritual reading of Scripture that he set out in the first four sections of the chapter, he argues that the verse 'Blessed are the pure in heart, for they shall see God' (Matt. 5: 8) means that God is known through a process of understanding. A careful study of scriptural imagery reveals that 'heart' signifies mind. There are two kinds of senses, the one mortal, corruptible, and human, and the other immortal, intellectual, and divine.[64] In accordance with his reading of Proverbs 2: 5 'You will find a divine sense ($αἴσθησιν θείαν εὑρήσεις$)',[65] he concludes that the 'pure in heart' will come to know God with the mind.[66]

Once again the essentially theological intent of Origen's metaphysical analysis is apparent. In the course of his proof for the intellectual nature of God, and his simplicity, he has 'moved into place the central pieces of his soteriological program.'[67] He ends the chapter where he began, demonstrating the philosophical attributes of God from the epistemological basis of Scripture and drawing out the soteriological significance of the spiritual meaning of the biblical verses he has used.

References to God as good and as 'he who is' are common

---

[62] *DP* I. 1. 7.

[63] *DP* I. 1. 9.

[64] Underlying this is the Platonist distinction between the perception of sensible reality and the understanding of intelligible reality, which Origen outlines in *C. Cel.* VII. 46.

[65] *DP* I. 1. 9; *C. Cel.* I. 48, VII. 34; and often elsewhere. The Septuagint reads: 'You will find the knowledge of God' ($ἐπίγνωσιν θεοῦ εὑρήσεις$).

[66] *DP* I. 1. 9.

[67] Torjesen, 'Hermeneutics and Soteriology', 343.

throughout Origen's writings. But unlike the ideas of God as incorporeal and as a simple intellectual existent, though like the word Father, they are not discussed in the context of the systematic presentation of the nature of God in the first chapter of *De Principiis*. Comments on the attributes of goodness, 'he who is', and fatherhood appear mainly in relation to discussions about the doctrines of creation and redemption, often as part of trinitarian formulations. Although Origen does not spell out the relationship in his theology between the two attributes of goodness and 'he who is', and their relationship to God's fatherhood, the ideas of God as good and as 'he who is' are bound up with each other, and he thinks about both in much the same way that he thinks about the attribute of fatherhood.

Origen derives the ideas of the goodness of God and God as 'he who is' from the Bible, but his understanding of them also reflects Middle Platonist influence. The verse that he repeatedly quotes to establish that God is good is Mark 10: 18, and he frequently includes the reference to Father: 'No one is good but God the Father alone.' The title 'he who is' comes from Exodus 3: 14. Along with these biblical ideas, Origen inherited the commonplace assumption of Middle Platonist tradition in which the form of the good of the *Republic* was understood to refer to God.

Origen defines God's nature as good. This is of critical importance, for the one who is the creator, the source of existence, and the one to whom we are to ascend must necessarily be perceived to be good. Origen's entire conception of the world, its inherent goodness and moral order, depends on the supposition that God is one and that he is good. Much of his thinking about the idea is worked out in opposition to Marcionism. Marcion, as Origen portrays him in *De Principiis* II. 5, maintained that there was a distinction between the creator God of the Old Testament who is just but not good, and the New Testament Father of Christ who is good but not just.[68]

In his discussion of the meaning of the statement that the Son is

---

[68] For a recent reinterpretation of Harnack's analysis of Marcion's view of God, see Catherine Osborne, *Rethinking Early Greek Philosophy: Hippolytus of Rome and the Presocratics* (London, 1987), pp. 100ff.

the image of the Father's goodness in *De Principiis* I. 2. 13, Origen, quoting Mark 10: 18, argues that God is the sole source of all goodness. There is no 'secondary' goodness existing in the Son that does not already exist in the Father. He describes the generation of the Son as a birth from the goodness of the Father. In a fragment from Justinian's letter to Mennas,[69] the Son is characterized as good, though in contrast to the Father he is not good without qualification, ἁπλῶς ἀγαθός. According to the fragment, the Son is not the sole genuine embodiment of goodness; he is not αὐτοαγαθός. By implication it is the Father alone who is αὐτοαγαθός.[70] There is only one fount of goodness, just as there is only one fount of intellectual existence. While Origen is willing to say that the Father is greater than such realities as truth, life, light, and being, he is never tempted to suggest that God is greater than the characteristic of goodness, unlike Albinus who is prepared to say of God that he is neither good nor evil.[71] Such a statement would have been unthinkable for Origen.

But if the Father is the only source of goodness, that goodness, like the attribute of incorporeal intellectual existence, is also a unique characteristic of the Trinity. Origen makes a contrast between the goodness found in the Trinity and that found in other entities. He notes that various things in the Bible are called good, such as an angel, a man, or a treasure, but they are not good in the same way as the Trinity. They are not good *substantialia*, whereas the Trinity is.[72]

Origen's doctrine of creation is based on the idea of the divine goodness. God's being is not only defined as good; God always acts to fulfil that being. Both the Son, whose generation and place

---

[69] *Acta Conciliorum Oecumenicorum*, iii, ed. E. Schwartz (Berlin, 1940), p. 210, fr. 7.

[70] John Dillon, 'Logos and Trinity: Patterns of Platonist Influence on Early Christianity', in Godfrey Vesey (ed.), *The Philosophy in Christianity* (Cambridge, 1989), pp. 6–7, thinks that this detail was 'almost certainly borrowed from Numenius', who makes a distinction between the αὐτοαγαθός and the ἀγαθός in fragment 16.

[71] *Epitome* X. 4.

[72] *DP* I. 2. 13. Raoul Mortley, *From Word to Silence*, ii, *The Way of Negation, Christian and Greek* (Theophaneia 31: Bonn, 1986), p. 73, suggests that if *substantialis* is a translation of οὐσιώδης, then Origen is predicating essential goodness of the Trinity and accidental goodness of lesser beings.

in the act of creation will be discussed below, and the created order come into existence in their differing ways through the goodness of God. The divine goodness, according to Origen, is a goodness that always and continuously gives itself for the creation and for the care of that which is other than itself. He writes of God: 'Now when "in the beginning" he created what he wished to create, that is rational beings, he had no other reason for creating them except himself, that is, goodness.'[73]

It is to this goodness that creation, once it too has been remade as good, returns. Origen makes this clear in a passage directed against Marcionism in the *Commentary on John* I. He suggests that the contention that the creator God is just while the Father of Christ is good could be turned on its head, and he concludes:

And it is without doubt by his justice that the Saviour prepares all things, by favourable circumstances, by his word, by his government, by his chastisements, and, if I might so speak, by his spiritual remedies, to receive in themselves at the end the goodness of the Father.[74]

He notes that it was in respect of this goodness that Jesus said, 'No one is good but God the Father alone' (Mk. 10: 18). Having been perfected by the Son, whom he frequently refers to elsewhere as the 'image' of the goodness of the Father,[75] the rational creatures are made ready to receive the perfect goodness of the Father from whom they came. The goodness of God has a central place not only in Origen's doctrines of God and of creation, but also in his soteriology.

Origen's concept of the goodness of God works in close harmony with his concept of God as 'he who is' or 'being itself' (ὁ ὤν). The use of ὁ ὤν to describe God had had a long history in Alexandrian thought prior to Origen. From Philo onwards, the description of God as ὁ ὤν is associated with the phrase τὸ ὄν of *Timaeus* 27D.[76] But in contrast to earlier Christian writers, Origen

---

[73] *DP* II. 9. 6. The attribute of goodness is discussed further in relation to Origen's understanding of the eternal generation of the Son and in relation to his doctrine of creation, pp. 71ff. below.

[74] I. 35. 254.

[75] e.g. in *DP* I. 2. 13.

[76] J. Whittaker, 'Moses Atticizing', *Phoenix* 21 (1967), 196–201, repr. in his

neither uses the neuter form of the participle, as for instance Justin did in the *Dialogue with Trypho*,[77] nor, unlike Pseudo-Justin, where the title ὁ ὤν is linked with *Timaeus* 27D–28A,[78] does he refer to *Timaeus* 27D where the neuter occurs. The absence of this apparently conventional Platonic reference suggests either that Origen assumed the traditional parallel and felt that there was no need to make explicit reference to it; or that he felt that the Exodus phrase was completely comprehensible, requiring no such reference to elucidate it; or that he wanted to keep right away from the impersonal neuter language.

Origen frequently uses ὁ ὤν to describe God, and he uses it exclusively of God.[79] It has a particular significance for him because not only is it one of the names recorded of God in the Bible, but more than that, it specifically is God's self-designation.[80] Origen refers to its occurrence in the book of Exodus several times. In *Commentary on John* II, for instance, conflating Exodus 3. 14 and 15, he observes that God is named: Εἶπε γὰρ κύριος πρὸς Μωσῆν· Ὁ ὤν τοῦτό μοί ἐστιν τὸ ὄνομα.[81]

The idea that God is 'he who is' is integral to Origen's conception of God as the source of creation and as the one who gives renewed life to those who return to him. In his exegesis of 1 Samuel 2: 2, he remarks that the text 'there is none holy like the Lord, and none beside thee' is equivalent to saying that 'there is no other God beside thee', or 'no other Creator beside thee'. It teaches that none of the things that exist have their existence by

---

Studies in Platonism and Patristic Thought (London, 1984), outlines the history of the relation between the two terms from Philo to Numenius.

[77] *Dialogue* 4.

[78] *Cohort.* 22, PG 6, 280C–281B.

[79] In a fragment on the Apocalypse, *Der Scholien-Kommentar des Origenes zur Apokalypse Iohannis*, ed. C. Diobouniotis and Adolf Harnack, TU 38, 20. 29, the Son is referred to as '"He who is", in his very substance', but the authenticity of the fragment is doubtful. Neither E. Skard, 'Zum Skolien-Kommentar des Origenes zur Apokalypse Iohannis', *Symbolae Osloenses* 16 (1936), pp. 204–8, nor P. Nautin, *Origène: Sa vie et son œuvre* (Christianisme Antique i: Paris, 1977), p. 449, includes it among those they regard as authentic. The analysis of the title which follows in this chapter will demonstrate that it is highly unlikely that Origen would have used it as a title for the Son.

[80] Its status as a name for God is discussed below, pp. 58–60.

[81] II. 13. 95; also *On Prayer* 24. 2 and *Hom. in 1 Reg.* I. 11. 20–1.

nature, except God, who alone has being without having received it from some other, and alone has always had it. Origen concludes that God chose to reveal to Moses his name as 'he who is' because that name could not be given to any other than the one who exists of himself, and from whom all other creatures have received their existence.[82] It is thus a fitting title for the one who is first principle. The Son and the Holy Spirit have also received their existence from God. The Son 'draws his being from [the Father]'.[83]

The importance of the Exodus 3: 14 title in Origen's doctrine of God and in his soteriology is well illustrated in *De Principiis* I. 3. 6–8, where Origen explains the distinctive role of the Father in the threefold activity of the divine in the process of regeneration, which is signified in the baptismal formula. The Father, who is being, grants being to all that exists; the Son, who is Logos, gives reason to all reasonable beings; and the Holy Spirit is the agent of sanctification. Of the Father he writes:

And all things that exist derive their share of being from him who truly exists, who said through Moses, 'I am he who is', which participation in God, God the Father extends to all, both righteous and sinners, rational and irrational creatures, and absolutely everything that exists.[84]

It is the characteristic of God as 'he who is' which allows God to give being to others, and to encompass and act upon the whole of creation, in contrast to the Logos and Holy Spirit, whose spheres of influence are limited.

If the existence of all things has its beginning with the God 'who is', it also finds its proper end in him. In *De Principiis* I. 3. 8, the concluding section of his explanation of the process of sanctification, Origen writes that through the activity of the Son and Holy Spirit, God brings us to a perfection of existence which is worthy of the God who caused us to exist. The Christian will receive power to 'exist forever'. Through Wisdom and the Holy Spirit, 'those who were made by God may be unceasingly and inseparably present with him who really exists'. This last phrase, *ei qui est*, may

---

[82] *Hom. in 1 Reg.* I. 11. 20–1.
[83] *DP* I. 2. 2.
[84] *DP* I. 3. 6.

be a reference to Exodus 3: 14.[85] The life in which man is called ultimately to share is the life of the one who is being itself and, as we have seen, is goodness itself. No less than the attributes of incorporeality and mind; the goodness of God and God as 'he who is' are of significance for Origen's understanding of God and of the process of salvation. *De Principiis* I. 3. 6-8 shows clearly the three-stage process by which the soul ascends to its perfect knowledge of God.

The relationship between of the titles 'good' and 'he who is' and their soteriological role is further illustrated by the use Origen makes of them in his solution of the problem of evil. He deals at length with the existence of evil in his discussion of John 1: 3 'without him nothing was made' in the *Commentary on John* II. 13. 91–9. He links the idea of God as being with the idea of God as good and uses this link in his explanation of the process by which man turns away from, and back to, God. Arguing in reply to those who conclude that the verse means that the Logos is responsible for the creation of evil, Origen maintains that the word 'nothing' (οὐδέν) is a synonym for 'non-being' (οὐκ ὄν).[86] He finds biblical warrant for the equation of non-being and evil in Paul's statement in Romans 4: 17 'God has called the things that are not', which Origen takes to be a reference to sinners,[87] and in Esther 4: 17 'Deliver not the sceptre to those who are not', which refers to the enemies of Israel.[88] Evil is non-being and thus cannot be thought of as created by God, who, as ὁ ὤν, is being itself.

Origen confirms his case for the contrast between God and evil by demonstrating the interconnection of God's nature as being, his nature as good, and his nature as Father. He cites the conflation of Exodus 3: 14 and 15 in conjunction with the verse from the Gospels 'No one is good but God the Father alone' (Mk. 10: 18), thereby bringing into one passage three of the primary attributes of God. Those who desire to belong to the church (presumably in

---

[85] P. Nautin, '"Je suis celui qui est" (Exode 3, 14) dans la théologie d'Origène', in *Dieu et l'être: Exégèses d'Exode 3, 14 et de Coran 20, 11–24* [no ed.] (Paris, 1978), p. 113.

[86] 13. 94.

[87] 13. 94.

[88] 13. 95.

contrast to the Marcionites), he explains, perceive that the God of the Old Testament, who names himself as 'he who is', is the same as the God whom Jesus describes as good alone, God the Father. This conjunction of the three verses allows Origen to do two things. He is able to show that the source of existence is the good God, the Father of Christ; and he is able to conclude, on the basis of Scripture, that 'the good is identical to "he who is"' and that 'evil and vice are non-being'.[89] The existence of evil is attributed to the free choice of rational creatures.

This has important implications for Origen's thinking about the process by which man is redeemed. (As will become apparent later, he describes the process in much the same way that he describes the way in which we come to be sons of God and know God as Father.) Participation in the Logos, and thus participation in the being of God, is something from which we may 'turn away' (ἀποστρέφω). Non-beings are those who are thus deprived of God, sinners, who have no knowledge of God. Those who do not turn away from God, but remain participant in 'he who is', may correlatively be called 'those who are'. These Origen identifies as 'the saints' (οἱ ἅγιοι).[90]

He continues with the theme in his exegesis of John 1: 4. He argues that those who do not live for God live lives of sin; in effect, they are dead. In support, he cites one of his favourite descriptions of God, Mark 12: 27 'He is not the God of the dead, but of the living', which he thinks is equivalent to saying that God 'is not the God of sinners but of saints'. He concludes that 'the saints are living, and the living are saints'.[91] In the *Commentary on Matthew*, he uses the Exodus title 'he who is' directly to confirm his interpretation of Matthew 22: 32, a parallel of Mark 12: 27. After quoting Matthew 22: 32, he remarks that God is the God 'of those who are' (ὄντων), and not 'of those who are not' (οὐκ ὄντων). Inasmuch as God is the God who gave his name as 'he who is' and thus is the God 'of those who are', so, in the words of Matthew, he

[89] *Com. Jn.* 13. 95–6.
[90] 13. 98.
[91] II. 16. 115–17. 118.

is the God 'of the living' (ζώντων).[92] 'He who is' grants being and true life to those who do not sin.

In at least two other places in his writings Origen returns to this theme. In his *Commentary on the Letter to the Ephesians*, with reference to his wording of Ephesians 1: 1, τοῖς ἁγίοις τοῖς οὖσιν καὶ πιστοῖς ἐν Χριστῷ Ἰησοῦ; which he interprets to mean 'to the saints who are and to the faithful in Christ Jesus', he writes:

It is not only with reference to the Ephesians that we find the expression 'to the saints who are', and we ask what, if it is not superfluous to add the phrase 'those who are' to the phrase 'to the saints', the phrase might mean. See then if it is not that just as he who named himself to Moses in Exodus gave his name as <ὁ> ὤν,[93] so likewise those who participate in 'he who is' become those who are (οἱ μετέχοντες τοῦ ὄντος γίνονται ὄντες), named as though they have passed from non-being to being. For, as the same St Paul says, 'God has chosen the things that are not' [1 Cor. 1: 28].[94]

Here Origen again uses Exodus 3: 14 as proof that God as being itself is the the source of true existence. The transition from non-being to being is brought about by God's initiative. Again it is the saints, those who live morally pure lives, who share in God's life.

In the *Commentary on the Epistle to the Romans*, Origen makes the moral aspect more explicit. With reference to Romans 4: 17, he asks:

What are 'the things that are not' except those who are deprived of 'he who is' (τοῦ ὄντος) and who do not participate in him? They are so named in opposition to those who participate in the one who said 'I am he who is'

---

[92] *Com. Matt.* XVII. 36.

[93] In the GCS edition of *On Prayer* 24. 2, Koetschau amends the manuscript reading of ὤν to ὁ ὤν in line with the Exodus text. Maurice Wiles, 'Eunomius: Hair Splitting Dialectician or Defender of the Accessibility of Salvation?', in R. Williams (ed.), *The Making of Orthodoxy: Essays in Honour of Henry Chadwick* (Cambridge 1989), 171 n. 31, citing the use of ὤν by Basil of Ancyra in Epiphanius, *Panarion* 73. 12, and by Eunomius, *Apologia apologiae* 17, concludes that the emendation is unjustified.

[94] 'The Commentary of Origen upon the Epistle to the Ephesians', ed. J. Gregg, *JTS* 3 (1901–2), p. 235.

('Ἐγώ εἰμι ὁ ὤν). But he 'calls the things that are not' in order that he might grant being to those who have been obedient.[95]

Although the fragment is brief, it demonstrates the way in which Origen links ethics and ontology. Our ontological status is directly related to our moral status; only as we are obedient are we called from non-being into a life of true existence.

The tendency in Origen's thought to collapse the language of being and willing into each other creates a tension that runs throughout his thinking about sonship and the fatherhood of God. In that context, the tension lies between a completed state of moral perfection, which he sees as concomitant with our rebirth as sons, and his sense that the process of adoption as sons is accompanied by an ongoing moral struggle. This will be discussed at length in Chapter 4 on the knowledge of God as Father and adoption as sons.

But notwithstanding the importance for his theology of the descriptions of God as 'he who is' from Exodus 3: 14 and as mind, Origen can also describe God as 'transcending mind and being'. He does this six times, once in *De Martyrio*, twice in *Contra Celsum*, and three times in the *Commentary on John*. His use of this idea has been much discussed in the recent studies of Mortley,[96] Nautin,[97] and Williams.[98] It is difficult to assess the weight that this description should be given in the context of Origen's thought as a whole. Its occurrence is rare; but the co-existence of two such contrasting descriptions, that God is both mind and being itself, and that he transcends mind and being, might be perceived to reflect at best an unresolved tension in Origen's thought or, at worst, a contradiction. Neither, however, is the case. Origen is not interested in working out the metaphysical implication of saying that God transcends being and mind. He employs the concept primarily for theological reasons: to support

[95] 'Commentary on the Epistle to the Romans', ed. A. Ramsbothan, *JTS* 13 (1911–12), p. 361.

[96] *From Word to Silence*, ii. 73 ff.

[97] Above, n. 85.

[98] Rowan Williams, *Arius: Heresy and Tradition* (London, 1987), pp. 140, 204–5.

his affirmation of the role of the Logos as the definitive revelation of the truth about God.

The phrase 'beyond being' recalls the words of *Republic* 509B, 'the Good is not the same thing as being, but even beyond being, surpassing it in dignity and power' (οὐκ οὐσίας ὄντος τοῦ ἀγαθοῦ, ἀλλ᾽ ἔτι ἐπέκεινα τῆς οὐσίας πρεσβείᾳ καὶ δυνάμει ὑπερέχοντος). The Middle Platonists, and particularly the Neo-Pythagoreans, reading this phrase in conjunction with the discussion of first principles in the *Parmenides*, took it to signify the possibility that God transcended both being and mind.[99]

Origen makes comments that suggest he was aware that the question of whether or not God transcended being and mind was a matter of discussion among the Greek philosophers. He introduces his study of John 4: 24 in the *Commentary on John* by observing:

Many people have said many things concerning God and his being. While some say that he also is of a corporeal nature, subtle and ethereal, some say that he is of an incorporeal nature, and others that he transcends being by his dignity and power (καὶ ἄλλους ὑπερέκεινα οὐσίας πρεσβείᾳ καὶ δυνάμει).[100]

Similarly, in *Contra Celsum* VI. 64 Origen acknowledges that the question of God's relationship to being is difficult and properly requires lengthy treatment. In such an investigation it would be necessary 'first to discover whether God transcends being in rank and power'. But he does not in fact set out to make this discovery, and the question of God's transcendence of being and mind is never made a subject of analysis at any point in his writings. Nevertheless, his use of *Republic* 509B reveals much about how he conceives of God's transcendence, the relationship between the Father and the Son, and his attitude to Greek thought.

The two instances in *Contra Celsum* occur in the course of replies to Celsus' charge that the Christian conception of God is

---

[99] J. Whittaker, in a series of articles reprinted in his *Studies in Platonism and Patristic Thought* (London, 1984), has marshalled the evidence. See especially his '*ΕΠΕΚΕΙΝΑ ΝΟΥ ΚΑΙ ΟΥΣΙΑΣ*', originally published in *VC* 23 (1969), 91–104. For a brief summary of the issue and the secondary literature, see J. Dillon, *The Middle Platonists: A Study of Platonism 80 B.C. to A.D. 220* (London, 1977), p. 351.

[100] XIII. 21. 123, following the reading of the Sources Chrétiennes edition.

corporeal. In *Contra Celsum* VI. 64, in response to Celsus' complaints about biblical anthropomorphisms, Origen agrees with Celsus that God does not participate in shape, colour, or movement. 'What is more,' he says, 'God does not even participate in being.' This leads on to the question of God's relationship to being:

However, there is much to say which is hard to perceive about being, especially if we take 'being' in the strict sense to be unmoved and incorporeal. We would have to discover whether God 'transcends being in rank and power' and grants a share in being to those whose participation is according to his Logos, and the Logos himself, or whether he is himself being, in spite of the fact that he is said to be invisible by nature in the words that say of the Saviour 'Who is the image of the invisible God' [Col. 1: 15]. That he is incorporeal is indicated by the word 'invisible'. We would also enquire whether we ought to say that the uniquely begotten and first born of all creation is being of beings and idea of ideas, and beginning and that his Father and God transcends all these.

A number of the themes which we have already seen in Origen's doctrine of God occur in this passage. He is concerned to eliminate any Stoic-inspired notion that God's being is corporeal; and he wants to ensure that God should be understood to be the single source of existence, even if he transcends being. A share in that being is granted through participation in the Logos, an idea we encountered in the context of Origen's discussion of God as 'he who is'.

Origen often assigns the term 'being' to the Son. In *On Prayer* 27. 9, he says that the Logos, as heavenly bread, gives οὐσία to those who partake of the bread. Here in *Contra Celsum* VI. 64, he canvasses the possibility that if as 'being of beings' and 'idea of ideas' the Son is identical with the realm of ideas, where intellect reigns, then the Father must be above both being and intellect, the order of intelligible reality. In an allusion to *Republic* 509B in *De Martyrio* 47, he states that God 'transcends the intelligibles' (ἐπέκεινα τῶν νοητῶν).

In *Contra Celsum* VII. 38, denying Celsus' contention that the bodily resurrection of Christ indicates that God is a body, knowable through the senses, Origen writes:

Since we affirm that the God of the universe is mind (νοῦν) or that he transcends mind and being (ἤ ἐπέκεινα νοῦ καὶ οὐσίας) and is simple and invisible and incorporeal, we would maintain the God is not comprehended by any other being than him made in the image of that mind.

This is the one instance where Origen uses the full phrase 'transcends mind and being'. Elsewhere he uses either 'mind' or 'being'.

There is evidence in *Contra Celsum* VII that Origen thought that *Republic* 509B parallels biblical teaching. Commenting on Celsus' interpretation of the discussion of the good in *Republic* 508B–509B, which he records in *Contra Celsum* VII. 45, Origen responds to Celsus' statement that God transcends (ἐπέκεινα) all things, with an attack on the adequacy of the Greek philosophers' knowledge of God, an attack in which he weaves together the Middle Platonic interpretation of the *Republic* with its stress on the transcendence of God, and Romans 1: 20. In *Contra Celsum* VII. 46, he describes the stages through which we must progress in order to come to the knowledge of God in terms of the Platonic doctrine of ascent.[101] It is only Christians, he implies, who are capable of successfully making the ascent. The disciples of Christ use the things that are 'becoming' as stepping-stones to the contemplation of 'the nature of intelligible things'. But they do not stop there.

'For the invisible things of God', that is, the intelligible things, 'are understood by the things that are made' and 'from the creation of the world are clearly seen' [Rom. 1: 20] by the process of thought. And when they have ascended from the created things of the world to the invisible things of God they do not stop there. But after exercising their minds sufficiently among them and understanding them, they ascend to the 'eternal power' of God, and, in a word, to his 'divinity' [Rom. 1: 20].[102]

Although he does not directly link *Republic* 509B and Romans 1: 20, Origen sees the Middle Platonist conception of the transcendence of God and the ascent of the soul to the highest reaches of God's being as more correctly expressed in Paul's statement. He

---

[101] The image is found in *Symposium* 211C. See below, pp. 44–5, where it is discussed in the context of Origen's epistemology.

[102] VII. 46.

may well have taken Paul's 'eternal power' and 'divinity' to be equivalent to Plato's 'dignity and power'. We go beyond the realm of the intelligibles to that which is above them, the eternal power and divinity of God. For Origen, the statement that God transcends mind and being is fully consistent with the biblical understanding of God's transcendence.

The focus of both of the passages in *Contra Celsum* where Origen discusses *Republic* 509B is not specifically the issue of whether or not God transcends mind and being. Indeed, the tenor of the comments, in which Origen can move easily from the statement that God is mind to the statement that God transcends mind, suggests that he does not perceive a metaphysical disjunction between the two. He has two purposes in the passages: first, a defensive intention of ensuring that Christians do not become labelled with promoting the notion of a corporeal God, which as we have seen is of fundamental importance to the whole of his theological enterprise; and second, a positive intention of establishing that the knowledge of God revealed through the Logos is definitive. In his polemic against Celsus, he is arguing that however high a notion of God Greek philosophy puts forward, the Christian conception is higher. In effect, he is indulging in a species of metaphysical one-upmanship. He is not embarking on a precise analysis of how to express transcendence in relation to being; rather, he is using the language of his philosophical contemporaries to support his theological assertion of God's exalted nature, and thus to establish that man is incapable of coming to a knowledge of God except through the Logos, as the succeeding sections of *Contra Celsum* VI show. The broader epistemological context of these passages of the *Contra Celsum* will be discussed in the next chapter.

The phrase of *Republic* 509B is alluded to three times in his *Commentary on John*, twice in Book XIII and once in Book XIX. His analysis of John 4: 24 in Book XIII begins and ends with a reference to the phrase. The whole of the treatment of the Johannine verse, which runs from XIII. 21. 123 to XIII. 25. 153, is a carefully crafted study of the divine nature, in which Origen makes the most of the rhetorical power of the phrase from the *Republic* to establish the correct understanding both of God's relationship to the created order and of his relationship to the Son and to the Holy Spirit.

As noted above, Origen opens the passage by outlining three possible ideas concerning God's being: that he is corporeal, that he is incorporeal, or that he transcends being by his rank and power. He begins by stating that it is worthwhile to see what the Scriptures have to say about the issue. After having studied the relevant biblical evidence, and having shown that John 4: 24 speaks of God as an *incorporeal* spirit, he turns his attention to the view that he attributes to Heracleon, namely that those who are 'spiritual' are of the 'same nature' as the Father, indeed that they are ὁμοούσιος with the Father. He develops his argument by a carefully ordered series of propositions designed to establish God's transcendence of all things. He first states that it is impious to suggest that anything is ὁμοούσιος with God, who is by nature ἀγέννητος, for those things which are ὁμοούσιος share the same predicates.[103] He appears to have understood ὁμοούσιος 'to designate co-ordinate members of a single class, beings sharing the same properties'.[104] But he is not prepared to countenance the placing of God in the same categories of existence as the rest of reality. The unique superiority of the Father was signified by the Saviour when he said that the Father who had sent him was 'greater than me' (Jn. 14: 28) and when he refused the appellation 'good' (Mk. 10: 18). Origen rebukes those, presumably like Heracleon, who glorify the Son excessively. The Son and the Holy Spirit, he contends, transcend all of the creatures by an absolute transcendence, but the Father transcends the Son and Holy Spirit by proportionately more than they transcend all other beings.[105]

---

[103] *Com. Jn.* XIII. 25. 147–50. The significance of the ὁμοούσιος in patristic thought is a major issue connected with the theme of divine fatherhood, but it does not impinge directly on the analysis of fatherhood given in this study and so a general discussion of the term has not been included. Further comment on the term is made below, pp. 141 ff., with reference to Arius' attitude to it.

[104] Williams, *Arius*, pp. 134–5, who points out that Origen is concerned to refute what he perceives to be entailed in Valentinian thought, the notion that God is divisible and thus that he is material.

[105] This is part of the anti-Marcionist, anti-Gnostic theme that runs throughout the *Commentary on John* and is especially prominent in the early books. To stress the transcendence of the Son might allow the possibility that there is a God over

He follows this in 25. 152, the climax of his rebuttal of Heracleon's position and of the entire exegesis of John 4: 24, by returning to *Republic* 509B. He writes of the Son:

However, although he transcends by his being, his rank, his power, by his divinity—for he is the living Word—and his wisdom so many beings and so great, he is comparable in nothing with his Father.[106]

Origen has returned to the phrase from the *Republic*, but in an unexpected manner, doubly unexpected because he has subtly altered the wording of the phrase with the result that at first it might not be realized that the phrase echoes the question with which he begins his exegesis of the verse, and because he no longer applies it to the Father, but instead applies it to the Son. The Son does not transcend being, he transcends 'by' his being, which confirms the pattern we saw in the *Contra Celsum* passage, where the Son is 'being of beings'; and Origen adds to the phrase a number of the qualities which he commonly uses of the Son. Because the reader expects the phrase to be used once again of the Father, the attribution of it to the Son makes its impact even greater.

By applying the phrase to the Son, Origen avoids answering directly the question of whether or not God transcends being, which he had posed at the beginning of his analysis. It is notable that most of his exegesis of John 4: 24 is devoted to proving that God is incorporeal and does not touch on the question of the transcendence of being. Origen is able to make effective use of the phrase without committing himself to its appropriateness as a description of God. He skilfully manipulates it for his own purposes, in this case to refute the Gnostic materialist abuse of 'God is spirit'. The precise meaning of the phrase is not of direct interest to him, and he is not averse to altering it radically. It is a useful stick with which to beat the dog Heracleon.

whom the Son is superior, the creator God of the Old Testament. In *Com. Matt.* XV. 10, the distances are inverted; there Origen says that the Son transcends the creatures by much more than the Father transcends the Son.

[106] Ἀλλ' ὅμως τῶν τοσούτων καὶ τηλικούτων ὑπερέχων οὐσίᾳ καὶ πρεσβείᾳ καὶ δυνάμει καὶ θειότητι – ἔμψυχος γάρ ἐστι λόγος – καὶ σοφίᾳ, οὐ συγκρίνεται κατ' οὐδὲν τῷ πατρί.

The third instance of a reference to *Republic* 509B is in the *Commentary on John* XIX, where Origen is commenting on John 8: 19 'Jesus answered, "You know neither me nor my Father; if you knew me, you would know my Father also."' In contrast to the instances already studied, Origen does not here use the phrase for immediate polemical purposes; but, as with the instances in *Contra Celsum*, he does link it with the revelatory function of the Logos. His analysis of John 8: 19 takes up the first six chapters of the book. Chapter 5 contains one of the most important of his discussions on the fatherhood of God, which will be taken up later. In the sixth and concluding chapter, Origen develops the theme that it is only through the Son that one comes to know God.

In chapter 6, he outlines the stages in the knowledge of the Logos through which we pass in order to come to a knowledge of God. Our contemplation of the Son as the Logos brings us to the contemplation of God. Our contemplation of the Son as Wisdom brings us to know the Father of Wisdom. And our contemplation of the Son as Truth brings us 'to see being, or that which transcends being, namely, the power and nature of God' (ἐπὶ τὸ ἐνιδεῖν τῇ οὐσίᾳ ἢ τῇ ὑπερέκεινα τῆς οὐσίας δυνάμει καὶ φύσει τοῦ θεοῦ).[107] Origen then draws a parallel between the revelatory functions of Logos, Wisdom, and Truth, which he calls the higher degrees of the only-begotten, and those which he calls the lower, which are those associated with the Son's humanity.[108] The phrase from *Republic* 509B is thus embedded in a complex exegesis of Scripture, and it is used in support of the assertion of the exclusive nature of the Son's role as revealer of God. The words and general sense of the Platonic description have passed into Origen's theological vocabulary and he uses them virtually without reference to their philosophical context.

On the basis of these allusions to *Republic* 509B, Mortley claims that Origen demonstrates an 'unwillingness to decide on whether God is within or beyond being'. He describes this unwillingness as 'peculiar', and he concludes that the issue of 'God's relationship with οὐσία . . . is an embarrassment for Origen'.[109] Similarly,

---

[107] 6. 35–7.
[108] 6. 38–9.
[109] *From Word to Silence*, ii. 73–4.

Nautin writes of Origen's 'indecision' about whether or not God is above being, which he says was affected by the importance for Origen of Exodus 3: 14.[110] But these are anachronistic judgements, made in the light of later Neoplatonic speculation. They suggest a degree of self-consciousness about the relationship between God and being possessed by few, if any, of Origen's contemporaries.

Williams presents a more subtle interpretation of Origen's use of the idea that God transcends mind and being. He writes that Origen's use of the idea 'is a particularly clear instance of the rather uneasy relationship between the two controlling factors in Origen's thought: the given constraint of Scriptural metaphor and the assumptions of Platonic cosmology'.[111] But this still suggests that Origen had a greater and more systematic sense of issues that only later became important than is warranted by the evidence of his usage. Williams' language is guarded, but he implies that Origen's understanding of God's relationship to being developed over time: in his later years Origen 'might have wanted to emphasize the Father's transcendence of "being" (so that he would be *beyond ho ōn*)'.[112] Williams does not cite the evidence on which he bases this suggestion, but it presupposes a greater degree of deliberateness on Origen's part than the chronology of the texts permits.[113] The first instance of Origen's allusions to *Republic* 509B may be as early as 232, since *Commentary on John* XIII and XIX were probably written between 232 and 238. *De Martyrio* was probably written between 235 and 238. Only the two examples in *Contra Celsum*, which was probably written in 249, can be dated from his later years. Moreover, Origen uses the expression ὁ ὤν without qualification, and in a manner consistent with his earliest citations of the title, in the *Commentary on Matthew*,[114] which is thought to have been composed at the same time as *Contra Celsum*. Williams links Origen's use of the idea that God is above mind and being with the possibility that Origen believed that the

---

[110] '"Je suis celui qui est" (Exode 3,14) dans la théologie d'Origène', p. 119.
[111] *Arius*, p. 140.
[112] Ibid. 143.
[113] For the dates of composition see Nautin, *Origène*, pp. 410–12.
[114] *Com. Matt.* XVII. 36.

Son did not have a perfect knowledge of the Father. The discussion of the Father's knowledge of the Son, he says, 'trembles on the brink of the radical Plotinian solution'—the dropping of the idea of 'knowing' where the first principle is concerned.[115] But while Williams manages to show that in one passage, *Commentary on John* XXXII. 28, Origen seems to suggest that the Father's knowledge of himself is greater than the Son's, this is only one unclear example, and Origen does not refer to it in conjunction with the statement that God transcends mind and being. Williams' attempt to find a pattern in Origen's use of the idea that God is above mind and being which places Origen on the 'brink' of the Plotinian solution fails to appreciate the actual function of the idea in Origen's thought.

This is part of the larger question of how the overall shape of Origen's theology is to be characterized. There are themes that run throughout his writing and act to give it a general unity and coherence; God's incorporeality, his nature as Father, and the Logos as revealer are among the most important. But he does not systematically work out the relationship between the various elements in his understanding of the divine nature; the focus of any given discussion of God's transcendence of mind and being, as with many other issues, is greatly influenced by the particular context of the discussion. Origen never mentions Exodus 3: 14 and *Republic* 509B in the same passage. He never uses the noun οὐσία when he discusses Exodus 3: 14, and he never uses the participle ὁ ὤν when he refers to the Platonic phrase. He tends, rather, to use the words provided by the text he is citing. If the interpretation given here is correct, then Origen would not have seen a tension between the statement that God is 'he who is' and the statement that God 'transcends mind and being'. Indeed, it is possible that he thought of both as biblical concepts, the one found in Exodus 3: 14, and the other in Romans 1: 20. The infrequency with which Origen employs the phrase from *Republic* 509B, and the lack of specific analysis of it in his writings, suggest that it is not a major issue in his conception of God. It acts as a handmaiden to his emphasis on the unique revelatory function of the Son.

[115] *Arius*, pp. 206–7.

2

The Revelation of the Son
and the Names of God

ORIGEN is certain that we may come to a saving knowledge of
God's transcendent nature. But the reader must take care to note
that he distances himself from what he considers to be the positive
evaluation of human reason in Greek philosophy. He employs the
sceptical arguments of his Middle Platonist contemporaries to
bolster his contention that the human intellect cannot apprehend
truth on its own merits unaided by God's grace. Only through the
mediation of the Logos, the Holy Spirit, and the Scriptures may we
come to know God's nature and to know his names. The issue of
knowledge is integrally related both to ontology and to soteriology: through the acquisition of the knowledge of God the soul is
perfected and it is saved. Part of that saving knowledge is the
knowledge of God as Father.

The framework of Origen's conception of how we come to a
knowledge of God is Platonic. In *Contra Celsum* VII. 46, he
describes the journey of the soul to the perfect knowledge of God
in much the same terms as the Platonic ascent to a knowledge of
truth,[1] and he acknowledges that this description is correct
teaching even though it has come from non-Christian sources. As
we have seen, the soul progresses from sensible knowledge to
intelligible knowledge, and finally to the knowledge of that which
lies beyond the intelligible, the knowledge of God.[2] Such an ascent
Origen thinks is described in 2 Corinthians 4: 18: 'we look not at
the things that are seen, but at the things which are not seen; for
the things that are seen are temporal; but the things which are not

---

[1] *Symposium* 211C.
[2] VII. 46.

seen are eternal.'[3] The ultimate felicity and perfection of man is to gaze upon God 'face to face'.[4] This conception too is indebted to the Platonic tradition, where the felicity and perfection of the soul is attained when the soul is able to know the good in a direct and immediate way.[5] Origen, however, modifies this tradition: the final happiness of the soul lies not in the contemplation of the forms, but in the contemplation of the divine hypostases.[6]

The possibility of coming to know God through the ascent is grounded, for Origen, as for his Greek contemporaries, on the likeness between God's nature and man's; as we have seen,[7] both are intellect.[8] He accepts the traditional dictum that 'only like knows like'.[9] He expresses this in the formula 'the rational soul recognizes that which is akin to it',[10] and by citing 1 Corinthians 2. 11: 'No one can know the things of God unless he is of the Spirit of God'.[11] The human soul, liberated from the body, perfected and made like God, is able then to know God, according to whose image it was originally made.

But while Origen's view of knowledge is Platonic in hue, he sharply distinguishes the heart of his theory of knowledge from that of the Greeks. He makes his strongly negative attitude to Greek epistemology clear not only in the polemical context of the *Contra Celsum*, but in such other writings as the *Commentary on John* and *De Principiis*. Although he accepts the notion of the ascent of the soul, he does not accept the traditional Platonist understanding of how we are able to effect it.

He ignores the doctrine of recollection and he dismisses the theory of the ideas. Self-subsistent forms do not exist.[12] The ideas

---

[3] *C. Cel.* VI. 19–20.
[4] *DP* II. 6. 7.
[5] *Republic* 490B; *Symposium* 211E.
[6] Berchman, *From Philo to Origen*, p. 190.
[7] Above, pp. 23–5.
[8] See the discussions in *DP* I. 1. 7 and *De Martyrio* 47.
[9] *Phaedo* 79D. M. Harl, *Origène et la fonction révélatrice du verbe incarné* (Patristica Sorbonensia 2: Paris, 1958), 92 n. 90, cites examples of the dictum in Middle Platonist writings.
[10] *C. Cel.* III. 40.
[11] *C. Cel.* IV. 30.
[12] *DP* II. 3. 6. This is in accord with his desire to ensure that the three divine

are only mental images and the soul does not rediscover them through the process of recollection.

In *Contra Celsum* VII. 42–6, Origen undertakes a thorough repudiation of the Platonist epistemology of Celsus. There he formally states and then rejects the three methods for gaining knowledge of God outlined by Middle Platonist writers. The discussion follows on from his statement in VII. 38, that God 'is mind, or transcends mind and being'. Celsus' sceptical statements about the possibility of knowing and describing God were based on an amalgam of Platonic passages familiar to the Middle Platonists. In *Contra Celsum* VII. 42, Origen quotes a passage from Celsus in which Celsus, describing God as ineffable and nameless, refers to *Timaeus* 28C and the three epistemological ways. In VII. 45, he quotes another passage from Celsus which is based on the discussion of the good in the *Republic* and on the *Seventh Letter* 341C. Celsus' view of knowledge may also reflect the influence of *Parmenides* 142A.[13]

The Middle Platonist attitude to the limitations of human knowing is a correlate of their emphasis on God's transcendence. Mortley argues that the thought of Classical and Late Antiquity exhibits a decline in confidence in reason and language, and he argues that a negative theological method began to take shape in the period after Plato's death. This negative theological method is clearly present, if not fully developed, in the Middle Platonists.[14] Mortley and Whittaker, among others, maintain that this trend was fostered by the bringing together of the Platonic texts just mentioned. The picture of God as an absolute one, not having being and not existing in time, which resulted from the conjunction of these passages, meant that God was not subject to human discourse. The Middle Platonists commonly described God as ἄρρητος and ἀκατονόμαστος.[15] Origen too, as we have seen,

---

intellects be understood as uniquely self-subsistent. He argues strongly against any theory about the existence of the Son and the Holy Spirit which would reduce them to mere ideas and deny them existence as independent hypostases.

[13] Whittaker, "Ἄρρητος καὶ ἀκατονόμαστος", *Platonismus und Christentum*, pp. 303–6; repr. in his *Studies in Platonism and Patristic Thought*.

[14] See the whole of Mortley's *From Word to Silence*.

[15] See the discussion in Whittaker, "Ἄρρητος καὶ ἀκατονόμαστος", pp. 303–6.

thought of God as one and simple, beyond being, time and qualification, and he describes him as ineffable and unnameable.[16] But God is not an unknown God for Origen. He is known both to the Son and to the Holy Spirit.[17] Although the human mind by itself is not capable of knowing God directly, it can know God through the mediation of the other two divine hypostases.[18]

In his rebuttal of Celsus in *Contra Celsum* VII. 42–6, Origen sets out to establish that the Christians put forward a more radical claim about the unknowability of God than do the Greek philosophers so that he may then assert the unique revelatory function of the Son. He rejects Celsus' claim, made on the basis of *Timaeus* 28C, that Plato was 'a more effective teacher of the problems of theology' than Christ.[19] He argues that although Plato's statement is 'noble and impressive', it is inadequate because it assumes that the acquisition of an adequate knowledge of God lies within the natural capacity of human reason.[20] He is not interested in the negative theological drift of the overall pattern of the Platonic passages Celsus has brought together. He focuses, rather, on Celsus' interpretation of the *Timaeus* phrase and maintains that Celsus has misread it, making Plato appear to be doubtful about man's ability to know God. But Origen, reading with characteristic accuracy, correctly points out that *Timaeus* 28C assumes that some may gain a knowledge of God: Plato does not say that God is ineffable; God can be described, though he can be *declared* to only a few; it is the multitude who are unable to gain a knowledge that is worthy of God.[21]

Origen posits a double contrast between the Christian understanding of the knowledge of God and the Platonist. On the one

---

[16] In *C. Cel.* VII. 43 Origen describes God as nameless, and echoes Celsus' use of both terms. The phrase πότε δὲ ἡ τῆς ἀρρήτου καὶ ἀκατονομάστου καὶ ἀφθέγκτου ὑποστάσεως τοῦ πατρὸς εἰκών, ὁ χαρακτήρ, <ὁ> λόγος ὁ "γινώσκων τὸν πατέρα" οὐκ ἦν occurs in *DP* IV. 4. 1, fr. 33 (*De Decretis* 27, Opitz 23. 27–9). In *Com. Jn.* XXXII. 28. 18, he says that it is only possible to speak of God with ineffable words.

[17] *DP* I. 1. 8.
[18] *Com. Jn.* II. 10.
[19] *C. Cel.* VII. 42.
[20] Ibid.
[21] Ibid. 43.

hand, not only do the Christians maintain that God is nameless, but they also maintain that there are lesser beings who are nameless, and on the other hand, they maintain that 'anyone who looks at the image of the invisible God will come to know the Father and Maker of this universe'.[22] Because of the revelation of the Logos, it is possible to come to an adequate knowledge of God and that knowledge is not restricted to the few.

Both of these claims are based on Origen's belief that 'human nature is in no way sufficient for the search for God, or for finding him in an unsullied way unless aided by him who is being sought'.[23] Earlier, Origen, playing on the meaning of logos, makes an explicit contrast between human reason and the Logos. He writes that the 'reason that is in us' cannot apprehend God; but

because we have understood that 'in the beginning was the Logos, and the Logos was with God, and the Logos was God', we affirm that God is attainable by this reason, and is comprehended by him alone, but also by any man to whom he reveals the Father.[24]

It is through the initiative of God's grace alone that God may be known. God reveals himself to man; man does not from his own powers attain the knowledge of God. It is because of this that the knowledge of God is potentially accessible to all.

Given this understanding of the role of grace in coming to a knowledge of God, we should not be surprised that in *Contra Celsum* VII. 44 Origen dismisses the three methods for attaining a knowledge of God which Celsus had cited in conjunction with *Timaeus* 28C. The three methods, synthesis, analogy, and analysis, are a systematization of elements in Platonic and Neo-Pythagorean epistemological reflection. Albinus gives an explanatory account of the three in the *Epitome*.[25]

Origen has a sufficiently good knowledge of the philosophical tradition to be able accurately to gloss Celsus' reference to the methods by observing that these methods arose among the geo-

---

[22] *C. Cel.* VII. 43.
[23] Ibid. 42.
[24] Ibid. VI. 65.
[25] *Epitome* X. 5–6.

meters.[26] But, in spite of his desire to emphasize the transcendence of God, he himself makes no use of analysis as a method for gaining a knowledge of God, a method used by Clement of Alexandria[27] and which, according to Mortley, plays a central role in the development of a negative theology.[28] He does not use the method, because he thinks that it, like the other two, presupposes that man's reason is capable by itself of bringing one '"to the threshold of the Good"'.[29] He concludes his rejection of the three methods by putting forward his theological alternative:

When the Logos of God says that 'No man has known the Father except the Son, and the man to whom the Son may reveal him', he indicates that God is known by a certain grace which does not come about in the soul without God's action, but with a sort of inspiration.[30]

Origen sets aside the Greek philosophical tradition and puts in its place his Christian vision of revelation through the Logos.

Origen's treatment of Celsus' Platonist epistemology illustrates his general approach to Greek philosophy, which we have already seen in his use of *Republic* 509B. He has a perceptive understanding of the background to contemporary Middle Platonist thought and is quite capable of giving an accurate reading of the *Timaeus* passage. But he is uninterested in dealing systematically with Celsus' theory of knowledge; his interests are theological. He maintains that the problem of gaining a knowledge of God and describing him is more profound than Celsus allows and that the solution is more radical and far-reaching. He employs *Republic* 509B to heighten the sense of the transcendence of God, and thus of God's inaccessibility, so that he may then highlight the epistemological role of the Logos.

---

[26] See the comments of Colin Macleod, '$ANAΛΥΣΙΣ$: A Study in Ancient Mysticism', *JTS* NS 21 (1970), p. 54, and also his 'Contra Celsum 7: 42 (Note)', *JTS* NS 32 (1981), p. 447. Mortley, *From Word to Silence*, ii. 78–82, provides a summary of the literature in which the mathematical background of the methods is discussed.

[27] *Stromata* V. 11. 71. 2.

[28] *From Word to Silence*, ii. 78–82, and throughout the book.

[29] *Philebus* 64C, quoted in *C. Cel.* VII. 44.

[30] *C. Cel.* VII. 44.

Origen confirms his case against Greek thought with an assessment of the actual moral and religious behaviour which it produced. This assessment is significant because of the close relationship in Origen's thought between epistemology and soteriology: true knowledge is saving knowledge; it brings moral perfection to the soul. Origen employs the argument of Romans 1: 19–32 both to explain how it is possible that the philosophers were able to obtain knowledge about reality and to deny the ultimate adequacy of their comprehension of God. Such thinkers have abandoned the great truths that God has revealed to them. According to his interpretation of the Romans passage, the Greek philosophers were those for whom the invisible things of God have been visible since the creation of the world, but who nevertheless 'became vain in their reasoning; and their senseless heart wallows in darkness and ignorance where the worship of God is concerned'.[31] Plato, and other wise men among the Greeks, were worshippers of idols,[32] and thus, for Origen, their claims to a proper knowledge of God cannot possibly be true. Knowledge of God that is not affective is not true knowledge. It is not enough to possess a sophisticated philosophical education. The Greeks may 'at long intervals have received a limited conception of God', but they are to be contrasted with the Christians who, regardless of their intellectual abilities, 'have been inspired to a greater degree and have always remained with God and are continually being led by the divine Spirit'.[33]

Origen gives a schematic analysis of the relative worth of the philosophers' knowledge of God in the second book of the *Commentary on John*. He divides the rational beings into four groups on the basis of whom they worship as God, and he parallels this with their response to the Logos. The lowest class are those who, having fallen away not only from the good, but from any trace of it, and thus having virtually placed themselves outside the

---

[31] *C. Cel.* IV. 30 and VI. 4.

[32] Origen cites the account of Plato's journey to Piraeus to worship Artemis (*Republic* 327A) and Socrates' request that a cock should be sacrificed to Asclepius (*Phaedo* 118A) as examples (*C. Cel.* VI. 4).

[33] *C. Cel.* VII. 51

Logos, worship 'soulless and dead idols'.[34] The third class are those who, giving themselves to reasoning, and thus having a share in the Logos, worship the sun and the moon. These Origen identifies as members of the philosophical schools of the Greeks. The second class are those who, thinking that the Word made flesh is all there is to know about the Logos, worship the Son of God. These are the great majority of faithful Christians. The first class are those who, having perceived that the Logos, because he was with God in the beginning, is eternal, worship the Father.[35]

It is evident that although Origen thinks that the Greek philosophers participate in the Logos, he is convinced that their share in the Logos is inadequate to bring them to a saving knowledge of God. One must go beyond their limited perception of the Logos and ascend to the perception of the eternal Logos, and so to a knowledge of God. This ascent can only take place as one's soul is made perfect, and as one consequently worships God in a manner that is worthy of him.

The Logos' ability to mediate saving knowledge of God comes from his unique status as the one who alone knows the Father and is himself the image of God. In *Contra Celsum* VI. 17, Origen gives a summary of the Son's unique knowledge of God: 'absolute understanding and knowledge of the Father is possessed by [the Logos] alone'. God is not comprehended by any other being than the one who is in the image of the mind which is God.[36] The Logos is 'God's wisdom and truth' who 'takes away from the Father what is called darkness'. Through 'participation in him . . . anyone whatever who has the capacity to know him may do so'.[37] It is as the 'image of God's substance or subsistence' that the Son mediates to man knowledge and understanding of God.[38]

Origen identifies three distinct forms of the mediating activity of the Logos: the pre-incarnate coming of the Logos, the incarnation itself, and the present self-disclosure of the Logos, all of which are

---

[34] He says that such people deny providence and he may have had the Stoics in mind.
[35] *Com. Jn.* II. 3. 27–33.
[36] *C. Cel.* VII. 38.
[37] *C. Cel.* VI. 17.
[38] *DP* I. 2. 7–8.

conveyed by the Bible.[39] He refers to all three in a passage in the *Homilies on Jeremiah:*

The coming of our Lord Jesus Christ recorded by history was a coming in the flesh, a coming for all, which illuminated the entire world, for 'the Word became flesh and dwelt among us', he 'was the true light that enlightens every man who comes into the world; he was in the world and the world was made through him, yet the world knew him not. He came unto his own home, and his own people received him not.' It is necessary also to understand that he came in the beginning, though not bodily, to each of the saints. And after his visible coming he again comes to us. . . . It is necessary for us to know these things because there is, especially for those who would profit from it, a coming of the Logos to each individual. For what profit is it to me, if the Logos comes to the whole world but I do not possess him?[40]

The incarnation is the central and paradigmatic form of the mediating activity of the Logos. But prior to the incarnation, the Logos revealed himself to the Old Testament saints. In the present, following the incarnation, the Logos discloses himself through the spiritual sense of Scripture.[41] The work of the Logos is the guiding of fallen souls back to their original state of perfect knowledge of God, and the scope of that work is universal.[42]

In taking on flesh, the Logos makes known God's divine nature in a way that is apprehensible to all:

God is absolutely one and simple, but our Saviour, on account of the multiplicity of things, whom 'God put forward as an expiation' [Rom. 3: 25] and the first fruits of all creation, became many things and perhaps everything that each creature capable of redemption needs from him.[43]

The Logos 'traverses the ontological distance between God and man'.[44] Through his pre-incarnate revelation, and especially

---

[39] See the discussion in Torjesen, *Hermeneutical Procedure*, pp. 113–18.

[40] *Hom. Jer.* IX. 1.

[41] Torjesen, *Hermeneutical Procedure*, p. 114.

[42] Ibid. 71–2. In the light of Origen's thinking about fatherhood, this statement needs qualification, as will become clear below. Origen seems to have thought that the knowledge of God as Father to which we ascend is greater than that which we possessed in our original state.

[43] *Com. Jn.* I. 20. 119.

[44] Torjesen, *Hermeneutical Procedure*, p. 115.

through the prism of the incarnation, the Logos refracts the undivided nature of God into many aspects (ἐπίνοιαι) so that they can be apprehended by us. Each of the titles of Christ conveys an aspect of God.[45] These aspects become clearly visible for the first time in the incarnation and thus it becomes possible to imitate God's attributes and to come to resemble him.[46] In his many aspects, the incarnate Logos accommodated himself as mediator to fit the spiritual condition of each person.[47]

As the Logos himself is eternal, so also is his mediatorship. The Logos who became incarnate is the same Logos who revealed himself to the Old Testament saints. This theme is found throughout Origen's writings and is part of his ongoing polemic against Marcion. The eternal continuity of the Logos' function as revealer of God testifies to the continuity of identity between the God of the Old Testament and the God of the New. The Old Testament saints possessed a knowledge of the Logos which is analogous to the knowledge of those who were present with Christ at the time of the incarnation. Origen argues that the saints of the Old Testament knew the teachings of God because, through their participation in the pre-incarnate Christ, on account of which they are called 'those who are', they had been taught by Christ before he came in the flesh.[48]

[They] received not only the appearance of Angels, but also the appearing of God in Christ, and perhaps having seen the image of the invisible God, since he who has seen the Son has seen the Father, they have known God and understood the words of God in a manner worthy of him. That is why it is written of them that they have seen God and they have understood him. . . . It is clear that Moses saw in his mind the truth of the Law and that he saw, according to the anagogical sense, the allegories of the histories that were recorded by him.[49]

Those among the people of the Old Testament who were morally

---

[45] Origen deals at length with the titles of Christ in *Com. Jn.* I. 20–39.
[46] *Com. Jn.* XIX. 23.
[47] *Com. Jn.* I. 20. 124.
[48] *Com. Jn.* VI. 4. 17.
[49] Ibid. 4. 19–22.

pure were able to see what the apostles saw when the Logos came in the flesh.

Before turning to the third of Origen's three forms of the mediation of the Logos—the present disclosure of himself to us in the spiritual meaning of the Bible—it would be helpful to give a brief description of Origen's doctrine of the Bible. It is for him the source of the saving doctrines of God; and it both describes God and gives us the names of God. He makes the central place that the Bible occupies in his doctrine of knowledge clear in the first sentence of the preface to *De Principiis*. He begins by stating the basic principle of his theology: truth comes from Christ alone, for he is the truth, and those who acquire the truth acquire it 'from no other source than the words and teaching of Christ'.[50] These words and teaching are found nowhere else than in the Old and New Testaments.[51]

The books of the law and the prophets are the record of the encounter of the Old Testament saints with the pre-incarnate Logos;[52] the writings of the New Testament are the record of the encounter of the disciples with the incarnate Logos.[53] 'Having drawn the intelligible from the historical,' the New Testament writers 'teach us through signs the things [concerning God] which they contemplated with their minds.'[54] They wrote with the intention of disclosing the Logos for our benefit.[55] The spiritual meaning of the Scriptures is the doctrines about God, which were communicated to the prophets and the apostles by the Logos and the Holy Spirit, and which we can now grasp through the proper reading of the biblical texts.

Both the Old and New Testaments were inspired by the Holy Spirit,[56] who revealed the 'unspeakable mysteries'[57] of God to their authors. The prophets and the apostles were able to

---

[50] *DP* Pref. 1.
[51] Ibid. 2.
[52] See the quotation from *Com. Jn.* VI. 4. 19–22 above.
[53] *Com. Jn.* X. 4. 15–17.
[54] *Com. Jn.* X. 5. 18.
[55] Torjesen, *Hermeneutical Procedure*, p. 111.
[56] *DP* IV. 2. 2.
[57] *Hom. on Josh.* XXIII. 4.

apprehend the mysteries of God's divine nature because of their moral purity and the constancy of the Holy Spirit's presence with them. Moses is the great exemplar of this: he had a 'pure and pious soul' in which 'dwelt a divine spirit which showed the truth about God far more clearly than Plato and the wise men among the Greeks and barbarians.'[58] The living of morally pure lives is correspondingly also a necessary precondition for coming in the present to a correct perception of the doctrines of God that are contained within the biblical text.

Origen's high view of the inspiration of Scripture, however, takes him beyond the affirmation that the Bible conveys a know-ledge of the doctrines of God. Notwithstanding his belief in God's ineffability, he is convinced that the words of the Bible actually describe God. His comments on the Bible and the describability of God, although numerous, are brief and unsystematic. Neverthe-less, it is possible to come to a general sense of his understanding of the relationship between language and the nature of God.

Origen, like his philosophical contemporaries, tends not to make a clear distinction between the question of God's describa-bility and that of his knowability.[59] Inasmuch as we may know God through the Logos, we may also describe him. But if we are to describe his nature accurately, we must describe him with the words he has given to us in the Scriptures. Mortley, however, reaches the opposite conclusion about Origen's attitude to God's describability. He maintains that while Origen thinks that God is accessible to the human mind, Origen also thinks that God is 'incommunicable in language'.[60] He acknowledges that much of the evidence he cites simply demonstrates that Origen believes that the mystical doctrines were intentionally hidden from the multitude of believers. But, he says, 'side by side with the idea that concealment is a deliberate practice, stands the view that the

---

[58] *C. Cel.* I. 19. The status of Moses as the inspired witness to the divine truths is an important theme in Origen's defence of the credibility of the Christian faith in *Contra Celsum*.

[59] In *C. Cel.* VII. 42, Origen treats Celsus' statement that God is unnameable and ineffable in terms of whether or not God can be known.

[60] *From Word to Silence*, ii. 84.

transcendence of things renders them inexpressible in any case'.[61]

In support of this, Mortley points to Origen's frequent references to Paul's statement in 2 Corinthians 12: 4 that the man caught up into paradise 'heard unspeakable words which it is not lawful to utter' (ἤκουσεν ἄρρητα ῥήματα ἃ οὐκ ἐξὸν ἀνθρώπῳ λαλῆσαι).[62] He argues, for example, that when Origen cites 2 Corinthians 12: 4 in *Contra Celsum* VII. 43 as proof that the Christian conception of God's ineffability is more radical than that of the Greeks and interpets 'heard' to mean 'understood', he does so in order not to imply that what Paul has experienced can be expressed in language.[63] But Origen's concern to gloss the Pauline phrase in the passage is more appropriately to be understood as an example of his attitude to biblical anthropomorphisms, and not as a negative comment on the capacity of language to express transcendent realities. A few sections earlier, in *Contra Celsum* VII. 35, he had been arguing that biblical references to man's 'hearing' and 'seeing' God are to be interpreted spiritually and not literally. This is a recurring concern for Origen.[64] Here in *Contra Celsum* VII. 43, he is not directly interested in the issue of language. He subsumes the question of God's ineffability under that of his knowability,[65] and ensures in passing that his Pauline proof text does not open him to the charge of being a naïve reader of the Bible.

Commenting on 2 Corinthians 12: 4 in *Homilies on Joshua*, Origen attributes the impossibility of speaking of the 'ineffable mysteries' to the fact that Paul's listeners would not understand them. They would fail, not because it is impossible to put such mysteries into human language, but because they do not live holy lives. By contrast, such figures as Timothy, Luke, and the other disciples, who did not live according to the ways of men, but lived

---

[61] Ibid. ii. 68.

[62] Origen assumes that it was Paul himself who was caught up to paradise. See e.g. *De Martyrio* 13.

[63] *From Word to Silence*, ii. 68.

[64] He refers to the issue when he discusses the voice of God in *C. Cel.* VI. 62, which will be considered below, pp. 57–8.

[65] This is true also of Origen's reference to 2 Cor. 12: 4 in *De Principiis* II. 7. 4, which Mortley, *From Word to Silence*, ii. 66–7, also cites in support of his argument.

lives of purity, were capable of receiving the 'ineffable mysteries'.[66] The capacity to understand the 'ineffable mysteries' is
dependent on our moral condition; it is not inherently impossible
for God to be described in the language of men.[67]

Through the Logos, then, man may know God's transcendent
being and describe it. But Origen goes further than this. He
suggests that the Son not only gives man the ability to describe
God, but that he also gives man the actual words with which to
make the description. Although he does not develop this line of
thought to a great extent, it follows from his understanding of the
status of the language of the Bible and the names of God which the
Bible contains.

Origen remarks that only God and the Son are capable of
thinking and saying the ineffable words concerning God; man's
attempts are inadequate.[68] But such ineffable words God gave to
the writers of the Bible. Origen gives us a glimpse of how he
imagines that God communicated to the prophets and apostles in a
charming, if not entirely conclusive, passage in which he discusses
the voice from heaven that spoke at the baptism of Christ and at
the transfiguration.[69] He is at pains to establish that the voice,
which he identifies as the voice of God, should not be considered a
physical phenomenon. He notes that the textbooks define speech
as 'vibrated air, or a percussion of air, or a kind of air', and
concludes that if this were the only way to define it, God could not
be said to have a voice, since God has no physical characteristics.[70]
But he is not prepared to abandon the idea that God has a voice.

He gets around the problem by arguing that God's voice is not a
physical phenomenon, but a spiritual one. He says of the transfiguration that 'the voice out of the cloud on the very high
mountain was heard only by the men who went up with him', not
because of their physical proximity to the voice, but because 'the

---

[66] *Hom. on Josh.* XXIII. 4.

[67] Henri Crouzel, *Origène et la 'Connaissance Mystique'* (Museum Lessianum,
Section Théologique 56: Paris, 1961), pp. 37–8 and 116, comes to a similar
conclusion.

[68] *Com. Jn.* XXXII. 28. 18.

[69] *C. Cel.* II. 72.

[70] *C. Cel.* VI. 62.

divine voice is such that it is heard only by those whom the speaker wishes to hear it'. He goes on to attempt to make clear how this speaking and hearing took place:

the utterance of God is heard by a superior sense, more divine than physical hearing. And since, when God speaks, he does not want his voice to be audible to all, a man who has superior hearing hears God, whereas a man who has become hard of hearing in his soul does not perceive that God is speaking.[71]

Elsewhere, quoting his version of Proverbs 2: 5 'You will find a divine sense',[72] Origen explains that there is a divine sense which the 'blessed', who are the prophets and the apostles, had on earth. This divine sense not only allowed them to hear spiritually, but also to see and taste spiritually. It was through this divine sense, 'a sense which was not a sense', that Isaiah and Ezekiel saw and heard what they recorded in the Bible as having seen and heard, and it was through this sense that Paul, because he was a disciple, saw the heavens opened and was caught up into them.[73]

In spite of the fact that Origen is forced to resort to a contorted account of the divine voice in order to protect the incorporeality of God, he refuses to give up his belief that God has a voice, that he spoke and was heard, and that his words are recorded in the Bible. He makes no suggestion that language has been superseded in the divine communication. However much Origen wants to protect the divine incorporeality, he is nevertheless certain that God's communication with the saints—those who participated in the Logos before and during the incarnation—was real, and that the Scriptures are an accurate testimony to that communication.

Origen's understanding of the relationship between God's self-disclosure and the words of the Bible is supported by a high doctrine of language and the significance of names. In the course of his discussions on the names of God in the Bible, he remarks more than once on the complexity of the issue of the status of names. He is aware of three theories of language, the Aristotelian,

---

[71] *C. Cel.* II. 72.
[72] Cf. above, p. 25 and n. 65.
[73] *C. Cel.* I. 48.

the Stoic, and the Epicurean, and he specifically rejects the Aristotelian theory that the relation between words and reality is a matter of arbitrary human convention.[74] He maintains that there is an intrinsic relationship between a name and the thing it names. Commenting on 'hallowed be thy name' in his analysis of the Lord's prayer, Origen says that a name manifests the individual quality of that which it names. Thus as the quality of a man changes, so also his name changes: Simon becomes Peter, Saul becomes Paul.[75] The same is true of the names of God. But since God, unlike man, is unchanging, so is his name. The name that Origen singles out in *On Prayer* is ὤν of Exodus 3: 14.[76] He allows that there might be more than one name for God, but the names must have the same meaning.

Because of the intrinsic relationship between a name and that which it denotes, and the ability of a name to manifest the particular quality that makes a thing what it is, it is important that we use the proper names for God. These names are found in the Bible: 'The supreme God ought not to be invoked by any name except those used by Moses and the prophets and our Saviour and Lord himself.'[77] Origen mentions various names in his writings,[78] and, with reference to Psalm 2: 2, he may have drawn up a list of the ten Hebrew names for God used in the Bible.[79] The name 'he who is' had particular significance for him, as we have seen, because he saw it specifically as a self-designation of God and because of the central place occupied in his doctrine of God by the concept of God as being itself. Except for 'he who is', he does not explain what the biblical names tell us about God. Nevertheless, he regards the names of God and the descriptions of God used by the saints of the Old and New Testaments as actual descriptions of God's essence, and not just descriptions of God's energies as they

---

[74] *C. Cel.* I. 24 and V. 45.

[75] *On Prayer* 24. 2.

[76] On the form of the reference to the Exodus verse in *On Prayer* 24. 2 see above, p. 33, n. 93.

[77] *De Martyrio* 46.

[78] For instance he defends the use of Adonai and Sabaoth in *C. Cel.* I. 24 and V. 45.

[79] Nautin, '"Je suis celui qui est"', pp. 109–10, thinks that this list can be reconstructed from Epiphanius, *Panarion* 40. 5 and Jerome, *Epistle* 25.

are revealed in history. The Logos truly mediates the truth of God's transcendent nature to us through the Bible and we may clearly apprehend it through a proper reading of the Bible. As we shall see when we come to his conception of God as Father, Origen also believes that the word Father is a name for God.

Origen, however, is not naïve about the difficulties involved in reading the Bible in such a way that one is able to perceive the spiritual meanings that lie behind its literal sense. As we have seen, he is acutely sensitive to the problem of over-simple readings of the text. He allows that while the prophets of the Old Testament and the writers of the Gospels recorded their encounters with the Logos, their knowledge of the Logos was conditioned by the limits of time and space and by the limits of their spiritual progress.[80] Their participation in him was only partial; consequently they were only able to give a partial presentation of the Logos in their writings, although they agree with each other in their witness to 'the true things about God and about his acts of goodness towards some'.[81] And just as the Logos accommodated himself to match the spiritual state of each soul, so also the language of the Bible is accommodated to the degree of spiritual understanding of men.[82] The very diversity of types of texts and the doctrines contained in them makes the Bible suitable to the diversity of spiritual needs among its readers.

Having looked at Origen's doctrine of Scripture, we are now in a position to understand more fully the third form of the Logos' mediating activity, the present disclosure of himself to us in the spiritual meaning of the Bible. The Logos revealed himself in history to the biblical saints, and he comes to us now through the Scriptures. Torjesen observes that for Origen, 'the content of Scripture is nothing other than the Logos incarnate in language, for the doctrines in Scripture disclose each in a partial and progressive or sequential way the nature of the Logos who is fully disclosed in his incarnation.'[83] The spiritual sense of the text is

---

[80] *Com. Jn.* X. 4. 15–17.
[81] X. 4. 17.
[82] *Hom. on Jer.* XVIII. 6.
[83] *Hermeneutical Procedure*, p. 120.

both teaching about the Logos and the present Logos teaching; he comes to the soul in the teaching of both the Old and the New Testaments[84] and offers himself in a form in which he can be received.

Origen follows a pattern of four steps in the exegesis of a passage of Scripture. The four steps are: first, the identification of the grammatical sense; second, the identification of the historical situation to which the grammatical sense refers—the first two steps together constituting the literal sense of the text; third, the identification of the spiritual teaching of the Logos, revealed to the inspired writer who recorded it in the figurative form of the narratives of events; and fourth, the incorporation of the reader into the spiritual meaning through the use of the first person plural or the second person singular or plural. The latter two constitute the spiritual meaning of the text.[85] The Christian's encounter with the Logos in the spiritual meaning of the Bible takes place within the context of the church as it is engaged in the exposition of Scripture.[86]

Through the progressive apprehension of the spiritual meaning of the Scriptures, and the saving doctrines that are contained in them, the soul is brought step by step to a knowledge of the divine mysteries. This progressive apprehension is accompanied by the three-stage development in the soul. The first stage in the soul's journey is marked by purification from sin. This allows the soul in the second stage to receive the wisdom and knowledge of the Logos through participation in him. The third stage in the journey is participation in God the Father. This participation in the perfection of God entails the perfection of the soul, its complete likeness to God, its divinization. The soul achieves this by the imitation of the virtues and knowledge of God.[87] The imitation of

---

[84] Ibid. 135. Torjesen demonstrates how this conception of the presence of the Logos in Scripture shapes Origen's exegetical procedure in *Hermeneutical Procedure*, pp. 124–38.

[85] Torjesen, 'Hermeneutics and Soteriology', pp. 343–4.

[86] *Hom. on Lev.* IX. 7.

[87] *DP* IV. 4. 10, and often elsewhere. Reference to similar passages will be made in the discussion of Origen's understanding of the relation between fatherhood and salvation.

God remakes the original likeness to God in which the soul was created and that likeness is the ground of a perfect knowledge of him.[88] Because God comes to us through the mediation of the Logos in Scripture, as Father, Son, and Holy Spirit, we are enabled to arrive at a full and immediate knowledge of God, a knowledge that is face to face.[89]

Origen is unclear about how far he thinks the soul is able to progress in the knowledge of God while it is in the body,[90] and he is not clear about whether it is possible to acquire the perfect knowledge of God in this life, or whether it is possible only once the soul has left the body.[91] Nevertheless, as the presentation in this chapter has shown, it is clear that Origen believes that through the agency of the Holy Spirit and the Logos, and their revelation in the Bible, God may be known, and that he may be known in no other way. Properly read, the Bible gives us a knowledge of God that ultimately is a knowledge of his transcendent nature. We may know the ineffable mysteries of God and the names of God; we may come to see 'being or that which transcends being, the power and nature of God'.[92]

---

[88] See the summary of Torjesen, *Hermeneutical Procedure*, pp. 71–2.

[89] *DP* III. 6. 1; *Com. Jn.* I. 16. 91–2.

[90] Harl, *Origène*, pp. 303–4, thinks that for Origen the saints, who live pure lives and love their enemies, are able to have a full vision in this life. She remarks that such people 'have arrived in spirit at the end of time'.

[91] e.g. Origen's discussion of Paul being caught up to paradise in *De Martyrio* 13. Those who die as martyrs will see greater mysteries than Paul, who was still in the body and returned to earth.

[92] *Com. Jn.* XIX. 6. 37.

3

Eternal Father and Eternal Son

THE fatherhood of God is integral to the overall pattern of Origen's theological vision. The title Father describes the divine being, and the divine fatherhood is something that we may come to know. More than that, such a knowledge is the promise of salvation. There are two points of particular focus for his understanding of God as Father: the relation between the Father and the Son, which will be discussed in this chapter, and the relation between the Father and those adopted as sons, the subject of the following chapter.

The Father–Son relation is the means by which creation is brought into being and it is also both the means and the model for the subsequent restoration of that creation to the knowledge of God, a restoration that entails our coming to sonship and the knowledge of God as Father. The Father–Son relation is distinct from the relation between God and his creation. Origen's thinking about God as Father is set against the background of the Marcionite claim that the creator God of the Old Testament is not the same as the God who is called Father in the New Testament.

It would appear that for Origen the fact that God is Father is a given datum of the Christian faith. Although he nowhere states that this is the case, such a supposition accounts for the fact that while references to God as Father abound in his writings and his writings are replete with biblical quotations in which God is called Father, he never engages in an attempt to establish the reality that God is Father. He does not discuss the nature of the divine fatherhood in abstraction from either his doctrine of the Trinity or his doctrine of salvation. The issues that arise for Origen concerning God's fatherhood mainly pertain to how that fatherhood is to be thought about in the light of two other accepted realities of the Christian faith: the generation of the Son and the adoption of Christians as sons.

There is, for instance, no discussion of the idea of God as Father in *Contra Celsum*, which suggests that the attribution of the word to God was not a matter of controversy between Middle Platonism and Christianity. The term is not treated as an anthropomorphism, needing to be explained, by either Celsus or Origen. Celsus himself had inherited the practice of describing God as Father in the words of *Timaeus* 28C,[1] and he does not include the use of the word Father for God among the instances of literalist readings of biblical images that he cites against Christianity. His difficulty with the Christian faith is not that it claims that God is Father, but that it claims that God has a Son who became incarnate.

Origen recognizes that both Christians and Greeks use the word Father to describe God and makes nothing of it. In the *Homilies on Genesis*, he observes that rational philosophy confesses that 'God is the Father of all' and goes on, without saying anything about the occurrence of Father in the phrase, simply to make the point that all right-thinking Greeks acknowledge the existence of God.[2] His presentation of God as Father, especially in relation to adoption, however, suggests that he distanced Christianity from what he took to be the meaning that the Greeks ascribed to Father as a title for God. We shall return to this when when we come to Origen's conception of fatherhood and salvation.

The common acceptance of the reality of the fatherhood of God may partly account for the fact that Origen does not discuss the topic in the opening chapter of *De Principiis*. The belief that God is Father is not one of the unresolved issues of Christian tradition that he says in the preface that he intends to clarify. As we have seen,[3] the more reliable title for the chapter is *De deo*, and not περὶ πατρός; God is referred to as Father only twice in the chapter, other than in biblical quotations, both times in conjunction with references to the Son.[4] The discussion of fatherhood is reserved for

---

[1] *C. Cel.* VII. 42.
[2] *Hom. on Gen.* XIV. 3.
[3] Above, pp. 10–13.
[4] *DP* I. 1. 1 and 8.

the second chapter, and it is only there that Origen begins as a matter of course to refer to God as Father.

The same pattern is also found in the credal summary in the preface to *De Principiis*. In setting out the 'doctrines which are believed in plain terms through the apostolic teaching',[5] Origen begins with a statement concerning the one God, the Creator, whom he identifies as the God of the Old Testament. But it is only with his first reference to Christ that he describes God with the word Father. With anti-Marcionite intent, he calls the creator God of the Old Testament 'this just and good God, the Father of our Lord Jesus Christ'.[6] He continues to describe God as Father in the second section of the summary, which deals with the Son, and in the third, which deals with the Holy Spirit.

The two instances of Origen's use of the expression 'the Father' in *De Principiis* I. 1, and his references to the Son and Holy Spirit, show that however sparingly he refers to God as Father in the chapter, the subject of the analysis nevertheless is the God who, for Origen, is indisputably Father. But it is also evident that he did not feel the need to discuss God's nature as Father in relationship to his nature as incorporeal, as mind, and as the simple and one immutable first principle, the topics that he deals with in the first chapter of *De Principiis*. Neither did he feel the need to relate the description of God as Father systematically to the description of him as good, as 'he who is', and as the one who transcends mind and being. This reflects the general shape of his theology. He works with a number of basic assumptions about God's nature, which he does not attempt to draw together into a comprehensive doctrine of God.

Origen makes his most systematic comments about the fatherhood of God in the course of his discussions of the Father–Son relation. The most concentrated of these discussions takes place in the second chapter of *De Principiis* and others are found scattered throughout his works. Just as the first had dealt with the metaphysical status of God, the second deals with the metaphysical status of the one who is God's Son. The Son's status is determined

---

[5] *DP* Pref. 4.
[6] Ibid.

by his relation to the Father. In *De Principiis* I. 2, Origen examines the nature of the Son's relation to the Father, his generation, and his existence. In the analysis given here, the structure of Origen's presentation of the generation of the Son will be looked at first, and then its significance for Origen's understanding of the divine fatherhood will be discussed. That will be followed by a discussion of his doctrine of the Son.

Origen's primary purpose in *De Principiis* I. 2 is not to prove that a divine Son exists, but rather 'to see what the only-begotten Son of God is'.[7] As with the fatherhood of God, the belief that there exists an only-begotten Son of the Father is not a matter for doubt for Origen. He claims that, although the philosophers, both Greek and barbarian, generally dismiss the belief that God has a Son, some, in their concept of a creative Logos, have held a belief in the existence of a Son.[8] As he conceives it, he has two purposes in the second chapter of *De Principiis*: to show that the Christian understanding of the generation of the Son is compatible with the attributes of God discussed in the first chapter of the work, and to show that this birth places the Son in a unique relationship to the Father, a relationship which is integral to God's nature as Father. In order to achieve the first of these purposes, he argues that the manner of the Son's generation is to be thought of as both incorporeal and eternal. The argument entails the affirmation of the eternity of God's fatherhood.

He begins his presentation of 'what the only-begotten Son of God is' by arguing that the existence of the Son is hypostatic. After having identified the Son with the figure of Wisdom in Proverbs 8: 22–5 and the first-born in Colossians 1: 15 in the first section of the chapter, he moves in the second section to preclude one erroneous conclusion that might be thought to follow from the identification of the Son with Wisdom: the conclusion that the Son does not have hypostatic existence. Wisdom, he maintains, is a 'living soul',[9] and

---

[7] I. 2. 1.

[8] *DP* I. 3. 1; *Hom. on Gen.* XIV. 3.

[9] Origen uses similar expressions elsewhere, e.g. *Com. Jn.* I. 19. 115, and I. 34. 244, where he describes Wisdom as living (ἔμψυχος). In the latter example he is arguing for the idea of Wisdom as an ἀσώματος ὑπόστασις.

not simply a device for bestowing the knowledge of truth.[10] He must then explain what characteristics this hypostatic existence has which allow it to be compatible with the nature of the Father.

He first eliminates the possibility that the recognition of the hypostatic existence of the Son could be taken to mean that the Son is a corporeal existent:

If then it is once rightly accepted that the only-begotten Son of God is God's wisdom hypostatically existing, I do not think that our mind ought to stray beyond this to the suspicion that this hypostasis or substance could possibly possess bodily characteristics, since everything that is corporeal is distinguished by shape or colour or size.[11]

Just as it is important that the incorporeal should not be denied substantial existence, so it is important that substantial existence should not be considered to be corporeal.

It is at this point in his discussion that Origen introduces the concept of the eternal generation of the Son.[12] The concept is crucial to his understanding of the fatherhood of God: it is essential to his argument for the eternity of the divine fatherhood, to his belief that the Father–Son relation is distinct from and metaphysically prior to the relation between God and creation, and to his affirmation of the eternity of God's goodness and creative power. In the immediate context of the discussion in *De Principiis* I. 2. 2, the concept demonstrates the closeness in nature of the Son to the Father while at the same time maintaining the Son's distinct existence.

The generation of the Son must be timeless. As we have already seen,[13] for Origen the concept of eternity is integral to the logic of incorporeality and immutability. Time applies to the realm of becoming and not to the realm of being. The Father, Son, and

---

[10] This statement matches the argument for the hypostatic existence of the Holy Spirit in *DP* I. 1. 3. His affirmation is directed against the Modalists and possibly also against the Valentinians. For a discussion of Origen's opponents, see Crouzel, *Traité des principes*, ii. 33 n. 6. The Son's real individual existence is one of the main themes of Origen's theology.

[11] *DP* I. 2. 2.

[12] *DP* I. 2. 2. See also the discussions in *DP* I. 2. 9; IV. 4. 1; *Hom. on Jer.* IX. 4; *Com. Jn.* I. 29. 204; II. 1. 8–9.

[13] Above, p. 24.

Holy Spirit, as incorporeal, are eternal and the relations that exist between them must also be eternal. But Origen acknowledges the difficulty in finding a way to speak about the eternal generation of the Son that does not imply temporality. Commenting on the statement 'there never was a time when he did not exist',[14] he attributes a non-temporal sense to tensed verbs when they are used of the Trinity:

For the very words, when, or never, have a temporal significance, whereas the statements we make about the Father and the Son and the Holy Spirit must be understood as transcending all time and all ages and all eternity. For it is this Trinity alone which exceeds all comprehension, not only of temporal but even of eternal intelligence. The rest of things, however, which are external to the Trinity, must be measured by ages and periods of time.[15]

He goes on to link this with the idea of the Son's incorporeality: to say that the Word was 'in the beginning' is not to be taken to mean that the Word is located in space, since that is impossible for an incorporeal existent.[16]

In the *Commentary on John*, Origen argues that the phrase 'in the beginning was the Word' should not be taken in a temporal sense. Rather, it means that the Son is in the beginning by virtue of his being in the Father. The Father is the absolute ἀρχή of all that exists; he is the ἀρχή of the Son; he is the creator, the ἀρχή of his works.[17] While this confirms the eternal generation of the Son and his closeness to the Father, it also testifies to the Father's character as the first principle who is the source of all existence.

---

[14] *DP* IV. 4. 1. Possible parallels to this phrase are found in the Hebrews fragment, Lommatzsch, xxiv. 328; in *De Decretis* 27, Opitz 23. 24–5; and in a fragment on Romans, Lommatzsch vi. 22–3. Williams, *Arius*, 296, n. 177, thinks that the third is the most suspect of the three. The phrase may be Rufinus', but it could plausibly be Origen's since it fits the logic of his argument for the eternal generation of the Son.

[15] Ibid. He remarks on the problem with reference to the Holy Spirit in *DP* I. 3. 4. Plato discusses the relation between eternity, time, and creation in *Timaeus* 37C-38B, where he says that it is only possible to employ expressions like 'was' and 'will be' once time has begun, but he finds it difficult to avoid them and freely uses them in describing pre-cosmic reality. See Sorabji, *Time, Creation and the Continuum*, pp. 114–15.

[16] *DP* IV. 4. 1–2.

[17] *Com. Jn.* I. 17. 102.

The assertion of the eternity of the Son's generation leads Origen directly on to the implications of this for the nature of God, and in particular the nature of God as Father. 'Can anyone', he asks, 'who has learned to regard God with feelings of reverence suppose or believe that God the Father ever existed, even for a single moment, without begetting this Wisdom?',[18] and he makes clear the disastrous consequences for the divine fatherhood entailed in the denial of the Son's eternal existence: 'Let him who assigns a beginning to the Word of God or the Wisdom of God beware lest he utters impiety against the unbegotten Father himself, in denying that he was always a Father.'[19] Fatherhood is part of God's eternal nature.

For Origen what is said of God must be eternally true. Given that God is Father, he must always have been Father. Basic to his argument is his assumption that Father and Son are correlative terms. As he explains in *De Principiis* I. 2. 10, 'one cannot be a father apart from having a son'. He is thus able to conclude in the *Dialogue with Heraclides* that to deny the distinct existence of the Son is tantamount to denying the existence of the Father.[20] God as Father must have a Son in order to be what *he* is, and the Son as Son must have a Father in order to be what he is. As Williams observes, 'If part of what is said about God is that he is one term of a relation, the other term must also be eternal.'[21] If the fatherhood

---

[18] *DP* I. 2. 2.
[19] *DP* I. 2. 3.
[20] *Dialogue with Heraclides* 4.
[21] *Arius*, p. 138. Origen's assumption of the correlative argument may reflect the influence of Aristotle's category of relation, πρός τι, which Aristotle discusses in *Categories* 7^{b}15 (quoted below, p. 131), and where he mentions the relation between lord and slave as an example. In *Metaphysics* 5. 15 he cites the relation between father and son as an example. The application of the category to the divine relation of the Father and the Son was to become a matter of controversy in the Arian debate. As we shall see in Part II, both Alexander and Arius employ terms in their remarks on the correlativity of the Father and the Son which occur in Aristotle's discussion. If Origen used such terms, they have been lost in Rufinus' translation. The correlativity of Father and Son, and lord and slave (*DP* I. 2. 10), has a parallel of sorts in Malachi 1: 6 'A son honours his father and a servant his master. If then I am a father, where is my honour? And if I am a master where is my fear?', a text which Origen quotes in the context of his discussion of the movement from the knowledge of God as Lord to that of God as Father. His use of the text will be discussed in the next chapter.

of God is eternal, then so also must the generation of the Son be eternal.

The correlative argument is supported by Origen's realist doctrine of language. In a passage in the *Commentary on John* directed against Modalism, Origen contends that there are biblical texts which 'definitely prove the Son to be another than the Father and that it is necessary for the Son to be the Son of a Father, and the Father to be the Father of a Son'.[22] He does not go on to specify what the biblical texts are, but he implies that the very words Father and Son indicate the actual (and distinct) existence of that to which each directly refers, and that as terms of relation, each simultaneously indicates the actual existence of the other.

Wiles has argued that the concept of the eternal generation of the Son serves to protect the immutability of God,[23] and this is certainly part of Origen's concern. He explains that denial of Wisdom's eternal generation would imply either that God had once not been able to generate Wisdom, or that being able, he had chosen not to generate her before he did. What the reader is to recognize from this 'absurdity'[24] is that 'for God, there is no gap between possibility and effective willing'.[25] He repeats this 'willing/able' form of argument in *De Principiis* I. 2. 9, where he links it to the idea that to have such a Son is a good: 'since God always had both the power and the will, there was never the slightest reason or possibility that he should not always have had this good thing that he desired.'

In a parallel passage in a Greek fragment of the *Commentary on Genesis*,[26] the only occasion on which he makes an explicit comparison between the fatherhood of God and the fatherhood of men, Origen observes that, unlike men who become fathers, having once not been able to be fathers, God, never having been hindered, has never begun to be Father. He goes on to say that God is eternally perfect, that he has present with himself the

---

[22] X. 37. 246.
[23] M. Wiles, 'Eternal Generation', *JTS* NS 12 (1961), 284–91.
[24] *DP* I. 2. 2.
[25] Williams, *Arius*, p. 138.
[26] In Eusebius, *Contra Marcellum* I. 4, GCS, p. 22, 11–18 (=*PG* 12, 46C).

ability to be a father, and that it is a good thing to be the Father of such a Son. He concludes the passage by asking, in the light of this, why God would delay and deprive himself of the good, since he is able to be the Father of the Son. Here again, as in *De Principiis* I. 2. 9, he links the generation of the Son to the idea of goodness.

But while it is true to say that the concept of the eternal generation of the Son protects the immutability of God, this concept, like that of the eternity of God's fatherhood, is more broadly integral to the whole of Origen's doctrine of God. In the logic of Origen's thought, given his belief in the distinct hypostatic existence of the Father and the Son, the idea of their eternal existence is bound up with the incorporeality of God and all that that entails for the definition of God's nature, and it is linked to God's goodness. As we have seen, Origen mentions the goodness of God in two of his discussions of the eternity of God's fatherhood: in the fragment of the *Commentary on Genesis*, and in *De Principiis* I. 2. 9. It is self-evident to Origen that for God to have such a Son is a good—καλὸν αὐτὸν εἶναι πατέρα τοιούτου υἱοῦ[27]—so, even though he does not make the connection explicit, it is fundamental to his thought that since the attribute of goodness is central to God's nature, God acts eternally to realize that which is good.

The concepts of the eternal fatherhood of God and the eternal generation of the Son also play an essential role in Origen's understanding of God's nature in another way: they are the key concepts in his understanding of the uniqueness of the Father–Son relation and its difference from the relation between God and creation. Creation, and the manner of God's relation to it, could, in his view, only come into existence through the metaphysically prior relation of the Father and the Son. This relation is prior both as cause and in its affective qualities. Before turning to look at the priority of the Father–Son relation and its contrast with the God–creation relation, however, we need to have a clear sense of how Origen thinks about the idea of eternity in reference to creation.

---

[27] *Com. on Gen.*, in Eusebius, *Contra Marcellum* I. 4, GCS, p. 22, 11–18.

Origen applies the belief that what is said of God must be timelessly true, not only to God's fatherhood, but also to God's attributes of omnipotence and beneficence as well. Just as the existence of a father necessarily entails the existence of a son, so too, according to Origen, the existence of a lord necessarily entails the existence of a slave, and the existence of one who is omnipotent requires creatures over whom he exercises his power.[28] Thus Origen argues that, lest it be supposed that God at some time progressed into omnipotence, there must always have been in existence creatures over whom he exercised his omnipotence.[29] By positing a necessarily eternal correlative relationship between God's omnipotence and creation, he protects God's immutability.

But as with the eternity of Father and Son, the idea of the eternal existence of all rational beings serves not only to protect God's immutability; it is equally important for the portrayal of God as eternally and continuously active in giving expression to every aspect of his nature, and especially to his goodness.[30] In *De Principiis* I. 4. 3–5, where he describes the activity of the Trinity, Origen explicitly links God's goodness and his creative power with the eternal existence of all rational beings. The passage is long, but deserves to be quoted in full, because it illustrates the passionate intensity with which he believes in a God who unceasingly and effectively cares for his creation.

This is the good God and kindly Father of all, at once beneficent power and creative power, that is, the power that does good and creates and providentially sustains. And it is absurd and impious to suppose that these powers of God have been at any time in abeyance for a single moment. Indeed, it is unlawful even to entertain the least suspicion that these powers, through which chiefly we gain a worthy notion of God, should at any time have ceased from performing works worthy of themselves and have become inactive. For we can neither suppose that these powers which are in God, nay, which are God, could have been thwarted from without, nor on the other hand, when nothing stood in their way, can we believe that they were reluctant to act and perform works worthy of

---

[28] *DP* I. 2. 10.
[29] Ibid.
[30] God's attribute of goodness is discussed at length above, pp. 25–8.

themselves or that they feigned impotence. We can therefore imagine no moment whatever when that power was not engaged in acts of well-doing. Whence it follows that there always existed objects for this well-doing, namely, God's works or creatures, and that God, in the power of his providence, was always dispensing his blessings among them by doing them good in accordance with their condition and deserts. It follows plainly from this, that at no time whatever was God not Creator, nor Benefactor, nor Providence.[31]

Here again we see Origen applying the 'willing/able' form of argument. God is the being that always and fully realizes his nature. As first principle, God can neither be thought of as constrained from without, nor as unwilling to be what he is. It is inconceivable to Origen that any of the divine attributes should ever not be actively expressed by God. The particular attribute that he sees manifested in God's relation to the eternal creation is his goodness, which eternally and fundamentally shapes the exercise of God's powers. God's goodness is a goodness that always and continuously gives itself for the creation and care of that which is other than itself. Later in *De Principiis*, Origen identifies this goodness as the motive power behind the act of creation. He writes of God: 'Now when "in the beginning" he created what he wished to create, that is rational beings, he had no other reason for creating them except himself, that is, goodness.'[32] As we have seen, God is the good Father who as 'he who is' brings all things into existence and, after they have fallen away, brings them to perfect existence through their participation in his Son. Were God not eternally and wholly active, he and the entire creation would cease to be.

Origen, foreshadowing the censure that Methodius of Olympus would bring against his work and the reason why Arius rejected the concept of the eternal generation of the Son, recognizes that the positing of eternal realities alongside God may create difficulties for maintaining the fundamental precept that the Father is the

---

[31] *DP* I. 4. 3. This passage is directed in part against Marcionism. The relation between the structure of the argument and its anti-Marcionite intent will be dealt with below.
[32] *DP* II. 9. 6; quoted above, p. 28.

first unique principle who precedes all other things, since it suggests that there are other unbegotten and eternal principles alongside God. His solution to the problem is the affirmation of the metaphysical priority of the eternal generation of the Son and the eternal Father–Son relation, an affirmation which allows for the fact that rational beings never began to be. At the conclusion of his discussion of the eternal nature of the Father's creative goodness and power in *De Principiis* I. 4. 4, he states that the question of how things that were created by God could have had no beginning, but existed always with God, is intractable to the human intelligence. The answer, which it should be noted he advances with some caution—it 'can be confessed without any risk to piety', it is 'probable'[33]—is 'that God the Father has always existed, he always had an only-begotten Son . . . who is called Wisdom':

In this Wisdom, therefore, who ever existed with the Father, the Creation was always present in form and outline, and there was never a time when the pre-figuration of those things which hereafter were to be did not exist in Wisdom. It is probably in this way that, so far as our weakness allows, we shall maintain a reverent belief about God, neither asserting that his creatures were not generated and co-eternal with him nor on the other hand that he turned to the work of creation to do good when he had done nothing good before.

Origen paints a picture of a set of metaphysical Dutch dolls. Only the Son receives his existence directly from the Father.[34] All other things, including the Holy Spirit,[35] receive their existence through the mediation of the Son. All things are created by (ὑπό) God, who is absolutely one and simple, through (διά) the Son.[36] The eternal relation of Father and Son is the key to the explanation of the relation between God and creation.[37] While the latter is

[33] The wording, of course, may reflect an attempt by Rufinus to make Origen look more respectable to his later readers on what came to be perceived as one of his most controversial ideas.

[34] *Com. Jn.* II. 2. 17–18.

[35] *Com. Jn.* II. 10. 76.

[36] Origen typically uses these two prepositions to distinguish between the roles of the Father and the Son in the act of creation. e.g. *Com. Jn.* II. 10. 72.

[37] Williams, *Arius*, p. 138, suggests that Origen's statement that God creates 'in'

a puzzle to the human understanding, the former Origen treats as an incontrovertible truth of the Christian faith. In his thinking, this truth maintains a proper conception of God as the first principle, while at the same time allowing for the eternal exercise of God's attributes. God does not undergo change; his nature as incorporeal first principle and as the one who always acts to realize his attribute of goodness is maintained through the prior Father–Son relation.

The idea of eternity, then, does not itself distinguish the relation of the Father and Son from that of the Father and creation. But Origen is certain that the two relations are distinct. The latter is dependent on the former. In *De Principiis* I. 2. 10, following the comparison he makes between a father needing a son to be a father and one who is omnipotent needing creatures over whom he can exercise his power, Origen focuses this distinction in a discussion of the difference between God as Father and God as Almighty, a discussion which suggests a difference in the affective quality of the two relations. He warns that it should not be thought on the basis of his argument for the eternity of God's almightiness that the 'title of Almighty belonged to God before the birth of Wisdom, through which he is called Father'. In support, he cites Psalm 104: 24 'In Wisdom thou hast made them all', and John 1: 3 'all things were made through him and without him was not anything made'. He concludes that 'the title Almighty cannot be older in God than that of Father, for it is through the Son that the Father is almighty'.[38] But more than that, the Son also shares in the Father's omnipotence, a truth that Origen sees confirmed by Revelation 1: 8, where the Son too is called Almighty. It is through Wisdom that God 'holds power over all things', and it is through Wisdom that the omnipotence of God is given its distinctive character: the almighty power of Father and Son is exercised not by 'force and necessity', but by 'word and reason'.[39]

---

the Word and Wisdom may be an attempt to avoid the idea of an automatic creation. 'God creates because he first (logically not temporally, of course) wills to be the progenitor of Wisdom.'

[38] *DP* I. 2. 10.
[39] Ibid.

Although Origen's comments about God's attribute of father-hood in this passage are brief, the line of his thought is clear. He is disallowing any suggestion that almightiness is a more defining attribute of God than fatherhood.[40] Rather, the title Father is logically prior to the title Almighty. Moreover, it is possible that Origen is tacitly assuming that the title Father logically precedes all other titles as well, for the Father–Son relation is the nexus through which all the divine attributes are expressed. As well, there is an implied distinction between the tenor of the Father–Son relation and the Father–creation relation, which is conveyed by the contrast between the two relations: that between a father and a son, and that between a lord and a slave. This contrast between the father–son and the lord–slave relations is a fundamental theme in his understanding of the process by which we come to the saving knowledge of God as Father.

Origen's conception of the distinctiveness of the Father–Son relation is confirmed by his understanding of what is implied in the relation between the words father and son. Each presupposes the existence of its own and of the other's referent in a way which cannot be the case for the relation of father and creation. He does not use the idea of the eternal existence of the rational creation to prove the eternity of God's fatherhood. To have done so would have destroyed the basis of the argument for the priority of the attribute of fatherhood. In terms of language, the eternal nature of God's fatherhood is logically related only to the eternal generation of the Son. In any case, although one of Origen's main concerns is to ensure that the Father of the Son and the Creator be recognized as the same, most of the biblical evidence to which Origen refers links God's fatherhood with the existence of the Son, and not with the existence of creation.

An important undercurrent in Origen's analysis of the eternity of the fatherhood of God and the generation of the Son is an anti-Marcionite polemic. Although he does not refer to Marcion's theology directly in the passages where he discusses the eternity of Father and Son, the 'willing/able' form of his argument, and some of its detail, suggest that Origen has Marcionism in mind. Marcion

---

[40] This too may be partly directed against Marcionism.

is reported by Tertullian to have used a similar argument as part of his case for the existence of the higher God:

If God is good and knowledgeable of the future and able to prevent evil, why did he allow man, who is in his own image and likeness—even his own substance through the origin of his soul—to be deceived by the devil and thus to fall into death from obedience to the law? For if he were good and unwilling that such a thing should happen, and if he were knowledgeable of the future and not ignorant of things to come, and if he were able and strong enough to prevent it, then given these three conditions of divine majesty this thing (the Fall) would never have occurred. But since it did occur, the contrary must be true, namely, that God is neither good, nor knowledgeable of the future, nor powerful. Inasmuch as such a thing would not have occurred if God had been of such nature, that is, good, knowledgeable of the future and powerful, this (the Fall) must have occurred because God was not of such a nature.[41]

Origen does not refer to the element of God's foreknowledge in the passages from *De Principiis* I. 2. 2 and the fragment of the *Commentary on Genesis*, but he does refer to the other elements of the argument. Later however, he explicitly attributes the 'willing/able' form of argument to 'those who come from the schools of Marcion, Valentinus, and Basilides', and he includes the idea of God's providence.[42] In the long passage from *De Principiis* I. 4. 3 quoted above,[43] he refers to God's providence in conjunction with the 'willing/able' argument. An implicit anti-Marcionite polemic helps account for the vigour with which Origen argues for the eternal exercise both of God's omnipotence and of his goodness. No gap is to be allowed to appear between the exercise of God's various attributes, least of all the attributes of goodness and creative power; they are exercised simultaneously.

In light of this discussion, when we turn back to the passages from *De Principiis* I. 2. 2 and the fragment from the *Commentary*

---

[41] *Adversus Marcionem* 2. 5. 1–2. J. Gager, 'Marcion and Philosophy', *VC* 26 (1972), pp. 53–9, believes that Epicurus is the likely source of Marcion's argument. He cites a similar argument from Lactantius, who attributes the argument to Epicurus (*De ira dei* 13. 20–1), and another from Sextus Empiricus (*Outlines of Pyrrhonism* 3. 9–11).

[42] *DP* II. 9. 5.

[43] See pp. 72–3.

on Genesis where Origen uses the 'willing/able' argument in his analysis of the eternal nature of God's fatherhood, it becomes evident why it is plausible to conclude that they were at least partly intended as a counter to Marcionism. This conclusion is supported by Origen's introduction of an anti-Marcionite comment into the midst of his statement that the Son, as well as the Father, is Almighty: he says that the omnipotence of the Father and of the Son are one and the same, just as God and the Lord are one and the same Father.[44] If by implication all of God's attributes, with the sole exception of fatherhood (which identifies God as origin of the Son), are shared by the Son, then there was no time when God was God without also being the Father of the Son. In his desire to show that there is only one God and Father to whom all attributes apply, and that there is no division between the attributes, Origen is edging towards the idea that the Father and the Son share the nature of divinity equally, and are differentiated only by the fact that one is Father and the other Son, and that it is the nature of the relationship that defines their difference. Origen will not allow the possibility that there was a time when God did not have a Son, for otherwise it could give rise to a radical separation of God as Creator and God as Father of the Son.

The idea of God as eternally Father and the correlative idea of the eternal generation of the Son protect the unitary identity of God. The one single subject of the Old and New Testaments, the one single subject who eternally creates from his goodness, is the one who is eternally the Father of the Son. The whole of Origen's doctrine of God, his understanding of the act of creation and the moral coherence of the created order, and, as we shall see, his doctrine of salvation, has its focus in the eternal Father–Son relation.

The primacy of the relation of Father and Son over that of God and Creation helps account for the relative infrequency of the expression 'Father of all', the Platonic phrase from *Timaeus* 28C, in Origen's writings. In second-century writers such as Justin Martyr and Theophilus the phrase appears frequently; indeed, in

---

[44] *DP* I. 2. 10.

the case of the latter's *Ad Autolycum* no references are made to God using the absolute form 'the Father'.[45] Origen, however, thinks of the fatherhood of God primarily in relation to the only-begotten Son, and then in relation to sons by adoption. The nature of the relationship between God and his creation is not defined by God's fatherhood, even if the impulse to create springs from his fatherly goodness. The small number of examples makes it difficult to establish a pattern in Origen's usage of 'Father of all'.[46] The phrase plays no conceptual role in his understanding of the Father–Son relation; nor does it have a role in his doctrine of creation. It is best understood as a terminological relic of an older form of theological discourse.

The preceding analysis shows that the idea of the fatherhood of God is central to Origen's thinking about the nature of God. Not surprisingly, it is also central to his thinking about the knowledge of God. His scepticism about our ability to apprehend God without the mediation of the Son finds a particular focus in relation to God's nature as Father: 'He is the God and Father of all, though for some he is God and not Father, while for others he is God and Father.'[47] Until our souls are made perfect through our participation in the Son, we cannot know God as Father, but only as Lord.

Origen thinks that there are different levels or stages in our knowledge of God. He explores the theme in the first six chapters of *Commentary on John* XIX, where he comments on John 8: 19 'Jesus answered, "You know neither me nor my Father; if you

---

[45] References to 'the Son' in *Ad Autolycum* are correspondingly rare. There appears to be a pattern in Justin's use of fatherhood language: he has a greater tendency to refer to God with a form of the absolute usage in the *Dialogue*, especially in his accounts of the Gospel narratives of the life of Christ, than in the *Apologies*, where the 'Father of all' phrase in various forms predominates. This will be discussed in a forthcoming article by the author.

[46] They occur at: *DP* I. 4. 3, in Latin; and in the Greek only, at *DP* I. 3. 3 (Justinian, *Ep. ad Mennam*, in *Acta Conciliorum Oecumenicorum*, iii. 210, fr. 8); III. 1. 14 (*Philocalia* 21. 13); IV. 2. 2 (*Philocalia* 1. 9); and IV. 3. 7 (*Philocalia* 1. 23); *Com. Jn.* I. 6. 35, 9. 57, 12. 75, 33. 243; *On Prayer* 5. 2; 8. 2; 15. 1 (twice); 33. 6; *Hom. on Gen.* XIV. 3; *Dialogue with Heraclides* 3. 21; *C. Cel.* II. 9; V. 53; VI. 69; VII. 43 (twice); VIII. 38, 53, 66; and *Com. Matt.* XII. 9. It is possible that Rufinus eliminated occurrences from *De Principiis*, though the instance at *DP* I. 4. 3 suggests that if this is the case his excision was not systematic.

[47] 'The Commentary of Origen upon the Epistle to the Ephesians', p. 413.

knew me, you would know my Father also."' In XIX. 5, he advances the idea that we may know God according to different ἐπίνοιαι; according to one ἐπίνοια we may know God as God, and according to another, we may know God as Father.[48] He illustrates this with Jesus' words to Mary from John 20: 17, 'Go to my brothers and say to them, I am going to my Father and to your Father, my God and your God'.[49]

Later, in XIX. 6, he extends the idea, maintaining that the Pharisees had no knowledge of God either as God or as Father, and possibly not as Creator.[50] He is sufficiently committed to this distinction in the knowledge of God to be prepared to run the risk (however fleetingly) of conceding the central Marcionite tenet by concluding that the idea which the heretics favour, namely that Moses and the Prophets did not know the Father, may well be correct. He justifies this on the grounds that the Son, by whom he means Christ, knows God as Father, while the servant, by whom he means Moses, knows God as Lord.[51] As corroborating evidence, he points to the fact that God is not addressed as Father in the prayers of the Old Testament.[52] He is careful, however, to distance himself from the fault of the heretics. He points out that it is the same God who is known as Lord and Father,[53] and takes back his claim about the ignorance of the Old Testament figures in the following sections of the commentary.[54]

He also suggests that these two types of knowledge are not commensurate with each other. The Son, who has had no experience of God as Master, only knows him as Father, and the servant only knows him as Lord. The fact that he goes on to assure his readers that to say this is not to utter an absurdity[55] is an indication that he felt some uncertainty about it.

[48] 5. 26.
[49] 5. 27.
[50] 6. 33.
[51] 5. 27.
[52] 5. 28.
[53] Ibid.
[54] 5. 28–32. The implications for revelation and the incarnation of this willingness to see a distinction between the knowledge of God available to the Old and the New Testament saints will be discussed below, pp. 110–15.
[55] 5. 27.

Origen gives a similar description of the stages in the knowledge of God as Father in a fragment of the *Commentary on Matthew*. He remarks that 'the knowledge of God is according to different aspects (ἐπινοίας)'.[56] In what remains of the fragment, he designates the words 'Creator' and 'Judge' as ἐπίνοιαι of God. He may have listed other ἐπίνοιαι, but there is a break in the text after the word 'Judge'.[57] He observes that one knows God as Father when one becomes a brother of the Son through the revelation of Jesus.

He also distinguishes between stages in our knowledge of God in *On Prayer*. After making a contrast between the prayers of the Synagogue and the prayers of the Church,[58] he says that if we pray as we ought, shutting every 'door' of the faculties of sense, we have the Father and the only-begotten Son present with us. Thus we 'shall make intercessions not only with the righteous God but also with the Father, as one who is not absent from his sons but is present in our secret place and watches over it, and increases what is in "the inner chamber" if we "shut the door" [Matt. 6: 6] of it'.[59] Origen does not suggest either in the fragment from the *Commentary on Matthew* or in this passage that the two types of knowledge are mutually exclusive.

It is clear from these several passages that Origen regarded the knowledge of God as Father as the proper goal and fulfilment of our knowledge of God. This is underscored by his linking of the discussion of the progression to a knowledge of God as Father with the statement of God's transcendence, and its allusion to *Republic* 509B, in the conclusion of his exegesis of John 8: 19 in *Commentary on John* XIX. 6. The discussion of the knowledge of God's aspects in XIX. 5 leads Origen on to an explanation of the means by which we come to know the Father in XIX. 6. After remarking on the limitations in the Pharisees' knowledge of the ἐπίνοιαι of God, he writes that 'those who know the Father ascend from the

---

[56] *Com. Matt.*, fr. 243.

[57] There is a close similarity in wording between the third line of the fragment and *Com. Jn.* XIX. 6. 33, where he discusses the extent of the Pharisees' knowledge of God.

[58] *On Prayer* 20. 1.

[59] *On Prayer* 20. 2.

knowledge of the Son to the knowledge of the Father'.[60] As we have already seen,[61] he then sets out a series of stages in the knowledge of the Logos through which we must pass in order to come to a knowledge of God: our contemplation of the Son as the Logos brings us to the contemplation of God; our contemplation of the Son as Wisdom brings us to know the Father of Wisdom; and our contemplation of the Son as Truth brings us 'to see being, or that which transcends being, namely, the power and nature of God'.[62] He ends with an affirmation of the Son's role as the mediator, who in his many aspects (ἐπίνοιαι) accommodates himself to the spiritual needs of each person.

Although Origen does not make an explicit link between our coming to know God as Father and our coming to know God's transcendent nature, he thinks of them in much the same way. The two images of the saving journey to the full apprehension of God's true nature complement each other, overlap, and become one. The Platonic ascent has been woven into the biblical account. The Son, who alone has known God as Father, and through whom we climb to that knowledge, is the one through whom we climb stage by stage to the perfect knowledge of God and his transcendent being. Both God's fatherhood and his transcendent power and nature represent for Origen the highest reaches of the knowledge of God.

The seeds of the distinction between knowing God as Lord and knowing him as Father are built into Origen's conception of the difference between the relation of a father and a son, and that between one who is omnipotent and those over whom he exercises his power. Although he does not discuss the question of whether or not this distinction in the knowledge of God is grounded in his cosmological distinction between the Son's relation to the Father and the rational beings' relation to God, it is consistent with it. It is not clear whether we ought to think of the pre-existent rational souls as having hypostatic existence; neither is it clear whether or not and in what way they may be said to have known God. Origen

---

[60] 6. 33.
[61] Above, p. 41.
[62] 6. 35–7.

gives little attention to the relationship between the pre-existent souls and God, and it is not a problem he looked at in relation to the knowledge of God as Father. But there is no evidence in Origen's writings that he thought that at the Fall we lost a knowledge of God as Father which we once possessed and now are called to reclaim.

In the foregoing analysis of the knowledge of God as Father we have seen Origen using the term ἐπίνοιαι to describe such divine titles as 'Father', 'Creator', and 'Judge', and it would be helpful to consider what specifically he may have meant the word to convey about the relation between these titles and the divine nature. He uses the word with reference to God only twice: in the *Commentary on John* XIX. 5. 26 and in fragment 243 of the *Commentary on Matthew*, two of the texts that we have just been considering. By contrast, the term occurs often in the general course of his writings, and has a specific application to the Logos.

Crouzel writes that the fundamental meaning of ἐπίνοιαι 'est celle de vue de l'esprit, de manière humaine de considérer les choses'.[63] The ἐπίνοιαι have a foundation in that which is real, where they are not separated; they are separated in the human mind. Thus Origen can perceive a tension between the ἐπίνοιαι and the real, which latter he designates by ὑπόστασις.[64] The kingdom of heaven and the kingdom of God are the same thing in reality (ὑπόστασις), if not in concept (ἐπίνοια).[65] The Modalists mistakenly maintain that in speaking of Father and Son, the Bible is referring to different ἐπίνοιαι, not to different ὑποστάσεις.[66] The term can be translated by 'imagination'.[67] It can also signify the attempt to acquire a correct understanding of an issue and be

---

[63] Henri Crouzel, *Origène et la 'Connaissance Mystique'* (Paris, 1961). The following discussion is based on Crouzel's analysis, pp. 389–91.

[64] Williams, *Arius*, p. 132, refers to the 'familiar philosophical distinction between what exists *kath' hupostasin* and what exists *kat' epinoian*, "conceptually"'. At 295 n.143 he gives a reference to Alexander of Aphrodisias, in *Aristotelis metaphysica* 230. 36, and to several patristic instances of this opposition. In a private conversation, however, Williams has suggested that it is unlikely that Origen would have been aware of this as a technical philosophical distinction.

[65] *Com. Matt.* X. 14.

[66] *Com. Jn.* X. 37. 246.

[67] *Com. Jn.* XIII. 61. 429.

translated by 'idea' or 'conception'. He writes of 'acquiring some idea' (ἐπίνοια) of the intention of the evangelists in order to interpret the discrepancies between the Gospels.[68]

Above all, it is the titles that the Scriptures give the Logos that Origen identifies with the word ἐπίνοιαι.[69] But although he is prepared to say that Christ is one by substance (ὑποκείμενον), and many by aspects (ἐπίνοιαι),[70] this does not mean that he thinks of all the ἐπίνοιαι of the Logos as merely assumed for our benefit and as not describing the Logos' real nature. When he asks which of the titles would remain if man had no need of redemption, he answers that perhaps the ἐπίνοια Wisdom would remain, and Word, and Life, and Truth,[71] titles which are fundamental to his presentation of the Son's nature.

In the two passages where Origen uses ἐπίνοιαι to refer directly to God, he specifies the words Father, Lord, Creator, and Judge as ἐπίνοιαι; and it is probable that he considered the word God to be an ἐπίνοια as well, since he identifies God as one of those elements, along with Father and Creator, which the Pharisees did not know about God. However, in the course of his discussion of the difference between knowing God as Father and knowing him as Lord in *Commentary on John* XIX. 5, Origen makes a comment that indicates that he regarded the word Father as a *name* for God. He does this obliquely. After admitting that Old Testament figures addressed God as Father, though in a secret fashion, he says that Jesus came 'to announce the name of God to his brothers and to praise the Father in the midst of the church, as it is written "I will tell of your name to my brethren; in the midst of the congregation I will praise thee" [Ps. 22: 22 and Heb. 2: 12].' That which has not been known by the majority of people before the incarnation is that God is Father; the name that will be announced is the name Father. Although the reference is oblique, and although Origen does not place the word Father on his list of names (which in fact

---

[68] *Com. Jn.* X. 37.
[69] Especially in *Com. Jn.* I–II, where he discusses the titles of the Logos, but also often elsewhere.
[70] *Hom. on Jer.* VIII. 2.
[71] *Com. Jn.* I. 20. 123.

are all from the Old Testament, and he plays down the presence of the word Father in the Old Testament), this passage at least suggests that he may have thought about the name Father in much the same realist terms as he thought about the name 'he who is'.

It is uncertain what exactly Origen intended by his use of the word ἐπίνοια in reference to the fatherhood of God. The signification of ἐπίνοια is fluid; it is used in various ways, and it does not appear to have been invested with a precise technical meaning. But it is unlikely that he intended to diminish the reality of fatherhood as a description of God's nature. The context of the two passages in which he uses the term of God is epistemological and the weight in the two discussions of fatherhood is on the question of our apprehension of God's nature. We apprehend him progressively under different aspects as we ascend to a full knowledge of him, but those aspects are true descriptions of God's nature. However inadequate our perception of God may be at any stage on our journey, God is eternally Father, and this we may come to know as the Son has always known it.

Origen's understanding of the Son's relation with the Father reveals much of how he thinks about the divine fatherhood, and it is to that relation that we now turn. The relationship of the Son to the Father is the model for the relationship that we are intended to have with the Father. In order to get a clear sense of that relation, however, we must first consider Origen's theology of the Son more generally. Origen thinks about the Son within the framework of two fundamental ideas: that the Son has a real individual existence, and that the Son shares in the divine nature of the Father. He strives to maintain a balance between these two guiding ideas throughout his theology and to defend them both against those who would erroneously emphasize one at the expense of the other. Some would make the Son and the Holy Spirit modes of being of the unique divine person, while others would deny the divinity of the Son. Origen summarizes his perception of the two mistaken extremes in the *Commentary on John*:

Either, while confessing as God the one they call Son at least in name, they deny that the individuality of the Son is different from that of the Father; or they deny the divinity of the Son, in admitting that his individuality and substance (οὐσία) are, in their proper characteristics, different from the Father.[72]

The same errors are denounced in a parallel passage in *Dialogue with Heraclides*.[73]

Origen is aware that the very words he uses to describe the Son, such as Wisdom, Word, and light, which emphasize the Son's closeness to the Father, are taken by some as grounds for denying the Son a distinct existence. But the Word is not to be thought of as existing only in the mind of God[74] or as a mere utterance of the Father, existing as syllables.[75] Such a conception of the Son fails to grant to him a distinct existence, ὑπόστασις.[76] While the Son shares in the nature of (incorporeal) light along with the Father,[77] it does not follow that the Son is not different in οὐσία from the Father.[78] In this latter instance, Origen differentiates between the two lights by stressing the Father's superiority to the Son. The Father is more than the true light.[79] Origen's task is to develop a theology and vocabulary that will allow him to honour both the distinct individual existence of the Son and the Son's divinity.

Origen insists that the Son is an ὑπόστασις or ὑποκείμενον.[80] In the *Commentary on John*, Origen replies to those who, misinterpreting the biblical language of the resurrection—the Father raising the Son—fail to distinguish 'numerically' between the Father and Son, and say that the Father and Son are 'one not only in οὐσία but also in ὑποκείμενον, distinct only according to certain ἐπίνοιαι, not according to ὑπόστασις'.[81] To counter such people he

---

[72] II. 2. 16.

[73] *Dialogue with Heraclides* 3.

[74] *Com. Jn.* I. 34. 243.

[75] *Com. Jn.* I. 24. 151.

[76] *Com. Jn.* I. 24. 151.

[77] As we have seen, Origen supports his argument for the incorporeality of God as light in *De Principiis* I. 1. 1, by referring to the Son's nature as light.

[78] *Com. Jn.* II. 23. 149.

[79] *Com. Jn.* II. 23. 151.

[80] He also uses ὑπόθεσις, but it is not one of his preferred terms. For a recent study of the origins and meaning of the ὑπόστασις language, see Alistair Logan, 'Origen and the development of Trinitarian Theology', in *Origeniana Quarta*, 424–9.

[81] X. 37. 246.

says 'one must pick out for them the texts which definitely prove the Son to be another than the Father'.[82] The words Father and Son identify distinct, subsisting realities; it is logically impossible in using them not to distinguish the Son from the Father. Thus when Origen asks Heraclides if the Son is distinct from the Father, he elicits the reply, 'Of course. How can he be Son if he is also Father?'[83] Origen clearly feels that this appeal to the commonplace way in which words are used carries weight.[84] In *Contra Celsum* I. 23, he requires that Celsus prove that the Greek gods have ὑπόστασις and οὐσία, and are not simply inventions, personified abstractions. He here treats ὑπόστασις and οὐσία as synonyms which mean 'real individual subsistence' in contrast to existence as a mere mental construct. Further on in *Contra Celsum*, he rejects the view of those who say that there are not two ὑποστάσεις in God. The Father and Son are 'two things (πράγματα) in subsistence (ὑπόστασις) but one in mental unity, harmony, and identity of will'.[85] In *On Prayer*, he says that he has 'proved elsewhere' that the Father and Son are distinct in οὐσία and ὑποκείμενον.[86] And at the conclusion of an argument in the *Commentary on John* to establish that the Holy Spirit has its own 'proper οὐσία', he states that there are three ὑποστάσεις: Father, Son and Holy Spirit.[87]

In *De Principiis* I. 2 Origen explains the manner by which this hypostasis, the Son, is generated from the Father. Arguing against Valentinian Gnosticism, he maintains that to think of the Son's generation as a bodily phenomenon plays into the hands of those who maintain that the Father becomes the Father of the Son by an act of προβολή (*prolatio* with Rufinus).[88] This implies a division in the divine substance, and violates the principle of the Father's incorporeality.[89] But if the generation of the Son is not to be

---

[82] X. 37. 246.
[83] *Dialogue with Heraclides* 2.
[84] This may reflect Origen's realist theory of language.
[85] *C. Cel.* VIII. 12.
[86] 15. 1.
[87] *Com. Jn.* II. 10. 75.
[88] *DP* IV. 4. 1. For a discussion of the translation of προβολή and its meaning for Origen, see Crouzel, *Traité des principes*, iv. 240, n. 3.
[89] *DP* I. 2. 6.

thought of as corporeal, in the manner of 'men or other animals',[90] how is it to be understood? It is, he says in *De Principiis* I. 2. 4, an 'exceptional process, worthy of God. . . an eternal and everlasting begetting, as brightness is begotten from light. For he does not become Son in an external way through the adoption of the Spirit, but is Son by nature.' Much of the second chapter is taken up with an examination of the images of the Son as ἀπόρροια and *vapor* and light from Hebrews 1: 3 and Wisdom 7: 25–6 and his use of the analogy between God and the human mind to explain the generation of the Son.[91]

Origen's concern in *De Principiis* I. 1 to demonstrate that God is mind, that he is one and simple, indivisible, and incorporeal, is evident here in *De Principiis* I. 2 in the use of this analogy. In *De Principiis* I. 1. 6, mind is portrayed as intentional, active, and effective in realizing its purposes. Given Origen's understanding of God's being as mind, will and substance language are complementary in his explanation of the generation of the Son. Thus, Origen's contention in *De Principiis* I. 2. 6 that the Son does everything just as the Father does, and consequently that the Son's 'birth from the Father is as it were an act of his will proceeding from the mind', is a statement both about God's being and how he acts.[92] When in *De Principiis* I. 2. 6 he says that 'the Father's will ought to be sufficient to ensure the existence of what he wills, for in willing he uses no other means than that which is produced by the deliberations of his will', he is affirming that God, in the act of begetting the Son, is the first principle, unconstrained by anything prior to himself, least of all corporeal reality.[93] In section 9 of the chapter, he draws on the terminology of Wisdom 7: 25–6, where Wisdom is called a mirror of God's ἐνέργεια or δύναμις, and portrays Wisdom as the *energeia* of a divine *virtus* or *dunamis*: Wisdom is the actualization of a divine potency.[94] But this argument creates a tension in his thought: a divine act is not a

[90] *DP* I. 2. 4.
[91] *DP* I. 2. 6 and 9.
[92] *DP* I. 2. 6 and 9.
[93] This will be discussed further below.
[94] *DP* I. 2. 9. Williams, *Arius*, p. 139, notes that Origen is using the Aristotelian order of potency and act.

subsistent reality - though here it is simply stated that it is - and Origen is insistent that the Son is a subsistent reality.

The conformity of the Son's will to the Father's will, which he refers to just before the statement of the 'proceeding of the will from the mind' in *De Principiis* I. 2. 6, is an important element in Origen's thinking about the relation of the Son to the Father. The divine nature of the Son is made evident in his perfect expression of the Father's will. In a passage from the *Commentary on John*, where he is commenting on John 4: 34 'My food is to do the will of him who sent me', he clearly distinguishes between the will of the Father and that of the Son. But at the same time he emphasizes that the will of the Son is in all respects the perfect image of the Father's, 'so that there are no longer two wills but one'.[95] Just as the Son is the image of the Father's goodness and his divinity is the image of the Father's divinity, so his will is the image of 'the first will'.[96] Similarly Origen stresses the constancy of the will in the human soul of Christ.[97] Both the ideas of will and of nature appear in his conception of how we come to a saving knowledge of God as Father.

Although the Father wills the Son into existence, he does not do so in the same sense that he wills the world into existence. Origen almost certainly called the Son a κτίσμα in the original text of *De Principiis*.[98] But it is unclear what he meant by it. Crouzel and Simonetti argue that κτίζειν, κτίσις, and κτίσμα do not have the strict sense of create for Origen: 'conformément aux récits de Gen. 1 et Gen. 2, ποιεῖν désigne la création spirituelle et πλάσσειν le "modelage" des corps. Donc κτίζειν s'applique à toute la "production" divine par génération ou par création'.[99] The gradation κτίσμα, ποίημα, πλάσμα is found explicitly in the *Commentary on John*.[100] Harl notes that Origen makes a distinction in various texts

---

[95] *Com. Jn.* XIII. 36. 228.

[96] 36. 234.

[97] *DP* II. 6. 5.

[98] *DP* IV. 4. 1. See Crouzel, *Traité des principes*, iv. 242–4 n.9, for a discussion of the issue and a review of the literature; see also W. Lowry, 'Did Origen style the Son a κτίσμα?', *JTS* 39 (1938), 39–42, and Williams, *Arius*, p. 141 and p. 298 n. 210.

[99] Crouzel, *Traité des principes*, i. 43.

[100] *Com. Jn.* XX. 22. 182.

between the κόσμος, the world of our fallen state, and the κτίσις, the primordial 'heaven and earth' of Genesis 1: 1, the realm of the rational spirits. The world that we inhabit is not 'created' by God; it is made or created by the choices of the creatures. The κτίσις alone is strictly the unimpeded expression of God's will.[101] Williams concludes that 'the Logos is without doubt formed by the Father, directly and uniquely, in a way that sets him apart at least from what later orthodoxy understood as "creation"'.[102]

The idea of the eternal generation of the Son is central to Origen's understanding of the tenor of the relationship between the Father and the Son. The relationship of the Father and the Son is a dynamic relationship, characterized by continuous activity. One of the images that Origen favours to illustrate the eternal and continuous generation of the Son is that of brightness from light. The image is drawn from Wisdom 7: 26 and Hebrews 1: 3. He argues that just as a source of light does not produce the light that flows from it at a particular moment only but continuously, so also the Son, being the effulgence of God's glory, is generated not momentarily but continuously.[103] The simile reinforces his ontological starting point: as light, the Son, like the Father, is incorporeal.[104] He maintains that the use of the present tense of γεννάω in Proverbs 8: 25, following a series of aorists, confirms that the generation of the Son is eternal and continuous.[105]

Corresponding to the Father's unceasing generation of the Son, the Son unceasingly turns towards the Father. As it is the Son's essence to be continuously generated by the Father, and to remain at the Father's side, so the Son gives expression to his life with the Father by 'remaining always in uninterrupted contemplation of the depths of the Father'.[106] The Son is divine by virtue of his

---

[101] M. Harl, 'La préexistence des âmes dans l'œuvre d'Origène' in *Origeniana Quarta*, pp. 244–5.

[102] *Arius*, p. 142.

[103] *Hom. on Jer.* IX. 4.

[104] It was pointed out above, p. 86, that Origen was aware that the simile of light from light was susceptible to misinterpretation. Unqualified, it could be taken as denying the distinction of the two persons. For this reason Justin prefers the simile of the two torches (*Dialogue* 128).

[105] *Hom. on Jer.* IX. 4.

[106] *Com. Jn.* II. 2. 18.

participation in the Father's being.[107] Referring to Proverbs 8: 30, Origen describes the Father's life as an eternal rejoicing in the presence of the Son, who is Wisdom.[108] It is the Father's nature to rejoice eternally.[109] The Father delights eternally in his only-begotten Son, and the Son turns unceasingly towards the riches of the Father. The Son is the model for our knowing and loving God,[110] and therefore must be a subject of knowledge and love and have a hypostatic existence comparable to ours. He is not just a cosmological principle connecting God to the creation. The Logos is Son, glorifying and being glorified by the Father.[111] He shares the Father's glory irrespective of his role in relation to the creation. His relation with God is of a personal nature: 'hence the appeal to the logic of relation (if a father, then a son too) serves, in the *Commentary on John*, to underline the real plurality and mutuality of the divine life. . . . Origen hints at a fundamental datum of later trinitarian thought, that the Father–Son relation is simply part of the *definition* of the word God, and so does not exist for the sake of anything else than itself.'[112]

One of the ways in which Origen seeks to highlight the unique status of the Son is through his description of the Son as 'Son by nature'. Of all existing things, only the Son is called Son by nature. It is a description that has particular importance for Origen's explanation of how we come to know God as Father. In *De Principiis* I. 2. 4, after comparing the eternal generation of the Son to the generation of brightness from light, Origen goes on to say

---

[107] Ibid. Williams, *Arius*, p. 142, refers to two exegetical fragments that suggest the opposite. One of these, 'A fragment on the Apocalypse', *Der Scholien-Kommentar des Origenes zur Apocalypse Iohannis*, TU 38, 20, 29 calls the Son '"He who is", in his very substance', but as I observed above, p. 29 n.79, the authenticity of the fragment is doubtful. The other instance Williams cites is the οὐσία–μετουσία antithesis of *Selecta in Psalmos*, on Psalm 134.

[108] As we shall see, Athanasius also quotes the verse and develops it further than Origen.

[109] *DP* I. 4. 4, IV. 4. 1, and *Com. Jn.* I. 9. 55.

[110] *Com. Jn.* I. 16. 92–3. Knowledge and love are the characteristics of sonship: *Com. Jn.* XX. 34. 305–9. We shall return to this with reference to Origen's idea of salvation and the knowledge of God's fatherhood. Williams, *Arius*, p. 297 n.186, points out that *On Prayer* throughout presupposes the same model.

[111] Williams, *Arius*, p. 139.

[112] Ibid.

that the Son 'does not become Son in an external way through the adoption of the Spirit, but is Son by nature (*natura*)'. A few lines later he repeats that the Son 'alone is Son by nature', and implies that it is because he is Son by nature that the Son is called only-begotten.[113] He makes use of the same idea in the *Commentary on John* in the course of outlining three opinions that might be held on the question of the origin of the Holy Spirit. He distinguishes the status of the Son from that of the Holy Spirit partly on the basis of the idea of sonship by nature. Referring to the Holy Spirit, he writes:

And perhaps this is the reason why he himself does not bear the name Son of God, for only the only-begotten is Son by nature (φύσει) from the beginning, and it seems that the Holy Spirit has need of him to minister to him his subsistence.[114]

The Son alone participates directly in the Father, and it is implied that it is the immediacy of the Son's relation to the Father which determines the Son's status as Son by nature. Again Origen links the idea of the Son by nature with that of the Son as only-begotten, a tendency which is also seen in three fragments of his *Commentary on John*, preserved in the *Apology of Pamphilus*.[115] Although he nowhere attempts to make plain his understanding of the two phrases or the relation between them, he seems to have thought of them as complementary terms, signifying the Son's unique closeness to the Father. They help fill out what he means when he describes the Son as being in the image of God.

Often, as in the quotation from the *De Principiis* I. 2. 4, Origen contrasts the idea of Son by nature with the idea of sons by adoption. The Pauline phrases 'adoption as sons' and 'spirit of adoption as sons' are repeatedly used in his discussions of our coming to know God as Father. The contrast and the similarity between the two types of sonship are central to Origen's thinking about how we gain that knowledge.

---

[113] *DP* I. 2. 5.
[114] *Com. Jn.* II. 10. 76.
[115] *Com. Jn.*, pp. 562–3.

4

The Knowledge of God as Father and Adoption as Sons

As we have seen, Origen thinks that although God is Father we can only come to know him as Father through our participation in the Son. We come to know God as Father through a step-by-step progression to the status of adopted sons and thus to a share in the eternal relationship of the Father and the Son. Origen portrays this progression as a spiritual pilgrimage from the condition of fear, servitude, and ignorance which characterizes the Lord–servant relationship to that of filial knowledge and love which character-izes the Father–Son relationship. This pilgrimage involves a cor-responding development in our moral behaviour: as we become morally pure, we grow in our knowledge of Wisdom and in our degree of sonship. The terms in which he thinks of the transforma-tion from servanthood to sonship are mainly shaped by the Pauline imagery of adoption and the Johannine imagery of rebirth.

Origen gives his most elaborate outline of the sequence of stages through which the Christian must pass in order to become a son of God in a passage in *Commentary on John* XXXII.[1] The Saviour, he says, speaks to his disciples as a father speaks to his children; but after the resurrection, the disciples become his brothers. Origen remarks that just as it is not possible for one who has previously been someone's child to become that person's brother, so the child of Jesus is not able to become Jesus' brother. However, following the resurrection, what was impossible be-comes possible: 'At any rate, after the resurrection of the Saviour,

[1] 30. 368–75.

these to whom he said "Little Children" become brothers of the one who earlier said "Little Children", even as they are endowed with a different quality (μεταποιωθέντες) as a result of the resurrection of Jesus.' As evidence for this Origen cites John 20: 17: 'Go to my brothers, and say to them, I am ascending to my Father and your Father, to my God and to your God.' He concludes by schematizing this process as a progression from being a servant to being a disciple, from being a disciple to being an infant, and from being an infant to being a brother (of the Son) and a son of God. A little later in the *Commentary on John*, paraphrasing Romans 8: 15–16, he describes the state that precedes being a child of God as one in which people are 'slaves of God, because they have received the spirit of servitude, which leads to fear'.[2]

Elsewhere, Origen does not make such fine distinctions in grades of pre-adoption existence. Commenting on Matthew 18: 10 'See that you do not despise one of these little ones', with Galatians 4: 4–7 in mind, he collapses the spiritual status of the infant into that of the servant. He observes that the infant, even as an heir, inasmuch as he is a child, 'has the spirit of bondage unto fear'; while the one who is no longer 'little' no longer has the spirit of bondage but already has the spirit of adoption as son when 'perfect love casts out fear' (1 Jn. 4: 18).[3]

Origen says very little in these passages about what accounts for the condition of servitude and the fear that goes with it, though in *Commentary on John* XX he makes the comment that those who do not attend to the words of God and do not comprehend their proper sense 'remain in the state which precedes that of the children of God'; such people 'do not strive to advance and progress, so that they might also receive the spirit of adoption, by which those who possess it cry Abba! Father!'[4] There is a hint that he thinks of the state of servitude as a state in which one encounters God as the one who both judges and punishes our misdeeds, and thus corrects the wayward. This idea may lie behind

---

[2] XX. 33. 289.
[3] *Com. Matt.* XIII. 26.
[4] *Com. Jn.* XX. 33. 289.

the statement in the *Commentary on John* that God 'demands' fear from bad servants,[5] for elsewhere he is careful to point out that God's severity towards human beings springs from his care for them,[6] and it also may lie behind the distinction Origen makes in *On Prayer* between knowing God as righteous and knowing him as Father.[7] Taken together these comments suggest that the condition of servitude is congruent with our wilful failure to grasp the significance of Scripture and with our sinfulness. Our progression to sonship, conversely, requires a desire for both moral and intellectual reformation; in this we will be aided both by God's punishment of us and by the gift of the Holy Spirit. How it is that we progress will be discussed at greater length below.

Against the spiritual condition of fear, Origen sets the condition of love as the fulfilment of our spiritual journey. In the *Commentary on John*, in the course of his analysis of the titles of Christ, he makes a distinction between those who know Christ as 'teacher' and those who know him as 'lord'. For the former, who strive for piety and wisdom, and are judged worthy of wisdom, Christ does not remain lord, but becomes their 'friend' ($\varphi i\lambda o\varsigma$). This is summed up by Jesus when he says, 'No longer do I call you servants, for the servant does not know what the master is doing, but I call you friends' (Jn. 15: 15).[8] Similarly, in *On Prayer* I. 1, Origen says that the Lord changes from being a lord to being a friend.[9]

Later, in *On Prayer*, Origen makes the contrast between our two spiritual states even bolder. In chapter 15, he argues that we should not pray to the Son, nor to both Father and Son, but to the Father alone through the Son. Through regeneration (1 Pet. 1: 3)

---

[5] I. 29. 203.

[6] Summed up nicely by Origen a little later in the commentary (I. 36. 263–4), where he remarks on the relationship between Christ's titles 'rod' and 'flower'. To those who have not responded to the love and gentleness of the Father, Christ is the rod of chastisement; to those who are perfect, he is a flower. At the end, he will be a flower to both.

[7] *On Prayer* 20. 2.

[8] *Com. Jn.* I. 29. 201–2. For an example of the conjunction of Romans 8: 15 and John 15: 15, see 'The Commentary of Origen upon the Epistle to the Ephesians', p. 237.

[9] For other references to friendship with God, see *C. Cel.* III. 28, III. 56, and IV. 6.

in the Son, we are given the 'spirit of adoption as sons' that we may be called 'sons of God' (Rom. 8: 14–15, Gal. 3: 26).[10] But it is not appropriate that those 'who have been deemed worthy to have one Father with him should pray to a brother'.[11] He concludes:

Let us pray, then, as to God, let us make intercession as to a Father, let us make supplication as to a Lord, let us give thanks as to God and Father and Lord, and by no means as to the Lord of a slave. For the Father might rightly be reckoned both as Lord of the Son and Lord of them who have become sons through him. As 'he is not the God of the dead, but of the living [Mk. 12: 27, and parallels],' so he is not the Lord of ignoble slaves, but of those who are ennobled, who at the beginning because of their infancy, lived in fear, but afterwards in love (ἀγάπην) serve a happier servitude than that of fear.[12]

Here, in his enthusiasm to stress the accessibility of God to those who stand before God as brothers of *the* Son, Origen ignores his careful distinctions of vocabulary with their relational logic. However we think of God, whatever titles we use for him in prayer, we are to be aware that our relationship with God is no longer defined by the fear that a slave has for his master; rather it is defined by love. The master–servant relationship has been redefined. In effect, for those who have become sons, the lordship of God has been transformed into fatherhood. God as Lord is not the Lord of ignoble slaves, but of sons. This is sealed by the fact that God is Lord also of the Son. Origen sacrifices the language of the Father–Son relation for the purpose of affirming that the essence of that relation is available now to all who are adopted as sons in Christ, whatever words we may use to describe our new relationship to God. The reference to Mark 12: 27 confirms our new status. As we have seen, Origen associates this verse with God as 'he who is', granting being through participation in Christ to those who are non-beings. The servitude of love is then a servitude given to those whose nature has been changed by the life of God found in the Son. The implication is that the 'noble slaves' are *in*

[10] 15. 2–4.
[11] 15. 4.
[12] 16. 1.

essence sons, because their big brother is Son before them! Sonship, being, and love are brought together here in a way which matches the nature of God as the good Father, 'he who is'.

The two agents who (under the Father's aegis) effect the transition from fear to love are the Son and the Holy Spirit, the Son as the eternally-begotten Son who is 'Son by nature', and the Holy Spirit as the 'spirit of adoption'. We become sons of God as we are incorporated into the Son of God. In the outline in *Commentary on John* XXXII. 30 of the sequence of stages through which we must pass in order to become sons of God it is the movement from being infants of Christ to being his brothers that is the critical moment in our becoming sons of God.[13] In *On Prayer*, as we have seen, it is as we are regenerated (1 Pet. 1: 3) in the Son that we receive his gift of the 'spirit of adoption' and may be called 'sons of God' (Rom. 8: 14–15, Gal. 3: 26). Thus as the brothers of Christ it is appropriate for us to address the Father in prayer.[14] In fragment 243 of the *Commentary on Matthew* he states that one knows God as Father when one becomes a brother of the Son.

Origen directly links our birth as sons in the Son with the idea of the eternal generation of the Son in *Homilies on Jeremiah* IX. 4. Here he uses the image of the generation of brightness by light to explain the eternal generation of the Son, and he then broadens the discussion to include the manner by which we become sons of God. He makes a contrast between the quality of the moral life of those who have the devil for their father and the quality of the moral life of those who have God for their father. Citing 1 John 3: 8 in the form 'Every one who commits sin is born (γεγέννηται) of the devil',[15] he suggests that as often as we commit sin we are born of the devil. He writes: 'Unhappy then is the one who is born unceasingly from the devil, and conversely, happy is the one who is born unceasingly by God.' In effect, he continues, God has not begotten justice once for all time, but is continuously generating

---

[13] 30. 368–75.
[14] *On Prayer* 15. 4.
[15] The text of 1 John reads: 'He who commits sin is (ἐστίν) of the devil', and there appears to be no variant. For a discussion of the significance for Origen of the differences in form of the verse, see below, pp. 103–4.

justice in each good human act. This is comparable to the eternal, continuous generation of the Son, which, he concludes, is the means by which we become sons of God:

If the Saviour is continuously begotten by the Father, so also, if you possess the 'spirit of adoption', God continuously generates you in him [the Saviour] according to each of your works, each of your thoughts. And being begotten, you thereby become a continuously begotten son of God, in Christ Jesus.

This continuous generation encompasses the whole of our lives, each deed and each thought: the eternal generation of the Son is of critical importance in Origen's conception of how our souls are perfected. The eternal generation of the Son has causal priority. It is through the 'spirit of adoption' and our concurrent participation in the Saviour that we become sons of God. Our relationship with God as sons is logically of a second order to that of the Son's relationship. The argument of the passage does not undermine the Son's status as *only*-begotten and Son by nature. Begotten by the Son, we receive a share in the continuous generation that the Father grants the Son, and we become sons of God. Origen thus extends the significance of the eternal relationship of Father and Son beyond the doctrine of God to encompass the doctrine of salvation.

In an analysis of Ephesians 1: 5 'He destined us in love to be his sons through Jesus Christ', Origen distinguishes between the Son and those who have been adopted as sons and explains how the Son brings about that adoption. There he points out that the name 'sons by adoption' stands in contrast to that of 'son by nature', and refers to those who have been predestined by God. Consequently, the name 'sons by adoption' should not be assigned to the Saviour, but to those who, having once been subject to the spirit of slavery unto fear, have now become worthy of freedom and worthy to hear Christ's words 'I no longer call you servants' (Jn. 15: 15), because of which they have received the 'spirit of adoption'.[16] The tacit assumption is that the Saviour is Son by nature. Origen goes on to make it clear that our sonship is granted by the Son, tying our

---

[16] 'The Commentary of Origen upon the Epistle to the Ephesians', p. 237.

reception of the Son tightly together with the granting of the 'spirit of adoption': when one receives the Son, one does not first possess the Son and *then* make room for the 'spirit of adoption'; rather, the 'adoption as sons comes into' (ἐπεισέρχεται) us through Christ. The whole of the process by which we become sons is grounded in the Son who is Son by nature.

Origen makes evident in fragment 73 of the *Homilies on Luke* his concern that the distinction between the Son by nature and the sons by adoption, and the priority of the former over the latter, should be maintained. Even after we have become sons of God, the difference between us and the Son remains. Lest there be any confusion, Origen advises his listeners that although the words of John 1: 12–13 testify to the fact that we may become sons, they do not mean that we are transformed into God's nature (φύσις); rather, it is through the grace of Christ that we are enabled to call God Father.[17]

If the Son has the pre-eminent role in bringing us to adoption as sons, Origen also assigns a prominent role to the Holy Spirit, albeit a less clearly defined one. His doctrine of the Holy Spirit is not as fully developed as his doctrine of the Son.[18] But, as we have seen, he includes the Holy Spirit with the Father and the Son in his discussion of the nature of God in the first chapter of *De Principiis*, and the Holy Spirit features significantly in the parallel discussion in *Commentary on John* XIII.[19] With the Father and the Son, the Holy Spirit is incorporeal and has hypostatic existence.[20] There are hints that Origen thought that the Spirit existed eternally. He is inclined to apply the 'willing/able' argument for the eternal nature of the Son's existence to the Holy Spirit as well: to say that the

---

[17] The contrast between the only-begotten Son by nature and those who have become sons by adoption is made explicit in a fragment of the *Commentary on John* in the *Apology of Pamphilus*. The text reads that those who receive the spirit of adoption 'are without doubt sons of God, but not as the only-begotten Son. The only-begotten is Son by nature, Son always, and indissolubly' (*Com. Jn.*, pp. 562–3).

[18] Part of the difficulty for Origen is that he is not always certain which biblical verses refer to God as spirit and which refer to the Holy Spirit. See e.g. *DP* I. 3. 6, where he discusses Genesis 2: 7.

[19] XIII. 20–5.

[20] *DP* I. 1. 3, *Com. Jn.* II. 10. 76.

Holy Spirit gained a knowledge he once did not possess through the Son would be to introduce time and change into the divine relationships.[21] This is confirmed in the Greek fragment of the *Commentary on Genesis*, where, after stating his argument for the eternity of God's fatherhood on the basis of the 'willing/able' argument with respect to the Son, he says, 'It is certainly necessary also to say the same thing concerning the Holy Spirit.'[22] The fragment ends at this point, and it is not possible to know whether he would have attempted to support the eternal existence of the Holy Spirit with an appeal to the logic of relation.

In quoting the phrase 'spirit of adoption as sons', Origen is placing the Holy Spirit at the centre of the process of adoption, along with the Son. He does not explain the relationship between these two agents in this transformation, but clearly both are essential and closely linked. In *Homilies on Jeremiah* IX. 4,[23] our continuous generation in the continuously begotten Son is contingent on our possessing the 'spirit of adoption'. There are suggestions that the Holy Spirit is the gift of the Son. For instance, in *On Prayer* we are described as receiving the 'spirit of adoption' through our regeneration in the Son.[24] The passage from the *Commentary on Ephesians* referred to above[25] states that we are given the Spirit 'through the Son'. Here Origen is concerned that our reception of the 'spirit of adoption' should not be thought to be subsequent to our possession of the Son. He implies that our reception of both, predestined by God and grounded in the Son by nature, is simultaneous: 'For only through Christ does the adoption as sons come into us.'[26] As we have seen,[27] the Holy Spirit, as the spirit of adoption, is portrayed as the purveyor of God's love,

---

[21] *DP* I. 3. 4. Origen accepts what he assumes to be the traditional Christian teaching, based on the Bible, that the Holy Spirit shares in the divine life with the Father and the Son. See the whole of *DP* I. 3.

[22] *Com. Gen.*, in Eusebius, *Contra Marcellum* I. 4, GCS, pp. 22, 11–18.

[23] Discussed above, pp. 97–8.

[24] 15. 4.

[25] p. 98.

[26] 'The Commentary of Origen upon the Epistle to the Ephesians', p. 237.

[27] Above, p. 94.

which is the 'perfect love' that 'drives out fear' (1 Jn. 4: 18).[28] As the agent of God's love, the Holy Spirit's place of activity is the human heart.[29] It is the love that the Spirit brings into our hearts which characterizes the spiritual condition of those who no longer stand before God as fearful servants, but who stand before God as loving sons and know him as Father.

But if our coming to the status of sons is something that God does for us through the Son and Holy Spirit, it can only take place if we live morally pure lives, and as we grow in our knowledge of Wisdom. This corresponds to the general pattern of Origen's conception of the three-stage progression of purification, knowledge, and perfection by which we come to a full and saving knowledge of God. The longest discussion of the issue occurs in *Commentary on John* XX, which is largely devoted to it, and the issue is also discussed at length in *Homilies on Jeremiah* IX. 4, Fragment 73 of *Homilies on Luke*, and *On Prayer* 22.

Origen's presentation of the moral and intellectual dimension of our coming to know God as Father exhibits the same tension between the concepts and language of being and of willing as we have already seen in his discussions of the transition from non-being to being through participation in God as 'he who is', and the place of ethics in that transition.[30] He maintains that our moral purification is made complete and final by our participation in the Son by nature and the Holy Spirit, but also that our moral and spiritual progression towards the knowledge of God as Father is a continuing, dynamic process. He wants both to say that when we become children of God we are no longer capable of sinning and to attribute the maintenance of our moral purity as sons to the ongoing exercise of our wills.

Origen's perception of the place of moral decision-making in the transition from servitude to sonship must be seen against the background of his adamant opposition to the Gnostic belief that one's spiritual and moral status is predetermined by one's nature. Properly understood, the transition is to be perceived to come about as the result of the kind of lives we choose to live. In

---

[28] *Com. Matt.* XIII. 26.
[29] *On Prayer* 2. 3, quoting Galatians 4: 6.
[30] See the discussion above, pp. 32–4.

Commentary on John XX, he takes Heracleon to task for maintaining that while some people are 'sons by nature', others are
'sons by adoption'.[31] He states that 'absolutely no one among men
is from the beginning a son of God' (οὐδεὶς ἀνθρώπων ἀρχῆθεν υἱός
ἐστιν θεοῦ).[32] This presumably is in contrast to the Son, who 'in the
beginning' was the Word and who is Son by nature eternally. To
fail to make plain the distinction between the Son by nature and
sons by adoption would be to allow the collapse of man's status as
a moral agent, as well as the destruction of the unique status of the
Son. Earlier in Book XX of the commentary, in his exegesis of
John 8: 42 'Jesus said to them, "If God were your Father, you
would love me, for I proceeded and came forth from God"', he
writes of the apostle Paul that there was a time when he hated
Jesus and during that time God was not his Father, for God is not
the Father of those who do not love Jesus. He concludes that
consequently it was not by nature (φύσις) that Paul became a son
of God.[33] It is only when one loves Jesus that God becomes one's
Father.

What determines our status before God is the quality of our
moral decisions. In the sections of *Commentary on John* XX
following his assessment of Paul's spiritual status, Origen asks the
question of the time at which God becomes our Father, and he
answers by linking the question with a discussion of our moral
conduct. If we choose to obey the commandments then God
becomes our Father and we become his sons. This he thinks is the
teaching of Matthew 5: 43–5. 'You have heard that it was said,
"You shall love your neighbour and hate your enemy." But I say to
you, Love your enemies and pray for those who persecute you, so
that you may be sons of your Father who is in heaven'.[34] We are
called to imitate our heavenly Father, who loves all things and
hates nothing that he has created. We come to resemble God

---

[31] XX. 24. 213.

[32] XX. 33. 290.

[33] XX. 17. 135–9.

[34] 17. 141–2, a text which he also cites in the parallel discussions in *Homilies on
Luke* and *On Prayer*, and which is one of the biblical texts he most often cites in his
discussions of the ascent of the soul to the knowledge of God.

through our moral perfection, and so make the transition from being God's servants to being his sons.[35]

But Origen also argues that no one who is born of God is capable of committing sin, a tenet he finds confirmed by 1 John 3: 8 'He who commits sin is of the devil', and 1 John 3: 9 'No one born of God commits sin; for God's nature (σπέρμα) abides in him, and he cannot sin because he is born of God'.[36] In fragment 73 of the *Homilies on Luke* he links 1 John 3: 9 to the reference to the imperishable seed in 1 Peter 1: 23, which he says one receives when one is born of God, and to John 1: 12–13. He appears to take 1 John 3: 9 literally, for the 'power of the seed' within one makes one 'no longer capable of sinning'.[37] In line with this contention, he posits a strict dichotomy between having God for one's Father and having the devil for one's Father. There is no intermediate position.[38] In so far as one commits sin, one is a son of the devil, and in so far as one is morally perfect one is a son of God.[39] One cannot be called both a son of God on the basis of one's good acts, and a son of the devil on the basis of one's evil acts.[40] He finds support for this idea in the words of John 8: 41 'You do what your Father did',[41] and John 8: 44 'You are of your father the devil, and your will is to do your father's desires'.[42]

Origen is apparently unwilling to entertain the idea that the sons of God might in fact commit even occasional acts of evil. He seems to assume that whoever becomes a son of God acquires a new ontological condition which is akin to that of God, a condition which makes one constitutionally incapable of sinning. Those who receive being from 'he who is' are not capable of sin. This accounts for the difference that Origen perceives between being 'of the devil' and being 'born of God'. In *Homilies on Jeremiah* IX. 4, he cites 1 John 3: 8 in the form: 'Every one who commits sin is born

---

[35] 17. 146–8.
[36] See his discussion in *Com. Jn.* XX. 13–15.
[37] *Com. Jn.* XX. 15. 120.
[38] See esp. *Com. Jn.* XX. 14. 111–15.
[39] e.g. *Com. Jn.* XX. 13. 107, and *Hom. on Jer.* IX. 4.
[40] *Com. Jn.* XX. 14. 111.
[41] XX. 13–15.
[42] XX. 21–4.

(γεγέν(ν)ηται) of the devil' and makes a contrasting parallel between that and being born from God. But in the *Commentary on
John* XX. 14, he cites the verse in the form 'He who commits sin is
(ἐστίν) of the devil',[43] and he thinks that it is significant that John
speaks of 'being born of God' and of 'being of the devil' rather
than 'being of God' and 'being born of the devil'. He maintains
that the very expression 'being born of God' in comparison with 'is
of the devil' indicates the superiority of the one who is a son of
God. In this context he maintains that to be 'born of God' is
superior to 'being of God'.[44]

But having established that those who have become sons are
incapable of committing sin, Origen is not prepared to abandon his
belief in the dynamic, progressive nature of salvation which
reflects the freedom of our wills. Surprisingly, in *Commentary on
John* XX, he argues that we may progress within the status of
sonship. We may become more and more sons of God. Just as,
according to Matthew 23: 15, when the Pharisees make a proselyte
they make him 'twice as much a child of hell as themselves', so it is
also possible for 'one to become a son of God two times more than
another'. While he employs the logic of his argument to affirm the
vastly superior status of *the* Son—if one may be more times a son
than another, how much the more is the 'first born of all creation'
Son of God than those who are 'sons by adoption'[45]—he also
applies it to our sonship. We progress from partial sonship to
perfect sonship the more we understand the 'ineffable' words of
God, until finally we become 'perfectly and unsurpassably a son of
God' (τελείως καὶ ἀνυπερβλήτως . . . υἱὸς θεοῦ).[46] The perfect son
knows 'all mysteries and all knowledge' (1 Cor. 13: 2), and 'along

---

[43] 14. 114. As observed above, p. 97 n.15, the Epistle of John reads 'He who
commits sin is (ἐστίν) of the devil', and the text does not appear to allow a variant.
Three times in *Com. Jn.* XX. 10. 78, 22. 176, and 28. 255, Origen has the verse in
the form ἐκ τοῦ διαβόλου γεγέν(ν)ηται.

[44] XX. 15. 116–22. This (implicit) understanding of moral constancy leading to a
change in one's being has affinities with his presentation of the soul of Christ.
Christ's soul only ever chose to love righteousness, and thus 'what formerly
depended upon the will was by the influence of long custom changed into nature'
(*DP* II. 6. 5–6).

[45] 34. 298–303.

[46] 34. 304.

with these things, accomplishes the works of perfect love'.[47] Even if we live the perfect moral life, but fail to understand the words of God, we are not of God.[48]

Origen acknowledges that the idea that we may progress in sonship appears to be paradoxical; certainly, the idea that we may become more and more adequately sons of God sits uneasily with the idea that our becoming sons brings with it a change in our nature that makes committing sin an impossibility. Wiles has noted that for Origen being 'in Christ' is something that has to be progressively realized; the 'development of consistently good actions is a slow and laborious business'.[49] But in the *Commentary on John*, Origen suggests that once we have become a son through our moral perfection, we cannot revert to being less than a son, and that having progressed to a better stage of sonship, we cannot fall back to a lesser sonship.[50] His ethics, as it is expressed in the course of his discussion of sonship, is perfectionistic, but it is also optimistic. Harl remarks that 'Origène est un optimiste, pour qui la lutte contre les passions est une première étape, vite dépassée, de la progression intérieure'.[51] Having become sons, we stand on an ontological plateau from which we can only go upwards; we can only progress, we cannot regress. Sonship then is a category of existence; but once we are within that category, it would seem that we realize it more and more as our knowledge of Wisdom increases.

Our progression to the status of sonship and the saving knowledge of God as Father finds particular focus for Origen in the ability to *address* God with the title Father. This ability is of signal importance for our understanding of Origen's thinking about the fatherhood of God because he perceives the addressing of God with the title Father as distinctively the activity of the Son, which

---

[47] 34. 305.

[48] 34. 309.

[49] M. Wiles, *The Divine Apostle: The Interpretation of St Paul's Epistles in the Early Church* (Cambridge, 1967), p. 117.

[50] W. Telfer, *The Forgiveness of Sins: An Essay in the History of Christian Doctrine and Practice* (London, 1959), pp. 56–60, discusses Origen's understanding of post-baptismal sin and penitence.

[51] Harl, *Origène*, p. 321.

arises from his unique relationship with the Father, and because this ability represents for him the climax of the practice of prayer, a practice in which we come especially close to God, and he to us. Only those upon whom the Son and the Holy Spirit have bestowed the intimate knowledge and love of the Father are able to emulate the Son's form of address. The two themes of the work of the Son and the Holy Spirit in bringing us to sonship, and the corresponding necessity of our living morally pure lives and striving to grow in the knowledge of Wisdom, are both fundamental to Origen's conception of how we become capable of calling God Father. His conception of the ability to call God Father is also especially significant because it is a principal indicator of his attitude to the question of the knowledge of the fatherhood of God in the two Testaments.

Origen's most thorough discussion of the ability to call God Father occurs in *On Prayer* 20, where he deals with the phrase 'Our Father' from the first line of the Lord's Prayer. His commitment to the significance of calling God Father in prayer is apparent when it is set against the background of his doctrine of prayer. He regards the practice of prayer as an activity in which we may come to an intimate knowledge of God. Prayer is not only an activity in which we engage when we are actually saying our prayers; it also encompasses the whole of our lives. The reference to praying without ceasing in 1 Thessalonians 5: 17, he says, can only makes sense if 'virtuous deeds or commandments fulfilled' are included as part of prayer. We must think of the 'whole life of the saint as one great unbroken prayer'.[52] As we live morally pure lives, and as we pray spiritually, we ascend from the realm of the senses to the realm of the divine, and concurrently the Son and the Father draw near to us, 'dwelling' with us in our 'secret place'.[53] We come eventually to 'make intercessions not only with the righteous God, but also with the Father'.[54]

But if the promise of prayer is great, so also are the difficulties involved in doing it well. The introduction to *On Prayer* is a

---

[52] *On Prayer* 12. 2.
[53] *On Prayer* 20. 2.
[54] Ibid.

statement of how weighty a task it is both to write on the subject of prayer, and to practice it adequately.[55] Prayer is one of the 'greatest themes [that] surpass man's understanding'.[56] It is impossible to write with true understanding on the subject of prayer unless one has the 'illumination of the Father . . ., the teaching of his firstborn Word, and the operation of the Spirit'.[57] Origen prays therefore that he might be granted spiritual insight by the Holy Spirit so that the prayers in the Gospels, which he intends to analyse, might be made plain.[58] The complexities of writing on prayer parallel those of the actual practice of prayer. The Father, Son, and Holy Spirit aided the biblical saints as they prayed. The Holy Spirit interprets the mind of God to us (1 Cor. 2: 11),[59] and he intercedes for us with the 'unspeakable words' which it is not possible 'for a man to utter' (2 Cor. 12: 4), so that our inability to pray adequately is overcome.[60] The Holy Spirit 'prays in the hearts of the saints', and thus their prayers are 'truly spiritual'.[61]

Prayer reaches its proper fulfilment when we are able to address God as Father. The Son is the model and the means, with the Holy Spirit, by which we are made capable of doing this. In *On Prayer* 20, Origen makes clear his conviction that Jesus' addressing God as Father marked a new departure in our relationship with God. He begins his analysis of 'Our Father' by stating that 'it is worthwhile examining with unusual care the Old Testament, as it is called, to see if it is possible to find anywhere in it a prayer in which someone calls God Father.'[62] But, notwithstanding the fact that the prayers of the Old Testament are 'truly spiritual', as he points out in the introduction to *On Prayer*,[63] such a thorough search reveals that there are no such prayers, a point he also makes in *Commentary on John* XIX. 5. 28. He concludes that he 'has not

[55] 2. 6.
[56] 1. 1.
[57] 2. 6.
[58] Ibid. The treatise is effectively Origen's prayer.
[59] 1. 1.
[60] 2. 3.
[61] 2. 5.
[62] 22. 1.
[63] 2. 5.

yet succeeded in finding in a prayer that confident affirmation in styling God as Father which was made by the Saviour'. He acknowledges that God is occasionally referred to as Father outside the context of prayer in the Old Testament, and that there are those in the Old Testament who are styled 'sons of God'. As evidence for this, he quotes three verses from Deuteronomy 32: 18 'Thou hast forsaken the God who begat thee', 32: 6 'Is not he thy Father that bought thee, and hath made thee and established thee', and 32: 20 'Sons in whom is no faith'; Isaiah 1: 2 'I have begotten and brought up sons, but they have rejected me';[64] and Malachi 1: 6 'A son will honour his father, and a servant his master: and if I am a father where is my honour? and if I am a master, where is my fear?'[65] But, he contends, there is no 'firm and unchangeable affirmation of sonship' among the figures of the Old Testament.[66] The verses from the Old Testament demonstrate the essential inadequacy of the relationship that those who are called 'sons' had with God.[67] They are 'blameworthy', since, in the words of Galatians 4: 1, although they are heirs, they are servants.[68]

Origen maintains that this state of affairs changed completely with the incarnation, the 'sojourn of our Lord Jesus Christ, when those who desire it "receive adoption as sons" (Gal. 4: 5)'. In support of this assertion, he cites Romans 8: 15 in conjunction with John 1: 12.[69] In Contra Celsum he observes that those who have within them the 'spirit of adoption' are able to cry 'Abba, Father', not only 'in words' but in reality.[70] Moreover, the addressing of God as Father is not only something we are enabled to do through the 'sojourn' of Christ, but it is something that Christ specifically enjoined us to do. As evidence of this, in On Prayer 22. 3 Origen quotes the opening words of Luke's version of the Lord's Prayer,

[64] As we shall see, the interpretation of these texts was a crucial issue in the Arian debate.

[65] On Prayer 22. 1.

[66] 22. 2.

[67] There is a lack of congruence between what he says about sonship here and what he says in Com. Jn. XX, where sonship is a condition from which the believer cannot fall back.

[68] On Prayer 22. 2.

[69] Ibid.

[70] C. Cel. VIII. 6.

Luke 11: 2 'When you pray, say, Father', and he says in fragment
73 of the *Homilies on Luke*, which deals with Luke 11: 2, that
Christ specifically enjoined us to call God Father. The implication
is that as a result of the incarnation of the Son, and the concurrent
gift of the Holy Spirit, we may become 'firm and unchanging' sons
of God and, like the Saviour, may address God 'confidently' as
Father.

The ability to call God Father too, as more generally with our
adoption as sons, is bound up with our moral behaviour and our
intellectual advance. In both fragment 73 of the *Homilies on Luke*
and *On Prayer*, Origen maintains that it is only possible to address
God with the title of Father if we live lives that are free of sin: 'A
son can give this title to God by glorifying him and observing the
commandment', by which he means Matthew 5: 44–5. He warns
that we should not address God as Father if we are not true sons. If
we are truly to know God as Father, we must live lives that
manifest the moral perfection of the heavenly Father. Just as those
who say Jesus is Lord in the Holy Spirit (1 Cor. 12: 3) must say it
from the heart, so also those who say 'Our Father who art in
heaven' must say it from the heart, through the presence of the
Spirit, who 'bears witness' with their spirit that they are 'children
of God' (Rom. 8: 16); those who have the 'seed' (1 Jn. 3: 9) within
them say 'Our Father' by their deeds, whose source is the heart.[71]
The words without the deeds of righteous living are not enough. In
a passage in *On Prayer* replete with the themes of his conception of
the journey of the soul, Origen writes of those who 'in everything'
say, 'Our Father which art in heaven':

Every deed and word and thought of theirs, having been formed by 'the
only-begotten Word' [Jn. 1: 14, 18] after his likeness, imitates 'the image
of the invisible God' [Col. 1: 15] and is 'after the image of the Creator'
[Col. 3: 10] who 'makes his sun to rise on the evil and the good, and sends
rain on the just and the unjust' [Matt. 5: 45], so that there is in them 'the
image of the heavenly' [1 Cor. 15: 49], who is himself 'the image of God'
[Col. 1: 15]. The saints, therefore, being 'an image' of an image (that
image being the Son), acquire an impression (ἀπομάττονται) of sonship,
becoming 'conformed' not only 'to the body of the glory' [Phil. 3: 21] of

[71] *On Prayer* 22. 3.

Christ, but also to him who is in 'the body' [cf. 2 Cor. 12: 2, 3]. They become conformed to him who is in 'the body of the glory', as they are 'transformed by the renewing of the mind' [Rom. 12: 2].[72]

Those who properly address God as Father imitate the Son, who is the image of God, in ethics and in thought. Thus they are to be identified as saints and described as being the image of an image, their original image having been restored. Our perception of the Son deepens as we progress through the knowledge of the incarnate Logos to a knowledge of the eternal Logos, and we become sons as we acquire the knowledge the eternal Logos.

Origen's attitude to the role of the incarnation in the revelation of the fatherhood of God is ambivalent, and the evidence needs to be discussed at length. In spite of the overall pattern of his theology, which stresses the continuity between the Logos' revelation of the knowledge of God in the Old Testament and that in the New, he is inclined to think that the transition from a knowledge of God as Lord to the knowledge of God as Father is brought about specifically by the incarnation. Indeed, on three of the four occasions on which he discusses the question of whether or not the saints of the Old Testament knew God as Father, he concludes that they did not.

In *Commentary on John* XIX, as in *On Prayer*, Origen maintains that God is not addressed as Father in any of the prayers of the Old Testament. Although he is sensitive in the commentary to the possibility that he is giving ground to the Marcionites, he is nevertheless sufficiently committed to the idea that it is the incarnation which reveals the knowledge of God as Father to be willing to entertain the possibility that the heretics might be right in their contention that 'Moses and the prophets did not know the Father'.[73] He adduces as evidence the fact that in the 'innumerable' prayers recorded in the Psalms, the prophets, and the Law, 'absolutely no one' prays to God as Father. He goes on to associate the ability to call God Father with the incarnation and the concurrent 'outpouring' (ἐκχέω) of the 'spirit of adoption as sons'

---

[72] 22. 4.
[73] 5. 27, discussed above, p. 80.

brought about by Christ.[74] The people of the Old Testament could not call God Father because they, like those who believe in God through the Son *after* his coming, awaited the 'outpouring' of the 'spirit of adoption of sons'.

However, having made this bold assertion of the definitive role of the incarnation in the ability to call God Father, he then qualifies it. There are those in the Old Testament for whom the *spiritual* coming of Christ had already happened, and who, being perfect, had already received the 'spirit of adoption' and consequently may have called God Father. But, Origen adds, if they used the word at all they used it in a secret manner so that they would not 'anticipate the grace that Jesus poured out on the whole world. Jesus calls all men to adoption as sons in order that he may announce the name of God to his brothers and to praise the Father in the midst of the church'. In support of this, he cites Psalm 22: 22 (Heb. 2: 12) 'I will tell of thy name to my brethren; in the midst of the congregation I will praise thee'.[75] The knowledge of the fatherhood of God is part of the Logos' revelation to the Old Testament saints prior to the incarnation. The distinctive contribution of the incarnation is thus not the making of a qualitatively new departure in the knowledge of God, but rather the making of a quantitatively new departure. Because of the incarnation, *all* may come to know God as Father. The point is the same as that which Origen makes generally about the knowledge of God when he corrects Celsus' reading of *Timaeus* 28C.[76] In *Commentary on John* XIX at least, Origen is prepared to harmonize his view of the ability to call God Father with two of his basic theological postulates: that, prior to the incarnation, the Son made God fully known to the saints of the Old Testament, and that, through the incarnation, the Son extends that knowledge of God to everyone.

However, as we have seen, in his interpretation of 'Our Father'

---

[74] 5. 28. The verb 'to pour out' ($\dot{\epsilon}\varkappa\chi\dot{\epsilon}\omega$) may be an allusion to the gift of the Holy Spirit at Pentecost. The verb occurs in Acts 2: 17 and 18, in Acts 2: 33 and 10: 45, and in Titus 3: 6. It may also be an allusion to Romans 5: 5, where the same verb is used to describe the process by which the Holy Spirit brings the love of God into our hearts.

[75] Discussed above, pp. 84–5, in reference to Father as a name for God.

[76] *C. Cel.* VII. 43. See the discussion of Origen's epistemology above, pp. 47–8.

in *On Prayer* 20, Origen makes no qualification of his attribution of the revelation of fatherhood to the incarnation. There he posits a sharp distinction between the experience of God in the Old Testament and that in the New. By identifying the 'sons' of the Old Testament with the 'servants' of Galatians 4: 1, and stressing their inability to call God Father in prayer, he effectively claims that no one in the Old Testament had succeeded in moving beyond a relationship with God that was defined by slavery and fear. Notwithstanding the fact that the prayers of the Old Testament are 'truly spiritual' and the fact that God is referred to as Father in the Old Testament, no one in the Old Testament had acquired the close relationship of knowledge and love with God which Origen thinks characterizes those who have been adopted as sons, and which issues in our ability to call God Father in prayer.

The positing of such a disjunction between the knowledge of God in the Old and the New Testaments reflects a tension in Origen's understanding of the nature of the relation between the two. The supposition that there is a continuity between the description of God in the Old Testament and that in the New is of critical importance for his development of a doctrine of God in contradistinction to that of the Marcionites. In his desire to maintain that continuity, he sometimes emphasizes the identical presence of the Logos in both Testaments. As we have seen,[77] it is a fundamental tenet of his theology that the Logos fully revealed the knowledge of God to the writers of the Old Testament, as well as to the writers of the New Testament. But at other times he risks creating a sense of discontinuity between the two. He does nothing in *On Prayer* to qualify the disjunction he has created between the knowledge of God in the two Testaments. Indeed, his stress on the thoroughness with which he has examined the evidence of the Old Testament prayers serves to heighten the sense of his commitment to the notion that there is a divide between the witness of the two. This is especially remarkable in the light of the fact that *On Prayer* contains anti-Marcionite argument,[78] and in the light of the

[77] Discussed above, pp. 51–4.

[78] It is one of the themes that runs throughout *On Prayer* 29, where Origen deals with the petition from the Lord's Prayer, 'Bring us not into temptation'. See especially sections 10–13.

sensitivity to the Marcionite issue that he plainly shows in his treatment in the *Commentary on John* of the absence of the word Father in Old Testament prayers.

But *On Prayer* 20 is not an isolated example of the incarnation being assigned an exclusive role in the revelation of the fatherhood of God. In the two other passages where Origen specifically discusses the question of whether or not the Old Testament saints knew God as Father, he concludes that they did not. In fragment 34 of *Homilies on Luke*, on the basis of the distinction between faith and knowledge, in which knowledge is deemed to be superior to faith,[79] he maintains that Abraham did not know God as Father. Although the Logos revealed himself to Abraham, Abraham was only enabled to *believe* in God as Father, he did not *know* him as Father.

More pointedly, in one of his last works, the *Commentary on Matthew*, Origen says that it was not until after the resurrection that the patriarchs knew God as Father. In *Commentary on Matthew* XVII. 36, commenting on Matthew 22: 31–2 and its reference to Exodus 3: 6 'And as for the resurrection of the dead, have you not read what was said to you by God, "I am the God of Abraham, and the God of Isaac, and the God of Jacob?" He is not the God of the dead, but of the living', he heightens the contrast between the knowledge of God before the incarnation and the knowledge of God after it by giving an extensive account of what he perceives to be the extreme closeness that existed between God, who as ὁ ὤν, is the God of the living, and each of the patriarchs, Abraham, Isaac, and Jacob[80] (and Elijah, on the basis of a phrase from 2 Kings 2: 14, 'the God of Elijah'), and then unfavourably contrasting their relationship with God to the relationship that exists between God and the Saviour, and the

[79] For the distinction, see e.g. *Com. Jn.* XIX. 3. 16–20. Wiles, *The Divine Apostle*, p. 111, discusses Origen's tendency to place knowledge above faith, and cites other examples. Origen does not make a formal and systematic distinction between the two.

[80] The particular closeness of God to these three Origen thinks is attested by the fact that the text assigns the word God to the name of each of the patriarchs. It does not read 'the God of Abraham, Isaac, and Jacob', but 'the God of Abraham, the God of Isaac, and the God of Jacob'.

Saviour's true disciples. However close God's relationship with the patriarchs was, for them God was only God, whereas for the Saviour, who is 'greater' than they, God is more than God, he is also Father. What is more, the Saviour gives his true disciples the grace of sharing in his relationship with God. They too may know God not only as God, but also as Father. Origen interprets the reference to the resurrection of the dead in Matthew 22: 31–2 in the light of the resurrection of Christ. He argues that it was only at the moment when Jesus said to Mary, 'Do not hold me, for I have not yet ascended to the Father; but go to my brethren and say to them, "I am ascending to my Father and to your Father, to my God and to your God"' (Jn. 20: 17), that Christ granted to Abraham, Isaac, and Jacob the favour that henceforth they should know God as their Father.

Origen regards John 20: 17 as a telling indication of the time at which the revelation of the fatherhood of God took place. It may have been an especially attractive verse for him because it draws together in one place references both to being Christ's brother and to being granted the knowledge of the fatherhood of God. As we have seen, he quotes the verse in *Commentary on John* XIX. 5. 27 in support of the argument that it is possible to know God as God and God as Father, according to different aspects.[81] Later, in *Commentary on John* XXXII, he puts the verse forward as proof that it is only after the resurrection that it is possible for those who have been children of Jesus to become his brothers, and so children of God. They are given a new 'quality' ($\mu\varepsilon\tau\alpha\pi\omega\iota\omega\theta\acute{\varepsilon}\nu\tau\varepsilon\varsigma$) after the resurrection.[82] It is possible that he thought that Matthew 22: 31–2 and John 20: 17, placed together as they are in the *Commentary on Matthew*, indicate that Christ has a role along with the Father in bestowing true being. The resurrection of Christ would then be perceived to testify literally to God's ability to grant new life. The passage from *Commentary on John* XXXII implies that Origen thinks that the resurrection of Jesus demonstrates a supernatural capacity for changing the natural categories of human existence.

---

[81] Above, pp. 80–1.
[82] 30. 368–75, discussed above, pp. 93–4.

The discussion of the transition to the knowledge of the father-hood of God in *Commentary on Matthew* XVII. 36 not only stresses the disjunction in the knowledge of God between the Old and the New Testaments, but it does so in part by making a contrast between the knowledge of God as 'he who is' and the knowledge of God as Father. Both of these, as we have seen, are for Origen cardinal characteristics of God's being. And elsewhere he takes particular care to hold both tightly together against those (Marcionite) heretics who would drive them apart. Thus, in *Commentary on John* II. 13. 95–6, he argues that the God who named himself in the Old Testament as 'he who is' is the same God whom Jesus describes as good alone, God the Father.[83] Here, in the *Commentary on Matthew* (a work which also contains anti-Marcionite comment),[84] he is prepared, at least in the order of knowing, to identify the fatherhood of God as the most significant of God's attributes, superior to God's attribute of being itself. This may simply reflect his characteristic approach to the interpretation of texts and his unsystematic development of doctrine. In the context of *Commentary on Matthew* XVII. 36 Origen's attention is given to the immediate task of interpreting the text of Matthew 22: 31–2. His exegetical creativity leads him to perceive a resonance between the statement of that text and the resurrection of Christ, which allows him to express a favourite idea: the distinctive knowledge of God as Father. The purpose of the passage of the commentary is not to relate his interpretation of the Matthean text to his doctrine of God. Had this been part of his purpose, he might well have been careful to ensure that his observations in the passage were plainly in accord with the larger shape of his thinking about the characteristics of God, though, as we have seen, he is more often inclined to suggest a hierarchy in the attributes of God in passages where he is discussing the manner in which we come to know God, a hierarchy that has fatherhood at its top, than he is in passages where he is writing about God's nature. Yet the passage

---

[83] Discussed above, pp. 31–2.

[84] For instance, Marcion is mentioned by name, with Basilides and Valentinus, as a teacher of false doctrine in *Com. Matt.* XII. 23, and Marcionite doctrine is rejected in XIII. 11.

in the *Commentary on Matthew* demonstrates again that in spite of his intense concern with the threat of Marcionite theology, he is willing to make a distinction between the knowledge of God in the Old Testament and that in the New, a distinction that is marked by the advance to a knowledge of God as Father.

Why, then, was Origen so inclined to link the revelation of the fatherhood of God to the incarnation, in spite of the general drift of his theology? There are a number of reasons. First, this inclination reflects the the actual content of the biblical texts on which he comments. He was keenly aware that the fatherhood of God is a major theme of the New Testament, as his use of New Testament references demonstrates, and he was equally aware that the word Father is seldom found in the Old Testament, and nowhere in prayer. Indeed, he was so aware of this that he was tempted to fudge what evidence there is. His thought was deeply imbued with the presentation in the Gospel of John of the themes of the fatherhood of God, the children of God, and the sharp distinction between those who know the Father and those who do not; these same themes are found in the First Epistle of John, on which he commented extensively. He also interpreted Paul's statement that through the spirit of adoption we may call God Father to mark a radical transformation in our lives. He wove the Johannine and Pauline themes together and gave them a central place in his theology.

Secondly, by far the most dominant person to use the word Father to address God in the Bible is the incarnate Logos. It is the Son as he inhabits space and time who consistently addresses God in the most personal terms. As we have seen, Origen perceived that Jesus' praying to God as Father is uniquely confident. His attempt to find a special element in Jesus' prayers to the Father places him in the company of many recent biblical scholars.

This is directly related to the final reason. Origen's piety was Christ centred. He saw the relation between the Son and the Father described in the Gospels as a personal, unchanging relation of warmth, trust, and confidence. He saw this also in the lives of the disciples and the New Testament church. *On Prayer* is a particularly fine example of his piety. It testifies to Origen's vision of the Christian life as a journey away from ignorance and fear and

towards the same intensely warm and unchanging personal relationship with God, a relationship of love, which is only possible
because God is Father and because we may become his sons. We
may know him as Father and become his sons, if we, like Paul,
love Jesus.[85] The weight of the biblical evidence constrained him
to identify the historical event of the incarnation as bringing to us
the decisive knowledge of God as Father. Although he is adamant-
ly opposed to the notion that there is an ontological disjunction
between the God of the Old Testament and the God of the New
Testament, he perceived an epistemological disjunction between
the two Testaments. The incarnation effects an ontological change
in human nature, remaking us as sons, and thus it essentially
transforms our relationship with God.

The vision of the fulfilment of our soul's journey which Origen
holds out to us is that we shall come to know and to contemplate
the Father as now only the Son knows and contemplates him. At
the 'restoration' (ἀποκατάστασις)[86] of all things

there will be one activity for those who have come to God by the Word,
who is with him, which is to contemplate God, so that they might all
become perfect sons of God, being thus transformed in the knowledge of
the Father, as now only the Son knows the Father.[87]

This perfect sonship and the single activity that is sonship's proper
activity is realized 'when we become one as the Son and the Father
are one'.[88] Although this takes place at the restoration of all
things, Origen never states that the knowledge of God as Father is
one of the things that has been restored. The logic of the
Father–Son and the Almighty–Creation relations effectively pro-
hibits him from describing the pre-fall, and thus pre-redemption,
relation of God and humanity as that between a father and sons.
While it is not a concern of his to work out the implications of this

---

[85] See *Com. Jn.* XX. 17. 135–9, and the discussion above, p. 102.
[86] *Com. Jn.* I. 16. 91.
[87] Ibid. I. 16. 92: μία πρᾶξις ἔσται τῶν πρὸς θεὸν διὰ τὸν πρὸς αὐτὸν λόγον
φθασάντων ἡ τοῦ κατανοεῖν τὸν θεόν, ἵνα γένωνται οὕτως ἐν τῇ γνώσει τοῦ
πατρὸς μορφωθέντες πάντες ἀκριβῶς υἱός, ὡς νῦν μόνος ὁ υἱὸς ἔγνωκε τὸν
πατέρα.
[88] Ibid., an allusion to John 17: 21.

for his understanding of the return to God, the logic of his thinking suggests that the end state is not a return to an original state of perfection[89]—it goes beyond that to bring us into a relation of love with the Father.

The Son is the model for our knowing and loving God. We share in the Son's continuous 'uninterrupted contemplation of the depths of the Father'.[90] Origen is suggesting that the Father's eternal delight in his only-begotten Son becomes ours as well, as we, with and in the Son, turn unceasingly towards the riches of the Father. If for Origen the Son's relation with God is of a personal nature and 'the appeal to the logic of relation (if a father, then a son too) serves to underline the real plurality and mutuality of the divine life', and if Origen 'hints at a fundamental datum of later trinitarian thought, that the Father–Son relation is simply part of the *definition* of the word God, and so does not exist for the sake of anything else than itself',[91] so too his picture of the journey of the soul to God as a journey from the servant's knowledge of God as Lord to the son's knowledge of God as Father hints at the possibility that our relation with God may be of a personal nature, and that through the Son and Holy Spirit we may be taken up into the plurality and mutuality of the divine life and share in the Father–Son relation that exists for nothing other than itself.

[89] As is often assumed. See e.g. Torjesen, *Hermeneutical Procedure*, p. 122, where she cites the passage from *Com. Jn.* I. 16. 92 just quoted.
[90] *Com. Jn.* II. 2. 18.
[91] Williams, *Arius*, p. 139.

5

Origen: Conclusion

THE continuity in Origen's thought about God as Father, over time and in various kinds of writings, reflects the fact that there is a continuity of theological intention, method, and themes in his work as a whole. His theology is worked out within the parameters of Middle Platonist philosophical assumptions, but the theme of the fatherhood of God is evidence of his biblical and theological orientation. The ideas of the priority of the Father–Son relation over that between God and creation, the latter conceived as a relation between the Almighty and those over whom he holds sway and also characterized as a Lord–servant relation, and the distinction between the Son by nature and sons by adoption, are reflected in the contrast between the knowledge we have of God as servants of a Lord and the knowledge we have of God as sons of the Father. These ideas are found in *De Principiis*, and the earliest parts of the *Commentary on John* which are contemporaneous with *De Principiis*, and they are found in the *Commentary on Matthew*, as well as in the writings in between.

The sense of the personal relation of Father and Son and of the plurality and mutuality of the divine life thus permeates the whole of Origen's writings and has a significant impact on his thinking about the nature of salvation. As creation arises from the Father–Son relation, so it returns to share in that relation. It may be that his intense feelings about the kind of relation we can have with God through his Son influence the way in which he presents the Father–Son relation; but in the event there is a strong correlation between metaphysical categories and moral and spiritual categories. Origen thinks of the process of God's salvation of man, and the end to which it is directed, in much the same terms as he thinks about the relationship between the Father and the Son.

There are several overlapping patterns in Origen's conception of the journey to the saving knowledge of God: a change from non-being to being, from evil to moral purity; a coming to know God as 'he who is', true being, as perfectly good; an ascent from the realm of body to that of mind, from the perceptibles to the intelligibles. But if this ascent is Platonic in hue, it is biblical and theological in thrust. It is affected only through the grace of God in the Logos, and the final happiness of the soul consists in the contemplation of the divine hypostases. This contemplation is undertaken ultimately by those whom Origen describes as perfected as sons, for the journey to a saving knowledge of God is also described as a journey from servant to son and from fear to love, a journey that takes place as we come to know and love the one who is Son, and share in his knowledge and love of the Father.

Williams writes of the 'uneasy relationship between the two controlling factors in Origen's thought: the given constraint of Scriptural metaphor and the assumptions of Platonic cosmology'.[1] Certainly, these are the two controlling factors in Origen's thought, but the relationship between them is not so uneasy as Williams thinks. Origen seems not to have perceived any tension between his different patterns of the journey to the knowledge of God. Of the two factors, it is scriptural metaphor which has the whip hand. It is the Bible that provides Origen with the basis for linking God as Father to God as good and as 'he who is', as well as to those attributes associated with God's incorporeality. Origen was prepared to identify the fatherhood of God as the highest level in our knowledge of God and to associate it distinctively with the incarnation, which he did with no other of God's attributes; he did this even at the risk of undermining his argument for the divine unity. Father and Son are the determinative subjects in his theology.

[1] *Arius*, p. 140.

Part II

The Fatherhood of God in the Alexandrian Tradition to 325

THE fatherhood of God continued to be a theme in Alexandrian theology after Origen. The argument from the correlativity of the Father and the Son and the idea of the eternal generation of the Son were taken up and modified by Dionysius, possibly by Theognostus, and by Alexander. Arius' rejection of both the argument from correlativity and the eternal generation of the Son is best understood against the background of third-century unease with Origen's use of the argument from correlativity to explain not only the relation of Father and Son as eternal, but also the relation between God and the rational universe as eternal. This unease was most clearly expressed by Methodius of Olympus.

6

After Origen

THE writings of Dionysius of Alexandria provide evidence of the occurrence in the Alexandrian tradition of the argument from correlativity, of the discussion of God's nature as ingenerate (ἀγέννητος), and of dissatisfaction with Origen's theory of the pre-existence of souls. We read in Athanasius' collection of extracts from the writings of Dionysius of Alexandria that in a letter sent to Euphration and Ammonius,[1] Dionysius maintained that the Son was a 'thing made' (ποίημα) and 'created' (γενητός), that he was not 'proper' (ἴδιος) to the nature of God, but 'alien in substance' (ξένον κατ' οὐσίαν), as the vinedresser is different from the vine, and the shipbuilder from the boat: 'for being a ποίημα he did not exist before he was generated'.[2] In reply to the letter, Dionysius of Rome denounced those who taught that there were three δυνάμεις or separate ὑποστάσεις or three θεότητες,[3] who taught that the Son was a work of God's hands (χειροποίητος),[4] a ποίημα,[5] and who taught a 'generation' of the Son and a time when he was not.[6] On the basis of Proverbs 8: 22, he maintained that the Son could be described as created (κτίζω) but not made (ποιέω);[7] he has been 'generated' (γεγεννῆσθαι) but not in the sense of 'deliberately produced' (γεγονέναι) by the Father.[8]

---

[1] So identified by Athanasius, *De Sent. Dionysii* 9, Opitz 52. 8–9.

[2] *De Sent. Dionysii* 4, Opitz 48. 20–3. The use of ἴδιος to describe the Son's relation to the Father will be examined in the course of the discussion of Athanasius' view of the Son's relation to the Father, below, pp. 193ff.

[3] *De Decretis* 26, Opitz 22. 3–4.

[4] Opitz 22. 20.

[5] Opitz 22. 26.

[6] Opitz 22. 20–5.

[7] Opitz 23. 1–4.

[8] Opitz 23. 4–7.

The Bishop of Alexandria defended himself, reports Athanasius, by writing two treatises, the 'interrogation' and the 'defence'.[9] In them he maintains that it is acceptable to call the Son a κτίσμα or a ποίημα on the grounds that a human being can be said to be the creator of his utterance (λόγος) and the doer of an inward quality.[10] His themes are close to Origen's. He makes much of the analogy of mental action, mind, and speech (for Origen mind and will), to explain the generation of the Son. The human λόγος is the ἀπόρροια of the mind, which assumes a distinct subsistence when it is uttered, but does not diminish the internal λόγος.[11] Mind is never without its utterance, and utterance depends for its existence on mind.[12] The Word is wisdom and truth, proceeding from God.[13] The generation of the Son is an eternal generation. Like Origen, he favours the image of a light and its radiance. Radiance is simultaneous with the source of light. Quoting Wisdom 7: 25, he states that as the Son is the ἀπαύγασμα of the eternal light, so the Son also is eternal,[14] and he also cites Proverbs 8: 30 as evidence of the eternal presence of the Son with the Father, as Origen had done.[15] He brings the image of the Son as radiance directly into conjunction with the argument from relation (something Origen did not expressly do), and associates it with the correlativity of parent and child:

Therefore, since the Father is eternal, the Son, being light from light, is eternal; for when there is a parent, there is also a child. And unless there is a child, how is it possible for anyone to be a parent? But both exist, and are eternal.[16]

The correlativity of parent and child he specifies as the correlativ-

---

[9] For a defence of the authenticity of Athanasius' citations, see Williams, *Arius*, pp. 151–2.

[10] *De Sent. Dionysii* 20–1, Opitz 61. 17–62. 14.

[11] *De Sent. Dionysii* 23, Opitz 63. 7–11.

[12] Opitz 63. 12–64. 2.

[13] Opitz 65. 8–9.

[14] *De Sent. Dionysii* 15, Opitz 57. 4–7. Williams, *Arius*, pp. 152–3, points out the oddity that Dionysius is not recorded as having made a reply to the allegation that he said that the Son 'did not exist before he was generated'.

[15] Opitz 57. 12–13.

[16] Opitz 57. 14–16.

ity of father and son. As Origen had done, he argues that to speak of the Father is also to designate the Son and to speak of the Son is to designate the Father; they cannot be separated. He then adds, perhaps to protect the priority of the Father, that 'the name [Father] is what provides the ground for the union [of Father and Son]'.[17] The term ὁμοούσιος he allows if it is taken only to mean ὁμογενής, in the sense that a human parent belongs to the same genus as his or her offspring.[18] Dionysius' trinitarian thought is close to that of Origen: 'the Origenian model of (a) eternal correlativity and (b) "emanation" conceived very carefully on the analogy of the concrete act of mind subsisting over against undifferentiated and continuous mental life of substance, clearly prevails in Dionysius' theology.'[19]

There are two other aspects of Dionysius of Alexandria's thought that are important for subsequent theological discussion about the status of the fatherhood of God. Eusebius records a discussion by Dionysius of the relationship between God and matter (ὕλη). Using the third-man argument, Dionysius insists that the attribute of unoriginateness (ἀγενησία) can only be ascribed to God, for to ascribe it to matter as well would necessitate the existence of a third 'older and higher than both' to account for the existence of ἀγενησία in both. Both could not be ingenerate in any case, given that God and matter are so unlike: God is ἀπαθής, ἄτρεπτος, ἀκίνητος, and ἐργαστικός, and matter is the opposite. But while he says that God is 'the fundamental principle (ὑπόστασις) on which the universe exists', he does not go on to say that matter was created from nothing; nor does he relate his claims about God's unique status as ἀγέννητος to God's nature as eternal first principle, or to the issue of the eternal generation of the Son.[20] Such developments would have to await the theologies of Methodius and Arius. Dionysius is also critical of Origen's teaching on the

[17] De Sent. Dionysii 17, Opitz 58. 15–25.

[18] De Sent. Dionysii 18, Opitz 59. 5–13.

[19] Williams, Arius, p. 153.

[20] Eusebius, Praep. Evang. VII. 19. References are to The Letters and Other Remains of Dionysius of Alexandria, ed. C. Feltoe, (Cambridge Patristic Texts: Cambridge, 1904).

pre-existence of souls,[21] as was Peter of Alexandria at the beginning of the fourth century.[22]

The influence of the Origenian trinitarian model is apparent in the theology of Theognostus, probably Dionysius' successor as head of the catechetical school. According to Photius, Theognostus set out a system of theology in seven books.[23] He is reported to have called the Son a κτίσμα.[24] He spoke of the Son as ἀπαύγασμα and ἀπόρροια, coming 'out of the Father's substance',[25] echoing Origen's discussion of Wisdom 7 and Hebrews 1, though perhaps with less caution about the materialist implications of talking about derivation from the οὐσία of God.[26] He denies that the Son is ἐκ μὴ ὄντων.[27] Reference to the idea of the Son as the utterance of the divine mind is found in a fragment,[28] and a few lines later the Son is described as an image or 'imitation' (μίμημα) of the Father, having complete likeness (ὁμοιότης) with him.[29] Theognostus may also have used the argument from correlativity. Photius says that in his first book Theognostus writes about the Father, showing that he is the creator, against those who postulate that 'matter is co-eternal with God' (συναίδιον ὕλην τῷ θεῷ)?[30] and that in his second he writes about the Son, putting forward proofs by which 'he says that it is necessary for the Father to have a Son' (δεῖν φησὶ

---

[21] See the texts published by W. Bienert, 'Neue Fragmente des Dionysius und des Petrus von Alexandrien aus Cod. Vatop. 236', *Kleronomia* 5 (1973), 308–14, and Bienert's discussion of them in his *Dionysius von Alexandrien: Zur Frage des Origenismus im dritten Jahrhundert* (Patristische Texte und Studien 21: Berlin, 1978), pp. 119–20.

[22] Texts in Bienert, 'Neue Fragmente'; see also a brief passage attributed to Peter in *Analecta Sacra*, ed. Jean Baptiste Pitra, iv (Paris, 1883), pp. 193–4; and the discussion in L. Radford, *Three Teachers of Alexandria: Theognostus, Pierus and Peter: A Study in the Early History of Origenism and Anti-Origenism* (Cambridge, 1908), pp. 76–82.

[23] *Reliquiae sacrae*, ed. M. Routh (Oxford, 1846), iii. 412. 18.

[24] Ibid. iii. 413. 1.

[25] Ibid. iii. 411. 1–11 (= *De Decretis* 25, Opitz 21. 1–6).

[26] Williams, *Arius*, p. 154.

[27] *Reliquiae sacrae*, iii. 411. 1–2. Williams, *Arius*, p. 303 n.321, points out that if this reflects post-Nicene alteration, one would expect ἐξ οὐκ ὄντων.

[28] F. Diekamp, 'Ein neues Fragment aus den Hypotyposen des Alexandriners Theognostus', *ThQ* 84 (1902), p. 483. 2; L. Radford, *Three Teachers*, pp. 21–2.

[29] Diekamp, 483. 16–17; Radford, 25–6.

[30] *Reliquiae sacrae* iii. 412. 20–2.

τὸν πατέρα ἔχειν υἱόν).[31] The conjunction of these two ideas in succeeding chapters suggests the possibility that Theognostus thought that the Son's eternity was necessary to God eternally being Father. But Photius gives no indication of whether or not Theognostus elaborated on the contrast between the Father's relation to the Son and his relation to matter, or what his attitude was to the pre-existence of souls.

The last figure to be considered before turning to the Arian debate is Methodius of Olympus.[32] Williams describes him as the most vocal critic of Origen in the pre-Arian period.[33] Methodius attacks Origen's doctrine of the eternity of creation on the assumption that it implies the eternity of matter as a rival self-subsistent reality over against God.[34] If God is not to be thought of as beginning to impose form on matter, since Origen's argument is based on the eternity and unchangeability of the divine creative act,[35] this means that God must be eternally imposing form on matter, and thus there is an eternal non-divine principle upon which God acts. Methodius thinks that this dualism is incapable of being logically articulated, and he puts forward a version of the third-man argument to demonstrate that the concept of two ἀγένητα is self-contradictory.[36] He remarks that Origen trifles when he says that if there was a time when creation did not exist God is 'stripped of his name of Father and Almighty';[37] however, at least in the materials available to us, he gives no sign of being aware that Origen linked the eternity of the name Father specifically to the eternal generation of the Son. He does not restrict the description of God as Father to the Father–Son relation; his writings contain very occasional references to God as 'Father of all'.[38] Williams concludes that Methodius was deter-

---

[31] Reliquiae sacrae, iii. 412. 20–413. 1.

[32] For a helpful study of the thought of Methodius, see Lloyd Patterson, 'Methodius, Origen, and the Arian Dispute', in E. A. Livingstone (ed.), Studia Patristica 17. 2 (Oxford, 1982), pp. 912–23; and see also Williams, Arius, pp. 168–71.

[33] Arius, p. 168.

[34] De Creatis VI, p. 497. 8–20.

[35] De Creatis IV–V, pp. 496. 13–497. 7.

[36] De Autex. V, pp. 157. 6–159. 4.

[37] De Creatis XII, pp. 499. 32–500. 2.

[38] Symp. I. 2, p. 10. 11; De Res. III. 18, p. 415. 14; De Creatis XI, p. 499. 10.

mined to establish that belief in creation *ex nihilo* demands belief in a temporal (that is, punctiliar) beginning . . . [His] criticisms of Origen's cosmology and anthropology turn upon the inability of Origen's scheme to provide a consistent account of the Christian belief that God is wholly sufficient to himself, and thus creates out of his freedom and his gratuitous love.'[39]

Methodius' stress on the creation of the world at a quasi-temporal point has affinities with the later Arian formulation with reference to the Son: ἦν ποτε ὅτε οὐκ ἦν.[40] But he says little that is distinctive about the generation of the Word. The Word exists 'before the ages' (πρὸ αἰώνων),[41] eternally and not adoptively Son,[42] remaining forever the same.[43] He is ἀρχή of all things, but distinct from the ἄναρχος ἀρχή, the Father,[44] who is greater than he.[45] Although this seems close to Origen, Methodius' language may only mean that the Word comes into existence before the visible creation, rather than that he is co-eternal in the strict sense. The term ἄναρχος is not always to be taken as 'timeless', and Methodius assumes that origination implies temporal beginning.[46] Williams argues that Methodius' abandonment of Origen's teaching on the eternity of rational souls raises Christological problems that could result in an Arian reading of scriptural imagery about the 'creation' of the Word in a temporal sense and in an ascription of the sufferings of Jesus directly to the Word.[47] Thus Methodius 'witnesses to the existense at this juncture of just such a broadly based and wide-ranging attack upon Origen's cosmology as would make sense of Arius' own many-sided critique of the Alexandrian consensus of his day'.[48]

[39] Williams, *Arius*, pp. 168–9.
[40] Patterson, 'Methodius, Origen, and the Arian Dispute', pp. 917–18, 920.
[41] *Symp.* III. 4, p. 30. 19; VII. 1, p. 7. 12.
[42] *Symp.* VIII. 9, p. 91. 4–17.
[43] *Symp.* VIII. 9, p. 91. 11.
[44] *De Creatis* XI, p. 499. 13–15.
[45] *Symp.* VII. 1, p. 71. 15–17.
[46] Patterson, 'Methodius, Origen, and the Arian Dispute', p. 917
[47] *Arius*, pp. 170–1.
[48] Ibid. p. 171.

7

Before Nicaea

METHODIUS' repudiation of Origen's theory of the eternal existence of the rational souls set the stage for the theological struggle
of the early fourth century, a struggle centred on the tension
between the affirmation of the divine attribute of ingenerateness
and that of the eternal generation of the Son. The focus of early
Arian debate was on the status of the Son and the nature of his
relation to the Father. It was not directly concerned with the
fatherhood of God, although Alexander, and also Athanasius
early on (assuming that he wrote the letter ἑνὸς σώματος),[1] had a
sense that the debate impinged on the nature of divine fatherhood.
Arius does not discuss the idea of God's fatherhood, but his
resolution of the tension between the two postulates of the divine
ingenerateness and the eternity of the Son by the denial of the
eternal generation of the Son meant that fatherhood could not be
perceived as an essential attribute of God's nature. For Arius, the
names Father and Son did not imply a natural continuity between
the two, but rather a relational continuity created by a free act of
God's will.

The documents that will be considered in this chapter are mainly
those of the Arian debate up to 325, namely Alexander's letter, ἡ
φίλαρχος, and the writings that can be securely attributed to Arius:
his credal letter to Alexander, his letter to Eusebius of Nicomedia,
the *Thalia* extracts in *De Synodis* 15, as well as the Confession of
Arius and Euzoius. The letter ἑνὸς σώματος will be discussed in the
context of Athanasius' writings. It is not possible to arrive at a

---

[1] Christopher Stead, 'Athanasius' Earliest Written Work', *JTS* NS 39 (1988),
76–91, has convincingly demonstrated that in language, structure, and theological
content the letter has greater affinities with Athanasius' writings than with
Alexander's ἡ φίλαρχος.

certain dating for the documents, but in any case the question of dating does not affect the interpretation given here. The dating adopted here is that put forward by Williams against the dating of Opitz.[2] Williams places Arius' credal letter at *c*.320, ἡ φίλαρχος at 321/2, followed by Arius' letter to Eusebius of Nicomedia shortly afterwards, and ἑνὸς σώματος early in 325.[3] The *Thalia* most probably was written some time after ἡ φίλαρχος, and before ἑνὸς σώματος; Williams suggests mid-323.[4] Such an ordering makes most sense of Alexander's apparent ignorance of the *Thalia* when he wrote ἡ φίλαρχος, an ignorance not reflected in ἑνὸς σώματος, and the evidence of Alexander's remarks about Colluthus in ἡ φίλαρχος and Colluthus' signature on ἑνὸς σώματος.

The importance of Alexander's letter ἡ φίλαρχος for understanding the shape of Alexandrian thinking at the moment of Arius' challenge is great. The letter is long and complex, dealing with a range of key theological issues loosely ordered around the central issue of the Son's status and his relation to the Father. It suggests that while Alexander had clearly perceived the Christological and soteriological implications of Arius' teachings, he had not fully understood the logic of Arius' argument. In the face of the challenge, Alexander reaffirmed an Origenian theology of God and salvation, failing to see that this theology had itself been put under question by Arius' ideas. He maintained the traditional Alexandrian ideas of the eternity of the divine fatherhood and the

[2] Hans-Georg Opitz, 'Die Zeitfolge des arianischen Streites von den Anfängen bis zum Jahr 328', *ZNTW* 33 (1934), 131–59.

[3] See *Arius*, pp. 48–61, and esp. pp. 58–9, where he gives a list of the documents and dates. Stead's rejection of Williams' dating of ἑνὸς σώματος, 'Athanasius' Earliest Written Work', p. 91, is unconvincing; his interpretation of the Colluthus evidence is obscure.

[4] *Arius*, pp. 62–6. The novel thesis of Charles Kannengiesser, *Holy Scripture and Hellenistic Hermeneutics in Alexandrian Christology: The Arian Crisis* (Colloquy 41 of the Center for Hermeneutical Studies in Hellenistic and Modern Culture: Berkeley, Calif., 1982), pp. 1–47, that the *Thalia* was written *c*.359, possibly by someone from Aetius' entourage, or Aetius himself, has not been widely accepted and is conclusively refuted by Rowan Williams, 'The Quest of the Historical *Thalia*', in Robert C. Gregg (ed.), *Arianism: Historical and Theological Reassessments* (Patristic Monograph Series 11: Philadelphia, 1985), 1–35.

co-eternity of Father and Son. But he was also sensitive to Arius' charge that this model of the Father–Son relation threatened God's unique status as ἀγέννητος, which he, like his Alexandrian predecessors, believed was fundamental to the preservation of the idea of God as first principle. His view of salvation was inspired by Origen but refocused in response to Arius.

Alexander's main concern in the letter ἡ φίλαρχος is to ward off what he perceived to be the threat to the divine status of the Son posed by Arius' theology. The gravamen of his rejection of Arius and his supporters is that they deny 'the divinity (τὴν θεότητα) of our Saviour' and reduce the Son to the 'same level as other men'.[5] Alexander focuses on what he claims to be the two determinative tenets of Arius' thought, that 'there was a time when the Son of God was not' (ἦν ποτε ὅτε οὐκ ἦν ὁ υἱὸς τοῦ θεοῦ),[6] and that God 'created' (ἐποίησε) all things 'out of nothing' (ἐξ οὐκ ὄντων), including the Son.[7] He thinks that these are complementary. The consequences for the status of the Son he considers to be disastrous, eliminating any distinction between him and men: the Son is necessarily mutable and his relationship with God is no different from that of anyone else; there is only one kind of sonship, that acquired by moral endeavour.[8]

He counters by arguing that the words of John 1: 18 'the only-begotten Son who is in the bosom of the Father' show that the Father and Son are 'two inseparable entities' (ἀχώριστα πράγματα δύο)[9]—Origen too had referred to the Father and Son as πράγματα[10]—and he goes on to explain that John 1: 3 establishes that the Son, as the source of existence, could never have not existed.[11] All things have their existence by the Father and through the Son.[12] He writes of the Son: 'For that which is (τὸ ὄν) appears to be the opposite of, and far removed from, the things created from

[5] U. 14, 20. 7–8.
[6] U. 14, 21. 8.
[7] U. 14, 21. 10.
[8] U. 14, 21. 11–22. 3.
[9] U. 14, 22. 4–8.
[10] C. Cel. VIII. 12.
[11] U. 14, 22. 8–15.
[12] U. 14, 22. 17–19.

nothing.'[13] His identification of the Son with the Father as the source of all existent things, signified by describing him as τὸ ὄν, may reflect the influence of Origen's idea that the Father as ὁ ὤν is the source of all existence, although Origen does not use τὸ ὄν to describe the Son. Of particular importance among the things made by the Son is time; there can be no 'interval' (διάστημα) between the Father and the Son.[14]

Alexander seals his argument by appealing to the idea of the correlativity of Father and Son. The argument from correlativity, as we have seen,[15] was ultimately derived from Aristotle's discussion of the category of relation in the *Categories* 7[b]15, where Aristotle writes:

Relatives seem to be simultaneous by nature (Δοκεῖ δὲ τὰ πρός τι ἅμα τῇ φύσει εἶναι), and in most cases this is true. For there is at the same time a double and a half, and when there is a half there is a double, and when there is a slave there is a master; similarly with the others. Also, one carries the other to destruction (συναναιρεῖ).

In the *Metaphysics* 5. 15, Aristotle cites the relation between father and son as an instance of this category, though it should be noted that he uses the example of father and son to illustrate the relation of agent and patient as it arises as a result of a *temporal* event, and that in the passage from the *Categories* he says that only in *most* cases are relatives simultaneous by nature. Such third-century commentators as Alexander of Aphrodisias,[16] Plotinus,[17] and Porphyry[18] were to make similar qualifications about the father–son relation.

There is evidence that Alexander was aware of the specific terms of Aristotle's statement of the argument, wherever he may have found them, but he gives no indication of having had reservations about the simultaneity of father and son. He twice uses the verb

---

[13] *U.* 14, 22. 15.
[14] *U.* 14, 23. 21.
[15] Above, p. 69, n.21.
[16] *Arist. Met.* 406. 8–10 (*CAG* i).
[17] *Enneads* VI. 1. 7.
[18] *Arist. Cat.* S. 119. 4 ff. (*CAG* iv. 1); so also Simplicius, *Arist. Categ.* S. 194. 28–195. 30 (*CAG* viii).

συναναιρέω, in a passage which will be quoted below,[19] and Arius uses the word ἅμα in his description of Alexander's teaching about the relation of Father and Son.[20] The passage in which Alexander appeals to the argument from correlativity comes immediately after his examination of the statements that the Son was 'created out of nothing' and that 'there was a time when he was not':

Since the supposition 'out of nothing' is clearly impious, it follows that the Father is eternally Father. And he is Father because of the eternal presence of the Son, on account of whom he is called Father. And the Son being eternally with him, the Father is eternally perfect, lacking in no good thing, for he did not beget his only-begotten Son in time, nor in any interval in time, nor out of nothing.[21]

Alexander retains the hallmarks of Origen's use of the argument from correlativity—the eternity of God's fatherhood and the eternal correlativity of the Father and the Son—though his statement of it is differently orientated. Origen's use of the argument was directed towards the establishment of certain truths about the nature of God, namely God's eternal immutability, goodness, and fatherhood, whereas Alexander's use is orientated towards the establishment of truths about the status of the Son, namely that he is eternally begotten from the Father. Alexander argues that the denial of the eternal generation of the Son imperils the eternity of God's fatherhood; he makes no reference to the 'willing/able' form of orgument.

In particular, the passage contains linguistic echoes of the fragment from Origen's *Commentary on Genesis* and *De Principiis* I. 2. 9.[22] The common references in Alexander and Origen to the 'perfection' of God and his not lacking in anything 'good' in relation to the eternal correlativity of Father and Son strongly suggest that Alexander is here directly dependent either on Origen

---

[19] *U.* 14, 24. 3 and 6. See below, p. 133.
[20] *U.* 1, 2. 1.
[21] *U.* 14. 23. 28–31: Ἀσεβεστάτης οὖν φανείσης τῆς ἐξ οὐκ ὄντων ὑποθέσεως, ἀνάγκη τὸν πατέρα ἀεὶ εἶναι πατέρα· ἔστι δὲ πατὴρ ἀεὶ παρόντος τοῦ υἱοῦ, δι' ὃν χρηματίζει πατήρ· ἀεὶ δὲ παρόντος αὐτῷ τοῦ υἱοῦ, ἀεί ἐστιν ὁ πατὴρ τέλειος, ἀνελλιπὴς τυγχάνων ἐν τῷ καλῷ οὐ χρονικῶς οὐδὲ ἐκ διαστήματος οὐδὲ ἐξ οὐκ ὄντων γεννήσας τὸν μονογενῆ υἱόν.
[22] Referred to above, pp. 70–1.

himself—*De Principiis* or a commentary *florilegium*, perhaps compiled in Caesarea—or some other source which retained Origen's words.

Arius' summary of Alexander's teaching in his letter to Eusebius of Nicomedia, then, seems accurately to reflect Alexander's commitment to the argument of the correlativity of Father and Son. The summary begins: 'God eternal, Son eternal, Father and Son always together' (ἀεὶ θεὸς ἀεὶ υἱός, ἅμα πατὴρ ἅμα υἱός).[23] As we shall see in a moment, Arius rejects the use of the category of relation to explain the relation between the Father and the Son.

Having used the argument from correlativity to explore the central metaphors of Father and Son, Alexander goes on to imply that the same logic pertains to all the terms by which the Son, and consequently the Father, are known: Wisdom, Power, Word.[24] Like Origen and Dionysius, Alexander cites Proverbs 8: 30 'I was daily his delight' in confirmation of the eternal presence of Wisdom with the Father.[25] But he also stretches the argument from correlativity to include both the conception of the Son as the 'brightness' (ἀπαύγασμα) of the Father, which we have already seen in Dionysius, and that of the Son as 'image' (εἰκὼν), which is unprecedented:[26]

To say that the brightness of the Father's glory did not exist destroys (συναναιρεῖ) the original light of which it is the brightness. And if also the image of God was not eternal, it is clear that neither is that of which it is the image (εἰκὼν) eternal. But also by the non-existence of the imprinted image (χαρακτῆρα) of God's subsistence the one who is entirely portrayed (χαρακτηριζόμενος) by it is destroyed (συναναιρεῖται) as well.

He concludes that this shows that the sonship of Christ has nothing in common with the sonship of men; indeed, that his subsistence (ὑπόστασις) is ineffable (ἄρρητος).[27] The apophatic theme in

---

[23] *U.* 1, 2. 1–2.

[24] Alexander does not use the activity of the mind as an analogy for the generation of the Son, perhaps because of Arius' emphasis on God's will as the ground of the Son's existence.

[25] *U.* 14. 23. 32–24. 1.

[26] *U.* 14. 24. 3–6.

[27] *U.* 14. 24. 8–11.

Alexandrian theology is woven into the fabric of the argument for the correlativity of the Father and Son. Alexander takes the Origenian logic of the eternal correlativity a step further: if the Father is unknowable, so also the manner of origin and the hypostasis of the Son is beyond the grasp of created minds;[28] the Father alone knows the divine mystery of the Son's generation.[29] Williams concludes that for Alexander, 'if the begetting of the Son is an eternal and "necessary" aspect of the divine life, part of the proper account of "what it is to be God", the Father cannot be more unknowable than the Son; what is incomprehensible is not the person of the Father but the pattern of the divine nature'.[30]

Alexander was aware that the concept of the eternity of the Son was held by his opponents to infringe God's nature as ingenerate. He recognized the force of the charge and was embarrassed by it. In the body of his letter, in answer to those who accuse him of teaching that there are two ἀγέννητα, because of his rejection of the creation of the Son from nothing, he says that the Father transcends the Son, and that the Son is intermediate between the absolutely self-subsistent and the wholly contingent.[31] In the credal part of the letter, he is clearly defensive and struggles ineffectually to find a definition of the Son's eternity that is compatible with the Father as alone ingenerate.[32] Arius' claim that Alexander described the Son as ἀγεννητογενής,[33] if it is not simply satirical, suggests that Alexander was prone to resort to novel and paradoxical expressions to resolve this tension in his trinitarian thought.[34]

Alexander's rejection of any notion that John 10: 30, 'I and my Father are one', means that the Son is declaring himself to be the Father, or that the two are actually one, may reflect more than an

---

[28] *U.* 14. 22. 15–19; 23. 6–11; 27. 8–10.
[29] *U.* 14. 23. 8–9.
[30] *Arius*, p. 155.
[31] *U.* 14. 26. 22–9.
[32] His defensiveness about such expressions in the creed as 'existed eternally' suggests that they have been introduced into the Alexandrian credal formularies by Alexander. See Williams, *Arius*, pp. 251–2.
[33] *U.* 1. 2. 2.
[34] See the comments of Williams, 'The Logic of Arius', pp. 66–7.

inherited concern with Sabellianism. Eusebius of Caesarea maintains that the idea of the coeternity of Father and Son would eliminate their individual identities as father and son. 'For how,' he asks, 'if they coexist will the Father be father and the Son be son? or how will there be on the one hand the first, and on the other, the second? and the ingenerate and the generate?'[35] Eusebius thinks that the very words father and son, rather than signalling a correlative relation involving simultaneity, do just the opposite; they are co-ordinate with the contrasting pairs first and second, and ingenerate and generate. When the Son says, 'The Father who sent me is greater than me' (Jn. 6: 44), he is testifying to the fact that the Father is another than he, and that the Son is lesser than, and inferior to, the Father.[36]

But for all of Alexander's concern to rebut the claim that his championing of the eternity of the Son leads to the destruction of the Father as uniquely ingenerate, he makes no connection between the issue of the Father's ingenerateness and the argument from correlativity. He is not prepared to abandon correlativity as the central argument in his defence of the eternal generation of the Son; indeed, rather than curtailing its applicability, he extends it. However sensitive he was to the challenge of Arius, he does not appear to have understood the full complexities of the problem that Arius' post-Methodian rigour posed for Alexandrian theology. If Alexander has failed to see the full force of Arius' logic, and is unable to anticipate the kind of argument Athanasius would employ, he is nevertheless committed to the Alexandrian tradition that places the eternity of God's fatherhood, the eternity of the Son, and their eternal relation at the heart of its trinitarian thought.

The description of God as Father is reserved exclusively for the Father–Son relation in the letter. There is no occurrence of the phrase 'Father of all'. Although it is not possible on the basis of one relatively short piece of writing to conclude whether this is typical of his manner of describing God, if it is typical, it suggests that early in the Arian debate, if not before, it was felt by the

---

[35] *U.* 3. 4. 4–6.
[36] *U.* 3. 5. 1–3.

'orthodox' that God's fatherhood could have no direct reference to creation. This will be discussed at greater length with reference to Athanasius.

Like Origen, Alexander closely conjoins his understanding of the Father–Son relation with his view of salvation. The way in which he does this has plainly been deeply influenced by Origen. Alexander's soteriological scheme[37] turns on the distinction that we have already encountered in Origen between the Son, who is uniquely 'Son by nature (φύσει)',[38] and those who, by virtue of God's grace and their own moral endeavour, become 'sons by adoption' (υἱοθεσίας):[39] 'Those who have put off the spirit of bondage and by brave deeds and progress in virtue have received the spirit of adoption, become sons by adoption (Rom. 8: 15), having received kindness through the Son by nature.'[40] Our becoming sons of God for Alexander, as for Origen, depends on the Son's status as Son by nature and our moral endeavour. But the point of emphasis in Alexander's presentation is different from Origen's. Whereas Origen presented the contrast between the two types of sonship mainly in relation to the coming to a saving knowledge of God as Father, and gave almost no attention to what the phrase 'by nature' meant, Alexander presents the contrast mainly in relationship to the status of the Son, and gives no attention to its consequences for the knowledge of God as Father. Following Arius' challenge, the issue around which the contrast revolves is the meaning of Son by nature.

Alexander cites several verses of Scripture to demonstrate that Christ's sonship is unique. He uses the occurrence of ἴδιος in Romans 8: 32, God 'did not spare his own Son (τοῦ ἰδίου υἱοῦ) but delivered him for us', to distinguish between us, who are not God's own (ἴδιος), and the Son who is. Matthew 3: 17 and Psalm 2: 7 confirm this by showing that the Son is a true (γνήσιος) Son, and that there are no other true sons;[41] other sons are sons by

---

[37] U. 14. 24. 8–25. 7; see also U. 14. 21. 11–22. 3.
[38] U. 14. 24. 24.
[39] U. 14. 24. 23.
[40] U. 14. 24. 22–4.
[41] U. 14. 24. 25–31. Alexander's use of ἴδιος will be considered further when the place of ἴδιος in Athanasius' thought is discussed below, pp. 193 ff.

adoption.[42] He establishes 'the natural sonship of the paternal birth'[43] by quoting (a version of) Psalm 110: 3 'from the womb before the morning',[44] for which he was duly censured by Arius. This he says proves that the Son is not son through moral progress. Unlike other rational beings, who are unstable because they have been created from nothing,[45] the Son is incapable of fall.[46] As evidence for the fact that all rational beings fall, he cites Isaiah 1:2 'I have begotten and brought up children, but they have rejected me'.[47] He claims that the Arians, having attended only to the first half of the verse, misinterpret the text to mean that all may become sons of God, and that they then go on to say that the Son has nothing by nature that makes him superior to other sons; he was chosen because God foresaw that though he was mutable he would be obedient.[48] But according to Alexander, what the text really shows, when the second half of it is noted, is that all rational beings fall away from God, and thus that the Son is distinctive.

Alexander has missed the Arian point, which presumably is to show that the language of generation is not used exclusively of the Son in the Bible.[49] He misses the point apparently because he is thinking within an Origenian soteriological framework. Origen too had cited Isaiah 1: 2, but for different ends. It was part of his argument to show that there is no 'firm and unchangeable affirmation of sonship' in the Old Testament and that the witness of Christ to the fatherhood of God is new.[50] Alexander does not make his defence of the Son's unique status as the saviour on the basis specifically of the language of generation, but on the Origenian language of nature. Confronted with the problem posed by the Arian denial of continuity of nature between the Father and the

---

[42] U. 14. 25. 3.
[43] U. 14. 25. 1.
[44] U. 14. 24. 31.
[45] U. 14. 21. 10–12.
[46] U. 14. 25. 2–7.
[47] U. 14. 25. 6–7.
[48] U. 14. 21. 15–22. 3.
[49] Early Arian exegesis of Scripture will be discussed in relation to Athanasius' exegesis, where it will be easier to see the points at issue.
[50] See above, pp. 107ff.

Son, this language appears anachronistic. Alexander does not succeed in making the language of Alexandrian tradition an effective bulwark against Arius' challenge. Yet he is convinced that only a saviour who shares in the divine nature can effect salvation and that such a saviour must be the Son who is eternally present with the God who is eternally Father. It remains to be seen whether Athanasius makes more effective use of Origen's trinitarian model.

The fatherhood of God plays little role in Arius' thought. He makes no direct comments about it. Writing in the light of the Methodian critique of Origen, his thinking about God and the generation of the Son cuts across the Alexandrian tradition of trinitarian language. In his concern to preserve the idea of God as the ingenerate first principle, above all limitations and absolutely free, Arius abandons the concept of the eternal correlativity of Father and Son.

Arius has no hesitation in accepting the traditional practice of referring to God as Father (or the Son as Son); the word Father for God occurs frequently in the documents. The expression 'Father of all' does not appear. Although the small amount of the extant writings, and the uncertainty about how representative they are, make it difficult to reach any definite conclusions, there are suggestions of a pattern in Arius' usage of fatherhood language. As Stead has pointed out,[51] while Arius, in his credal letter to Alexander, refers to God as ἀγέννητος, he also calls God Father eleven times. But Stead does not take note of the distribution of the occurrences. Arius does not mention fatherhood in his opening statement of the divine predicates. Nor does he refer to God as Father in the early part of the letter, even when he goes on to say that this God is the begetter of a Son, and begins his explanation of the Son's generation. It is only one-third of the way through the letter, in line 11,[52] in his summary of erroneous theories about the generation of the Son, that he first refers to God as Father. After that, in the rest of the letter, he refers to God either as God or

---

[51] Christopher Stead, 'The Platonism of Arius', *JTS* NS 15 (1964), p. 18; repr. in his *Substance and Illusion in the Christian Fathers* (London, 1985).
[52] *U.* 6. 12. 11.

Father, using the two terms interchangeably. It is unusual for credal statements of the period not to include a reference to God as Father in their opening statements; the 'Creed of Lucian of Antioch' is an exception, but it does refer to the Father early in its section on the Son.[53] The uncontroversial confession of Arius and Euzoius describes God as Father in the first clause.[54] In his letter to Eusebius of Nicomedia, Arius only refers to God as Father in his report of Alexander's teaching.[55] The letter is short; following the report, God[56] is referred to only three times: twice as God and once as the Ingenerate.[57] In Eusebius' letter to Paulinus, God is not referred to as Father at all, except in biblical quotations; rather, he is called God three times, Ingenerate twice, and Maker twice. God's οὐσία is once described as πατρική.[58]

If the *Thalia* as recorded in *De Synodis* 15 is a compilation of extracts, it is impossible to know how representative of the full text the distribution of the word Father in it is.[59] This is especially a problem given Athanasius' determination to attribute to Arius the idea that God was not always Father. The distribution is similar to that in the two letters. In the 41 lines of the text,[60] God is referred to as Father six times, God thirteen times, the Higher One twice, and the Monad once. The first reference to God as Father is in line 11, which comes after both the apophatic opening statement of God's nature and the description of the generation of the Son. Again we see that the word Father appears neither in the statement of the divine predicates, nor in the statement concerning the generation of the Son.

The evidence suggests that Arius was disinclined to call God Father either in his formalized descriptions of God's nature or in

---

[53] *De Synodis* 23, Opitz 249. 11–14.

[54] *U.* 30. 64. 5.

[55] *U.* 1. 2. 1.

[56] *U.* 1. 3. 4, 6.

[57] *U.* 1. 2. 10–3. 1.

[58] *U.* 8. 16. 16.

[59] On the structure of the *Thalia* see Charles Kannengiesser, 'Les "Blasphèmes d'Arius" (Athanase d'Alexandrie, *De Synodis* 15): Un écrit néo-arien', in E. Lucchesi and H. Saffrey (eds.), *Mémorial André-Jean Festugière: Antiquité païenne et chrétienne* (Cahiers d'Orientalisme 10: Geneva, 1984), 143–51.

[60] *De Synodis* 15, Opitz 242. 8–243. 23.

his discussions of the generation of the Son. The one exception to this is in the confessional creed that he wrote with Euzoius, which seems to have been intended to be as uncontroversial as possible. The other documents were written in a polemical context; their point was to stress that God was uniquely ingenerate and that the Son could not therefore be eternal. It is then perhaps not surprising that, wittingly or not, the pattern of Arius' use of fatherhood language suggests a de-emphasizing of fatherhood as a divine attribute. The substantive place of the fatherhood of God in his theology confirms this.

Arius' attitude to the subject of the fatherhood of God can only be understood within the context of his conception of God and the generation of the Son. Arius has as his primary concern the protection of God as alone ingenerate, a concern that was shared by his supporters. It is upon this that God's nature as first principle, indeed his very definition as God, depends. God is the uniquely self-existent and unconstrained source of all existing things who transcends all limitation and thus is inexpressible. References to the Father as ingenerate recur throughout his writings, often in conjunction with the predicates eternal and without beginning and the complementary idea that no existing thing can participate in the divine nature. It is a coherent doctrine of God that he thinks Alexander's trinitarian speculations put at risk.

The predicates of ingenerateness, eternal, and without beginning are the three with which Arius begins his credal formulation in the letter to Alexander: 'We acknowledge one God, the only unbegotten, the only eternal, the only one without cause or beginning.'[61] It is with these three predicates that he sets up the apophatic contrast between the Father and the Son in the opening section[62] of the *Thalia*,[63] and they occur variously together throughout his writings. The third-man argument that Methodius (and, earlier, Dionyius of Alexandria) had used of God's relation

---

[61] *U.* 6. 12. 4.

[62] Following Kannengiesser's division of the *Thalia* into six sections, as explained in his article, 'Les "Blasphèmes d'Arius"'.

[63] *De Synodis* 15, Opitz 242. 11–13.

to creation Arius now applies to God's relation to the Son. There can necessarily be only one ingenerate first principle. If there are two distinct eternal and ingenerate substances, there must be a third which accounts for the existence of that which distinguishes them, and it too must be eternal and ingenerate; these in turn need to be distinguished by a fourth, and so on *ad infinitum*. 'The supposed class of ἀγέν(ν)ητα, then, is a conceptual nonsense. The ἀγέν(ν)ητον must be self-identical—simple and single, indivisible and without contingent attributes. It is what it is necessarily and eternally, and it is whatever it is *by definition*.'[64] There is no room for another eternal existent, even if he is the Son.

To attribute eternal existence to the Son is thus for Arius tantamount to maintaining that there are two ingenerate realities (δύο ἀγέννητα), an accusation which he makes explicitly in his letter to Alexander,[65] and which underlies his summary of Alexander's teaching in his letter to Eusebius of Nicomedia.[66] The accusation appears in Eusebius of Caesarea's letter to Euphration,[67] and it is the first of the dangerous teachings mentioned in Eusebius of Nicomedia's letter to Paulinus.[68]

Directly linked to this is Arius' denial that there is a community of οὐσία between the Father and the Son. In the *Thalia* Arius says that the Son is οὐδὲ ὁμοούσιος with the Father,[69] and is ξένος . . . κατ' οὐσίαν.[70] Twice in his letter to Alexander he rejects the idea that the Son is a 'consubstantial portion' (μέρος ὁμοούσιον) of the Father,[71] and in the letter to Eusebius of Nicomedia he rejects the idea that the Son is a portion of the ingenerate.[72] Eusebius of Nicomedia makes similar denials in his letter to Paulinus.[73] The term ὁμοούσιος appears to have had two meanings for Arius: it conveyed the sense of a compound and divisible substance, and so

---

[64] Williams, 'The Logic of Arianism', p. 70.
[65] *U.* 6. 13. 12.
[66] *U.* 1. 2. 1–3.
[67] *U.* 3. 4. 4–10.
[68] *U.* 8. 16. 1.
[69] *De Synodis* 15, Opitz 242. 17.
[70] Ibid.
[71] *U.* 6. 12. 11; 13. 18.
[72] *U.* 1. 1. 8–2. 3.
[73] For instance at *U.* 8. 16. 3–6.

had materialist implications, and it conveyed the notion that two or more subsistents were co-ordinate members of the same class. Arius rules out the first in his two letters, for like Origen he perceives that to think of God as material and compound is to undermine God's divine simplicity and immutability.[74] The second he particularly comments on in the *Thalia*. He makes it clear that the Son οὐδὲ . . . ἐστιν ἴσος, ἀλλ᾽ οὐδὲ ὁμοούσιος with the Father.[75] This phrase implies that such an equality would mean a total identity of attributes, so the Son, like the Father, would be ingenerate, eternal, and without beginning. Arius spells this out in the converse observation in the *Thalia*: 'The Father is other than the Son in substance (κατ᾽ οὐσίαν) because he is without beginning.'[76] The word God is not to be thought of as a generic term, the name of a substance in which the Father and Son equally share. There can be no substantial participation between them.[77]

Williams suggests that behind this lies the third-century shift in the understanding of the nature of participation.[78] The earlier Platonic ideas of paradigmatic causality and a 'realist' conception of participation, witnessed in the Origenian model, were replaced by an understanding that substantial similarity between two subsistents entailed only generic identity. The likeness between cause and effect in this conception of participation cannot be described as participation in the sense of substantial continuity. In Alexander of Aphrodisias' treatment of the category of relation, this shift in understanding of participation issues in the assimilation of paternity to other (irreversible) relations of making and being made. The causal relation was seen by some in the period as different from a relation of participation. The Son consequently cannot participate

[74] For a full discussion of Arius' interpretation of ὁμοούσιος as implying a materialist conception of God, see Williams, 'The Logic of Arius', pp. 63–6. On pp. 64–5 Williams finds a parallel for this understanding of the term in the writings of Iamblichus, who was roughly contemporary with Arius. See also the whole of the chapter 'Analogy and Participation' in *Arius*, pp. 215–29.

[75] *De Synodis* 15, Opitz 242. 17. See Williams, 'The Logic of Arianism', p. 67, for a comment on the two ways of reading the phrase.

[76] *De Synodis* 15, Opitz 242. 27.

[77] Williams, 'The Logic of Arianism', p. 67.

[78] 'The Logic of Arianism', pp. 67–73. Williams argues that this new understanding of participation is seen in the discussions of Porphyry and Alexander of Aphrodisias. See also his chapter 'Analogy and Participation' in *Arius*, pp. 215–29.

in a common essence with the Father by virtue simply of the logic of the terms introduced.

We are now in a position to see fully why Arius rejected the argument from correlativity. Although there is no direct evidence that Arius knew Alexander of Aphrodisias' interpretation of Aristotle, he is familiar with the technical term πρός τι, and in his credal letter to Alexander he uses it concisely to sum up and dismiss the Alexandrian reliance on the argument from correlativity:[79]

For [the Son] is not eternal or coeternal or equally ingenerate with the Father, nor does he have his being simultaneously (ἅμα) with the Father, [in virtue] some say [of] his relation with him (τὰ πρός τι), thus postulating two ingenerate first principles. But as monad and first principle of all things, God thus is before all things.

The application of the category of relation to the Father and Son, in order to establish the eternal existence of the Son, cannot but violate the basic postulate of God's unique status as ingenerate and unconstrained. It includes the Son in the same class as the Father, and it assumes a substantial continuity between father and son, whereas for Arius the relation between Father and Son is that of maker and thing made. Williams points out that Arius treats the words Father and Son as names identifying distinct and unique subsistences who do not share substantial attributes. The terms Father and Son do not mutually define each other because they name two individuals whose essential properties are different.[80] The word Father, though it tells us about an inalienable characteristic of God, is not part of the essential definition of God. Accordingly, the statement in the *Thalia* that 'the Father is God [even] when the Son does not exist' (υἱοῦ μὴ ὄντος ὁ πατὴρ θεός ἐστι)[81] could appropriately be taken to signify that 'God was not always Father'.[82] Fatherhood is not essential to God's being God.

---

[79] *U.* 6. 13. 10–13.
[80] Williams, 'The Logic of Arianism', p. 61.
[81] *De Synodis* 15, Opitz 243. 2.
[82] *CA* I. 5, *PG* 26, 21A. Stead, 'Athanasius' Earliest Written Work', p. 86, points out that the phrase may have meant only that the Father was in existence before the Son, but it could easily have been taken in the sense in which it is translated here.

Thus for Arius it is logically possible to talk about God without talking of him as Father, and this is consistent with the low profile given to the description of God as Father in his writings.

Similarly, the metaphor Son does not characterize the Son's essence. The Son is not generated from the Father's being; rather, his existence is the result of a punctiliar act of God's free will. The freedom of God from all limitations, his essential independence of all contingencies, and the essential contingency of the Son's status as Son are brought into sharp focus in the assertion made in the *Thalia* that God could create an 'equal' to the Son.[83] The Son then is begotten *de facto*, and not by nature. The relation of the Father and the Son 'is not unique, exclusive, and necessary to their being what they are'.[84] By definition Arius is neither concerned to explore a relation (of Father and Son) within the divine nature; nor is he concerned to explore what particular significance the language of Father and Son might have, an enterprise which, in any case, might have run the risk of implying that there was a natural continuity between the Father and the Son.

For Arius it is true that God has chosen to create the Son as Son and that this may tell us much about how God chooses to reveal himself to his creation and about the kind of relationship that he would choose to have with his creatures, a relationship of love and trust. But what it does not tell us is anything directly about the divine nature. Whatever this saviour's efficacy, he does not bring us to a knowledge of God as Father by virtue of his participation in a divine life eternally lived as a relation of love and knowledge between the Father and himself. While Arius forced the Church to come to a self-conscious appreciation of what it meant when it called God Father, he did so in a manner that undercut the Alexandrian tradition that, at least since Origen, had made the fatherhood of God central to its conception of the Trinity, and to its soteriology. Like Athanasius, Origen too would have found the notion that God is free not to express himself as Father of the Son incomprehensible.

---

[83] *De Synodis* 15, Opitz 243. 9.
[84] 'The Logic of Arianism', p. 62.

Part III

Athanasius: Father, Son, and Salvation

THE words Father, Son, and begotten are the metaphors which shape and define Athanasius' doctrines of God and of salvation. While the logic of Arius' conception of God could allow him to think of God's being in abstraction from the attribute of fatherhood, this was not possible for Athanasius. For him it was only possible to think of God existing as Father and Son. The image of begetting as the manner of the generation of the Son from the Father is the image in relation to which all other biblical and Platonic images which describe the relation between the first and second divine principles are to be interpreted. His writings abound with biblical quotations—many from the Gospel of John—in which God is referred to as Father, and the Johannine idea of rebirth and the Pauline idea of adoption are fundamental to his soteriology. No reference, however, is made in his writings to *Timaeus* 28C or to any other non-biblical source in which God is called Father.

With Athanasius, for the first time in the Christian tradition, the concept of God's fatherhood, and his relation to the Son is made the subject of explicit and systematic analysis. Confronted with the challenge which he believed Arian theology posed to the Church's largely unreflective acceptance of the common practice of using the language of fatherhood to refer to God, Athanasius attempted to clarify and to determine specifically what that tradition of usage meant for a coherent theology of the divine nature and a coherent theology of salvation. He takes up key elements from the Origenian-Alexandrian understanding of the fatherhood of God: the centrality of fatherhood to the nature of God, the eternal correlativity of the Father and the Son, the idea of the Father–Son relation as rooted in God's eternal goodness, the existence of that relation for its own sake. But he extends and refines these elements, making them the structural pattern of his theology.

Athanasius develops a theological structure and a theological vocabulary which allow him to distinguish sharply and systematically between the relation of Father and Son and the relation of God and creation. In his theology, the language of God as Father describes, in the first order, relations internal to the divine nature, and, in the second, through the Son, God's relation to those adopted as sons. The word Father is a trinitarian and soteriological term. In its description of the divine nature as the Father–Son relation, a relation inherently generative, it identifies the divine nature as the source of creation as well. It is as Father of the Son that God is who he is and it is as Father of the Son that God expresses himself in relation to all things.

Athanasius wrote within a very different cosmological and theological context from Origen, and his language of fatherhood and sonship reflects this. Methodius, as we have seen, argued against the eternity of the rational creation and attributed the existence of created reality strictly to God's will. Arius applied the radical disjunction between God and the world to the relation between God and the Son. He attributed the Son's existence, like the rest of creation, to God's will and not to his being. In contrast to this, Athanasius maintains that the relation of the Father and the Son is not a relation based on God's will but rather one based on his being. This, he believes, is encapsulated in the description of the Son as begotten. Like Arius (but unlike Origen, who divided reality into spirit and matter), he accepts without reservation the division of reality into two distinct realms: the divine and that which has been created out of nothing. But unlike Arius, he places the Son within the divine realm. Only in this way, he argues, can the language of biblical tradition and the Church's practice of worship be maintained, and a satisfactory doctrine of salvation be sustained. Only if the one who became fully human in the incarnation was fully divine could salvation be effected. Only a Son whose being was one with that of the Father could make men sons by adoption. The language of God as Father of the Son, properly understood, is the appropriate expression and guarantee of the Son's divinity. Thus Athanasius argues consistently throughout his mature works for the affirmation of the fundamental theological proposition that the Son is eternally begotten from the being of the God who is eternally Father.

The fatherhood of God, the sonship of the Son, and their soteriological significance are the central topics in many of Athanasius' writings. The most important for understanding his thinking about them, as for understanding the shape of his theology as a whole, is *Contra Arianos* I, II, and III, written around 340.[1] It is mainly on *Contra Arianos* that this chapter is based. The general theological orientation of the three orations stands in continuity with his two earlier writings, *Contra Gentes* and *De Incarnatione*[2]

---

[1] Charles Kannengiesser, *Athanase d'Alexandrie évêque et écrivain: Une lecture des traités contre les ariens* (Théologie historique 70: Paris, 1983), has put forward the suggestive thesis that the third oration was written not by Athanasius but by the young Apollinarius; see especially pp. 405–16. His argument is based on a painstaking examination of the perceivable contrast in style and structure between the first two orations and the third. Christopher Stead, in a review of *Athanase d'Alexandrie*, JTS, NS 36 (1985), 220–9, acknowledges that there is a difference between the first two and the third orations. But he points out that the dissimilarity in word usage is not nearly as great as Kannengiesser's thesis requires, and that parallels for the usage in the third oration can be found in other writings of undisputed Athanasian authorship, but not to any extent in the writings of Apollinarius. Stead thinks that the differences may indicate that the third oration was written by the same author, Athanasius, at a later date and for a different purpose than the first two. If this is true, the questions of when and why the third was written remain unanswered. It is assumed in the present study that the three orations were written by Athanasius. Kannengiesser's dating of the first two orations to 340 (*Athanase d'Alexandrie*, 374–403) is accepted and the third oration will be analysed in conjunction with the first two.

[2] Placed in this study before 325. The complete absence of any sign of anti-Arian shaping to the central theme of *De Incarnatione*, namely, the necessity for the Son to be both fully divine and fully human, a shaping which was so characteristic of his later writings, makes it highly unlikely that *Contra Gentes* and *De Incarnatione* could have been written after Athanasius had begun to think concertedly about the theological implications of the Arian teachings. If Athanasius wrote ἑνὸς σώματος, and if it is to be dated to early 325, then it is even more probable that *Contra Gentes* and *De Incarnatione* were written sometime before 325. Stead, 'Athanasius' Earliest Written Work', p. 91, in the light of his attribution of ἑνὸς σώματος to Athanasius, dismisses the argument that it is improbable that such a young man could have composed a work of the theological maturity of the *Contra Gentes* and *De Incarnatione*. Timothy Barnes, *The New Empire of Diocletian and Constantine* (Cambridge, Mass., 1982), p. 35, places *Contra Gentes* 'some years before 324'. For a thorough statement of the opposite position, see Charles Kannengiesser, 'Le Témoignage des *Lettres festales* de Saint Athanase sur la date de l'Apologie *Contre les païens – Sur l'incarnation du verbe*', RSR 52 (1964),

(though in them he does not discuss the idea of God's fatherhood), and his treatment in *Contra Arianos* of the three central topics establishes the terms within which he deals with them in the writings that come after *Contra Arianos*. In his desire to refute Arian misconceptions, Athanasius pursues the topics of Father, Son, and salvation in *Contra Arianos* with a relentless thoroughness which borders on the obsessive. His presentation of the divine fatherhood is consistent throughout the work and, so far as his polemical and catechetical purposes allow, systematic. However, before we look at Athanasius' concept of the fatherhood of God, we need to make clear the philosophical assumptions with which he worked, and, more briefly, his view of the authority of Scripture.

91–100, and 'La Date de l'Apologie d'Athanase *Contre les païens* et *Sur l'incarnation du verbe*', *RSR* 58 (1970), 383–428.

8

Background: Philosophy;
Doctrine of Scripture

IT is against the background of his theory of *creatio ex nihilo* and the division of reality into two orders that Athanasius' trinitarian thought is best understood. The underlying assumptions of his cosmology follow those of his immediate predecessors, and they are much the same as those of Arius, though his understanding of their theological implications is very different from Arius'. His comments about cosmology are made in the course of theological discussion; he makes little reference to the tradition of debate among the Greek philosophers, and he does not undertake a speculative philosophical analysis of the question of creation from nothing. What he does is to employ his cosmological assumptions in relation to the theological questions of God, the Son, and the world with a rigour and thoroughness not previously seen.

In *De Incarnatione*, Athanasius outlines several Greek philosophical theories about creation. Among them is the theory that 'God made the world from pre-existent and uncreated matter'.[1] He attributes this to Plato and rejects it. God, he says, created the matter from which all things come into existence—he 'makes everything from nothing',[2] and this includes the soul.[3] All existing reality (except the Son) is called into existence by God through the Son and is sustained in existence by God. As we have seen, Dionysius of Alexandria, Methodius, and Arius made explicit use of the third-man argument to deny the possibility of a second

---

[1] *DI* 2.
[2] *DI* 3.
[3] *DI* 4. For a discussion of the status of the soul in *De Incarnatione*, see Andrew Louth, *The Origins of the Christian Mystical Tradition: From Plato to Denys* (Oxford, 1981), pp. 77–80.

eternal and ingenerate first principle alongside God. But such a philosophical reference is absent from Athanasius' discussion of creation in *De Incarnatione*, though later in *Contra Arianos* he does use a form of the third-man argument to help to explain the relation of the Father and the Son.[4] Instead, having apparently absorbed the lesson of Methodius, he makes the more simple point that to posit the existence of matter coeternal with God necessarily suggests a limitation of God's power, since his ability to create is dependent on something other than himself. The single overriding question for him is whether the Son is to be thought of as generated from the being of God or as brought into existence from nothing by God's will.

The distinction between God and the world is expressed by Athanasius as the distinction between the unoriginate and the originate, between 'he who is' and the things which have been created from nothing. He frequently identifies God with true being. In *Contra Arianos* III. 63, he suggests that this identification is self-evident: 'it is enough only to hear about God for us to know and understand that he is he who is ($\acute{o}$ $\check{\omega}\nu$)',[5] eternal and immutable. By contrast all originate reality is inherently unstable and subject to dissolution. No creature is of a 'constant' ($\check{\varepsilon}\mu\mu o\nu o\varsigma$) nature.[6] 'For the things with the potential to perish, even if they would not perish through the grace of their maker, have nevertheless come into existence from nothing, and they themselves testify that there was [a time] when they were not.'[7] Between the unoriginate and the originate, between God and his creation, there can be no similarity in being:

For what sort of resemblance is there between things which are from nothing and the one who brought the things which are nothing into being?

[4] This will be discussed in the next chapter.
[5] *PG* 26, 456B. This is not a theme on which Athanasius has much to say. Although in *CG* he also describes God as 'beyond all being and human thought' ($\acute{v}\pi\varepsilon\varrho\acute{\varepsilon}\varkappa\varepsilon\iota\nu\alpha$ $\pi\acute{\alpha}\sigma\eta\varsigma$ $o\dot{v}\sigma\acute{\iota}\alpha\varsigma$ $\varkappa\alpha\grave{\iota}$ $\dot{\alpha}\nu\theta\varrho\omega\pi\acute{\iota}\nu\eta\varsigma$ $\dot{\varepsilon}\pi\iota\nuo\acute{\iota}\alpha\varsigma$), he does not discuss the phrase and its Middle Platonist provenance. Meijering, *Orthodoxy and Platonism in Athanasius*, pp. 6–7, points out that elsewhere in *CG*, e.g. in sections 35 and 40, $o\dot{v}\sigma\acute{\iota}\alpha$ simply signifies 'created substance', and he thinks that this is probably what it means in *CG* 2.
[6] *CA* II. 48, *PG* 26, 249B.
[7] *CA* I. 58, *PG* 26, 133A.

Or how can that which is not resemble him who is, since it is inferior because once it was not, and has its place among things originated?[8]

This radical dissimilarity means that for Athanasius all originate things are to be thought of as ontologically the same, relative to the unoriginate. Thus, while he acknowledges that Genesis states that no creature is like another, he concludes that they are all fundamentally alike in that they are all creatures;[9] they all share the 'same condition',[10] having all had a beginning to their existence: 'the being of things originate is measured by their becoming.'[11] Consequently, Athanasius sweeps aside Arius' qualification of the creaturehood of the Son—a creature, but not like one of the creatures—and accuses Arius of teaching that the Son is like all the other creatures. From his point of view, Arius' qualification can have no validity because it makes no sense in a world in which intermediate realities cannot exist.

The concept of time is included by Athanasius among created things. His discussions of the concept are occasioned by the need to refute the two Arian slogans, 'there was [a time] when the Son was not' and 'the Son was not before his generation', which he thinks are equivalent in signifying that there was a time before the Word.[12] His speculation about time as a cosmological question goes little beyond that of Alexander; his predominant concern is with its importance for trinitarian thought, and he writes about it at much greater length than his predecessor.

His most extensive treatment of the subject of time occurs in the opening sections of his reply to Arius, in *Contra Arianos* I. 11–13. He begins with a brief discussion of the relation between the Father and time, and then turns to a longer discussion of the more contentious issue of the relation between the Son and time. To say that 'there was [a time] when the Son was not' is to apply temporal categories to God, since to use the word 'once' for a time when the Son did not exist, leaves the Father as the subject of that 'once'.

[8] *CA* I. 21, 56A–B.
[9] *CA* II. 20, *PG* 26, 188C–189C.
[10] 188C.
[11] *CA* II. 57, *PG* 26, 269B.
[12] *CA* I. 11, *PG* 26, 33C.

But God is eternal, and 'is himself he who is (ὁ ὤν)',[13] and so cannot be the subject of time. Athanasius does not dwell on the argument, perhaps because it would have been accepted by everyone, including the Arians, as self-evident. It lays the basis for associating the Son with the eternal status of the Father.

His argument for the eternity of the Son has two strands. He begins by arguing that the Bible never uses temporal terms to describe the Son. Rather, it uses such terms as 'always', 'eternal', and 'co-existent always with the Father', and he provides a collage of suitably interpreted texts to prove his case. He then goes on to attribute the creation of time to the Son, as Alexander had done before him. The slogan 'there was [a time] when the Son was not', Athanasius explains, means that there was a time prior to the Son's existence. But since the Scriptures attest that the Son is the creator of time, this cannot be so because he is metaphysically prior to it. Like Alexander, he cites as proof John 1: 3 'all things were made through him'[14] and Hebrews 1: 2 'by whom he made the ages',[15] and he adds Psalm 145: 13 'Thy kingdom is a kingdom for all ages'.[16] He maintains that it is therefore 'forbidden for anyone to imagine any interval (διάστημα) in which the Logos did not exist', for the Son is 'king and maker' of all ages.[17] Time is a creation, and if the Bible uses timeless expressions of the Son, it correspondingly uses temporal expressions of creatures.[18] He concludes his argument with a statement that demonstrates his belief that the notions of time and creation from nothing are closely interrelated: 'While it is fitting for the phrases "once was not" and "before it came to be" and "when" and the like, to be said of things originate and creatures, which have come into existence out of nothing, they are alien to the Word.'[19] The Son is eternal, never having not been and not having had a beginning to his existence.[20]

---

[13] *CA* I. 11, *PG* 26, 33B–C.
[14] *CA* I. 13, *PG* 26, 40B–C.
[15] *CA* I. 12, *PG* 26, 36C.
[16] 37A.
[17] 37A–B.
[18] *CA* I. 13, *PG* 26, 37C–40B. He cites several examples.
[19] 40B.
[20] *CA* I. 12, *PG* 26, 37B–C.

As with Athanasius' understanding of creation from nothing, there is no place in this conception of time for an intermediate condition. If the Son is not coeternal with the Father then he must be the subject of temporal categories, and so Athanasius also sweeps aside any Arian qualification about the Son's relation to time, that he was begotten before times and ages. This attitude to Arius' conception of time is illustrated by his comments on the wording of the two slogans which he thinks attribute temporality to the Son. The comments also give insight into what degree of accuracy Athanasius regarded as appropriate in the reproduction of the ideas of his opponents. At the end of his discussion of time, in *Contra Arianos* I. 13, Athanasius upbraids the Arians for what he considers to be their duplicity in the way they have worded the two slogans:

For why, when you mean time (χρόνον), do you not plainly say, 'There was a time when the Word was not' ('Ην χρόνος ὅτε οὐκ ἦν ὁ λόγος)? But, while you drop the word 'time' (χρόνον) to deceive the simple, you do not at all conceal your own thoughts, nor even if you did, could you escape discovery. For again you mean times (χρόνους) when you say 'There was when he was not' ('Ην ποτε ὅτε οὐκ ἦν) and 'He was not before his generation' (Οὐκ ἦν πρὶν γεννηθῇ).[21]

This does not simply represent polemical obstinacy on Athanasius' part. He feels constrained to acknowledge the Arian point, but he regards it as worthless. To say that the Son is not eternal, brought into existence out of nothing, is for Athanasius necessarily to say that he originated in time. It is inconceivable to him that there could be any other possibility. The absolute gulf that separates God from the world, the unoriginate from the originate, is mirrored in the separation of eternity and time.

The passage shows that Athanasius is faithful to what he thought was Arian usage. Although he occasionally strays into inserting χρόνος into his quotation of the slogans,[22] he usually quotes them in the form 'there was when he was not' (ἦν ποτε ὅτε οὐκ ἦν), even though this is not as conclusive as he would like. This latter form

---

[21] *CA* I. 13, *PG* 26, 40C.
[22] *CA* I. 11, *PG* 26, 33B.

had a set shape early in the tradition of controversy. Both ἡ φίλαρχος[23] and ἑνός σώματος[24] record it in this form, and Athanasius does not arbitrarily alter the phrase to suit his case. He seems to think of it as a genuine Arian expression. The discussion in section 13 also suggests that when he wrote *Contra Arianos* Athanasius did not have the *Thalia* of *De Synodis* 15 clearly in mind, since in the fifth line of his reproduction of the *Thalia*, he quotes Arius describing the generation of the Son as taking place ἐν χρόνοις.[25] This would have provided Athanasius with all the evidence he would have needed to clinch the argument of section 13.

For Athanasius as for Arius, there is no continuity of being between God and the world, and there are no intermediate realities. But for Athanasius, in contrast to Arius, the Son stands on the divine side of the ontological gulf. Athanasius sums up the fundamental dissimilarity of the Son and creation, and the Son's unique relation to the Father, in a passage in *Contra Arianos* I. 58, the opening lines of which were quoted above.[26] It leaves no doubt about which side of the divide the Son is on:

for [the Son] not having the potential to perish, as originated things (τὰ γενητά) have, but having eternal duration, it is foreign to him to have it said, 'He was not before his generation', but it is proper for him to be always, and to endure together with the Father. . . . The Son is offspring of the Father's being (γέννημα τῆς τοῦ πατρὸς οὐσίας), and he is fashioner, while other things are fashioned by him, and he is radiance and Word and image and wisdom of the Father, while originate things stand and serve below the Triad. Therefore the Son is different in kind and essence from originated things (ἑτερογενὴς ἄρα καὶ ἑτερούσιός ἐστιν ὁ υἱὸς τῶν γενητῶν), and on the contrary is proper (ἴδιος) to the Father's being (οὐσίας) and one in nature (ὁμοφυὴς) with it.[27]

Several of the expressions in this passage—'offspring of the Father's being', 'proper to the Father's being', 'one in nature with

[23] *U.* 14, 21. 8.
[24] *U.* 4, 7. 21.
[25] *De Synodis* 15, Opitz 242. 13.
[26] On p. 150.
[27] PG 26, 133A–B.

the Father's being'—are among Athanasius' favourites for describing the relation of the Son to the Father, and they will be considered when we come to look at his understanding of the nature of the generation of the Son. The passage demonstrates that in stressing the contrast in being between the unoriginate and the originate Athanasius does not shrink from describing the relation of the Son with the Father as a relation based on the οὐσία of God, but makes it the basis of his theology of the Son. Like Arius, Athanasius reflects the influence of the Methodian heritage. Both understood the relation between God and created reality in terms of the distinction between God's being and his will: the former refers to God in himself, and the latter to God's expression of himself to that which stands outside of himself. But unlike Arius, Athanasius is not concerned that basing the Father–Son relation on the Father's being compromises God's unique status as ingenerate. For him, as we shall see, the being of God is a being which eternally exists in relationship, a relationship by which the Son shares in the life and activity of the Father.

Athanasius holds a high view of the authority of Scripture as the source of revealed knowledge about God. This view has an important bearing on the way in which he develops his conception of God's fatherhood and the generation of the Son. He does not deal systematically with the question of biblical authority; his comments, many of which are directed against the Arian approach to the interpretation of the Bible, are few, brief, and scattered throughout his writings.

Athanasius regards the Bible as 'sacred and divinely inspired'.[28] It was 'spoken and written by God, through men versed in theology', who were 'witnesses to the divinity of Christ'.[29] The Scriptures are 'sufficient for the exposition of the truth'.[30] They speak authoritatively about philosophy—he cites Genesis 1: 1 as proof of the incorrectness of the Platonic theory of pre-existent matter[31]—and they speak authoritatively about the things of God,

---

[28] *CG* 1.
[29] *DI* 56.
[30] *CG* 1.
[31] *DI* 3.

providing 'more exact' (ἀκριβέστερα)[32] expressions of the true doctrines of God than any other source. They demand our obedience.[33]

But Athanasius is fully aware that it is not a simple task to read the Bible correctly so that it leads to the formulation of true doctrine. The reason for this is that the sense of some texts is not obvious, especially for the simple, and he is certain that biblical words and phrases can be given the wrong meaning.[34] Two basic principles underlie his approach to the reading of Scripture: the interpretation of the Bible must be in conformity with the church's tradition of faith, and it must be undertaken in moral purity.

In the introduction to the main body of Contra Arianos I, Athanasius accuses the Arians of using Scripture as a veneer. Those who think that the 'blasphemy' of the Thalia is turned into 'reverent language' by the use of biblical phrases must become aware that the Bible itself teaches that the devil uses the cloak of scriptural language in order to deceive the simple.[35] Much of Contra Arianos is taken up with providing a corrective reading of disputed texts. At the beginning of his first passage of sustained exegesis, in which he gives what he considers to be the proper reading of the second chapter of Philippians, he maintains that the Arians fail to explicate the Scriptures in an 'orthodox sense' because they read them in 'a private sense' (ἴδιον νοῦν).[36] They make their 'own' (ἰδίαν) doctrinal assumptions about the Son their 'canon' of interpretation, and force the whole of the Bible into conformity with it.[37] The correct alternative, according to Athanasius, is to interpret Scripture in the light of the 'scope' (σκοπός) of the Christian faith, using it as a 'canon' for the reading of Scripture. This scope the Arians do not know.[38] In Contra Arianos III. 58, he describes this scope as the 'ecclesiastical scope', which is the 'anchor of the faith'.[39]

---

[32] De Decretis 32, Opitz 28. 4.
[33] Apologia de Fuga Sua 2, Opitz 69. 3–4.
[34] De Synodis 40, Opitz 266. 5–12.
[35] CA I. 8, PG 26, 25C–D.
[36] CA I. 37, PG 26, 88B–C.
[37] CA I. 52, PG 26, 121A–B.
[38] CA III. 28, PG 26, 385A.
[39] 441A.

Athanasius places the 'scope and character' of the Bible itself in juxtaposition with this scope of the church's faith.[40] He identifies the 'scope and character' of the Bible as the 'double account of the Saviour',[41] a double account which is based on the distinction between the two spheres of theological discourse: God in himself, and God in relation to the economy. Some phrases and texts refer to the Son in his eternal relation to the Father, some refer to the incarnate Son. This 'scope' is present throughout the Scriptures[42] and must be recognized if one's exegesis is to be well grounded. Athanasius charges the Arians with the fundamental mistake of failing to observe this distinction. In practice, the determination of which texts belong to which sphere involves determining the type of literature in which the text occurs and then asking three questions about the text: to what time does the text refer, to what person, and to what purpose.

But Athanasius' use of the concept of the scope of the church's faith does not mean that there was an established ecclesiastical reading of the disputed texts. Williams observes that Athanasius had to work hard to develop an alternative reading. 'Arius' interpretations are "private" in so far as they undermine the actual faith and practice of the Catholic Church'.[43] As evidence of this, Williams points out that both Alexander and Athanasius appeal to the fact that Christ is worshipped as divine, and also that Athanasius challenges the Arians to make sense of the baptismal rite on the basis of their theological presuppositions.[44]

One of Athanasius' particular concerns in the interpretation of Scripture, a concern that is of importance for his evaluation of the Bible's use of Father to describe God, is the role of non-biblical terms in doctrinal formulation. It is a topic that recurs in both *De Decretis* and *De Synodis*, as he attempts to justify the introduction

---

[40] *CA* III. 28–9, *PG* 26, 384C–385A.

[41] 385A.

[42] Ibid.

[43] *Arius*, p. 110. He suggests that what lies behind the exegetical debate is tension between 'Catholic' and 'Academic' models of the Church, which he outlines on pp. 82–91 of the same book. This idea of two models of the church has been questioned by Robert Gregg in a review of *Arius* in JTS NS 40 (1989), 247–54. It is nevertheless a useful interpretative hypothesis.

[44] *Arius*, p. 110.

of the language of 'being' into the creed of Nicaea. Non-biblical words serve to protect biblical words and phrases from those who, while they use them, give them a wrong meaning. In *De Decretis* 19, he says that they make the meaning of the biblical words 'more distinct' (λευκότερος).[45] In any case, he implies, there is no possibility of avoiding the use of non-biblical expressions in the explication of the Bible and the development of doctrine from it. Competing explanations that use non-biblical terms can be examined to see which most closely represent the truth.[46] For Athanasius, this truth is the ecclesiastical scope of the faith.

Athanasius' comments on the necessity of moral purity in the reading of Scripture are brief. It is, he says, only as one comes to the text with a purity of 'mind and a life modelled on the saints' who wrote the words that one can apprehend the truths they contain. We must stand in the company of the saints, through our manner of life, if we are to understand the things revealed to the saints by God.[47] This principle intersects with the first: it is only as we place ourselves in the tradition of the church's teaching and practice that we may come to a proper interpretation of the Bible.

For Athanasius the exercise of a satisfactory biblical hermeneutics is a complex procedure. The development of true doctrines about the Father and the Son involves the interplay of metaphysics, theological reflection, detailed textual analysis, and the exegete's participation in the Christian life. How this hermeneutical procedure and doctrinal development works in Athanasius' theology will become more evident as we begin to examine his understanding of the Father–Son relation.

[45] Opitz 16. 6.
[46] *De Decretis* 18, Opitz 15. 25–35.
[47] *DI* 57.

9

God As Father

THE word Father in Athanasius' theology is the word that identifies God's being as fruitful, inherently generative, relational, and
dynamic; it is the word that indicates that the divine being exists
first as the relation of Father and Son. But while he addresses the
question of the divine fatherhood in a much more deliberate and
systematic way than his predecessors had done, he nevertheless
still seldom makes the question a specific topic of analysis in its
own right. The description of God as Father is for Athanasius, as it
was for Origen and succeeding Alexandrians, including Arius, an
irreducible given of the Christian faith. It was not as amenable to
deliberate and abstract analysis for Athanasius as the more
immediately problematical issue of the status of the Son, which is
the primary focus of Contra Arianos and of his theology generally.
Contra Arianos was written in response to what Athanasius
identified early in the work as the three central errors of the Arian
understanding of the Son—that 'there was [a time] when he did not
exist'; that 'before he was brought into being, he did not exist'; and
that the Son 'came into existence out of nothing'[1]—around which
he organized the work.[2] Discussions about God as Father arise
mainly in relation to his arguments for the eternal generation of
the Son and the Son's divinity.

While the most obvious threat that Arianism posed was to the
Son's status as divine, Athanasius considered that this threat was
necessarily also a direct threat to God's status as Father, and
ultimately to a proper conception of the nature of divinity itself.

---

[1] CA I. 5, 21A.
[2] For a thorough and persuasive discussion of the three slogans and the
organizing themes of Contra Arianos, see the whole of Kannengiesser, Athanase
d'Alexandre.

He assumes that the Father and the Son are correlatives and that to defend the divinity of the Son is to defend the fatherhood of God. Inasmuch as he was working towards a doctrine of God whose content is defined by the nature of the Son's relation to the Father, it was not possible for him to write about the Son without constantly making statements that he perceived to be full of significance for the fatherhood of God. His picture of the fatherhood of God must be built up both from explicit comments about the divine fatherhood and from his portrayal of the eternal generation of the Son and the Son's relation to the Father. *Contra Arianos* is not solely devoted to a negatively orientated polemic, and this is true of his other writings as well. In *Contra Arianos* Athanasius develops a positive conception of the divine nature as Father and Son, a conception of God that goes beyond mere refutation of errors.

The importance for Athanasius of the fatherhood of God is seen negatively in the fact that the denial of the eternal fatherhood of God is the first of the heretical doctrines with which Athanasius charges his Arian opponents in his numerous summaries of the Arian creed. Summaries appear in the letter ἑνὸς σώματος, *Contra Arianos* I. 5–6 and I. 9, *De Decretis* 6, and *Ad Episcopos Aegypti* 12. The opening article of each is a statement about the fatherhood of God.

ἑνὸς σώματος, *U.* 4. 7. 19–20
God was not eternally Father, but there was [a time] when God was not Father . . . The Word of God was not eternal, but came to be from nothing.

Οὐκ ἀεὶ ὁ θεὸς πατὴρ ἦν, ἀλλ' ἦν ὅτε ὁ θεὸς πατὴρ οὐκ ἦν . . . οὐκ ἀεὶ ἦν ὁ τοῦ θεοῦ λόγος, ἀλλ' ἐξ οὐκ ὄντων γέγονεν.

Contra Arianos I. 5, 21A
God was not eternally Father, but there was [a time] when God was alone, and was not yet Father; only later he became Father . . . The Son did not always exist, for everything is created out of nothing.

Οὐκ ἀεὶ ὁ θεὸς πατὴρ ἦν, ἀλλ' ἦν ὅτε ὁ θεὸς μόνος ἦν, καὶ οὔπω πατὴρ ἦν, ὕστερον δὲ ἐπιγέγονε πατήρ . . . οὐκ ἀεὶ ἦν ὁ υἱός πάντων γὰρ γενομένων ἐξ οὐκ ὄντων.

Contra Arianos I. 9, 29 A–B
God was not always Father, but became so later . . . the Son did not always exist.

Οὐκ ἀεὶ ὁ θεὸς πατὴρ ἦν, ἀλλ᾽ ὕστερον γέγονεν . . . οὐκ ἀεὶ ἦν ὁ υἱός.

De Decretis 6, Opitz 5, 23–6
Not eternal Father, not eternal Son. For the Son was not before he came into existence, but he too came into existence from nothing. In consequence, God was not eternally Father of the Son; but when the Son came into existence and was created, only then was God called his Father.

Οὐκ ἀεὶ πατὴρ, οὐκ ἀεὶ υἱός· οὐκ ἦν γὰρ ὁ υἱὸς πρὶν γεννηθῇ, ἀλλ᾽ ἐξ οὐκ ὄντων γέγονε καὶ αὐτός· διὸ καὶ οὐκ ἀεὶ πατὴρ ὁ θεὸς γέγονε τοῦ υἱοῦ, ἀλλ᾽ ὅτε γέγονε καὶ ἐκτίσθη ὁ υἱός, τότε καὶ ὁ θεὸς ἐκλήθη πατὴρ αὐτοῦ.

Ad Episcopos Aegypti 12, *PG* 25, 564B
God was not always Father . . . the Son did not always exist.

Οὐκ ἀεὶ ὁ θεὸς πατὴρ ἦν . . . οὐκ ἀεὶ ἦν ὁ υἱός.

It is not possible to determine whether these statements about the fatherhood of God, and their location, represent actual Arian wording and order of presentation, or whether they are extrapolations from Arian teaching about the Son. But there is a similarity between them and Arius' summary of Alexander's theology in his letter to Eusebius of Nicomedia. As we have seen, the summary begins 'God eternal, Son eternal, Father and Son always together' (ἀεὶ θεὸς ἀεὶ υἱός, ἅμα πατὴρ ἅμα υἱός), followed by 'the Son exists ingenerately with God' (συνυπάρχει ὁ υἱὸς ἀγεννήτως τῷ θεῷ).[3] The correlation of the first two terms, God and Son, matches the structure of the first phrase in the statement from *De Decretis* 6.[4] Athanasius may well have deemed it a reasonable conclusion that

[3] *U.* 1, 2. 1–2.
[4] The fact that Arius uses 'God' and not 'Father' suggests that this summary may reflect his usage as well as Alexander's.

if Arius rejected a positive statement of the eternal correlativity of
the Father and Son, that meant he accepted a negative one. Arius'
summary of Alexander's teaching at least might help explain how
such a perception of Arian belief became part of the anti-Arian
polemic.

In any case, there is a parallel of sorts between the portrayal of
fatherhood in Athanasius' credal versions of Arian teaching and
what Arius says in the writings that can be reliably attributed to
him. The denial of the eternity of God's fatherhood, the 'only
later' of *Contra Arianos* I. 5, and the 'only then' of *De Decretis* 6
could all be deduced from several lines of the *Thalia* of *De
Synodis*; for instance, the contrast between the one without a
beginning and the one with a beginning,[5] the contrast between the
eternal one and the one who had a beginning in time,[6] the contrast
between the Monad and the Dyad,[7] and especially the statement in
line 20 that 'the Father is God when the Son does not exist' (υἱοῦ
μὴ ὄντος ὁ πατὴρ θεός ἐστι).[8]

The way in which Athanasius expresses the Arian conceptions
goes beyond what Arius actually says, however, implying a change
in God, an implication which Arius would have have found
intolerable, and it suggests that God's 'fathering of the Son is a
pretty peripheral matter'.[9] While line 20 of the *Thalia* suggests that
the divinity of the Father is independent of the existence of the
Son, *Contra Arianos* I. 5 makes the fatherhood of God appear
incidental to God's nature.[10] The claim in the *De Decretis* formulation that only with the coming into existence of the Son was God
called Father corresponds to the charge that Athanasius frequently
brings against the Arians concerning the Son: that they ascribe
such words as 'Logos' and 'Sophia', and, in more direct parallel,
'Son' to him purely verbally.[11]

It is doubtful whether Arius would have been prepared to accept

---

[5] *De Synodis* 15, Opitz 242. 12.
[6] Opitz 242. 13.
[7] Opitz 243. 1.
[8] Opitz 243. 2. See the comment above, p. 143 n.82.
[9] Williams, *Arius*, p. 104.
[10] Ibid.
[11] *CA* I. 9, 29B.

that such conclusions about the fatherhood of God could be legitimately derived from his theology. And it is even more doubtful that, if he had been, he would have been prepared to state the conclusions in as forthright a manner as they appear in Athanasius' summaries, which presumably would have caused needless offence among the faithful and not helped the credibility of his theology.[12] The pattern of Arius' usage of the word Father to describe God in his two letters and in the *Thalia* shows that the word Father does not usually appear in the early part of his writings where he is formally describing God's nature, and he appears disinclined to give the word Father any particular attention. His attitude to the use of the word Father for God is revealed by omission rather than commission, an attitude which stands in marked contrast to that suggested in Athanasius' presentation of Arian beliefs and strengthens the impression that with reference to the topic of the fatherhood of God, if in no other way, Athanasius' summaries go beyond what Arius actually taught.

But whatever the relation between Athanasius' credal summaries of Arianism and what the Arians actually said, the summaries follow contemporary practice in placing an article about God as Father at the beginning of a statement of the faith and so enable Athanasius to highlight the heretical consequences of Arian christology. This placement also allows for the presentation of a neatly balanced correlation between the denial of the eternity of God's fatherhood and what Athanasius considers to be the crux of Arian thought, the denial of the eternal generation of the Son. This balance is seen in each of the summaries quoted above: the first article on the eternity of the fatherhood of God is followed by the second on the eternity of the Son, and the same words are used of the Father that are used of the Son. The simplest is the symmetrical opening phrase of the summary in *De Decretis* 6: οὐκ ἀεὶ πατήρ, οὐκ ἀεὶ υἱός.[13]

The structured balance of the first two articles not only serves the purpose of alarming the reader; it also expresses Athanasius'

---

[12] This of course may be one of the reasons why Athanasius reports Arius' teaching in this way.

[13] Opitz 5. 23–4.

fundamental belief in the eternal correlativity of the Father and the Son. Athanasius does not spell out the logic of the argument from the category of relation that underlies the summaries, but the negative form of the opening two articles of the summaries well exemplifies the principle of the argument from relations that 'one carries the other to destruction',[14] a principle which, as we have seen, Alexander had employed, using the technical philosophical terms.[15] In contrast to both Alexander and Arius, however, Athanasius does not use Aristotle's terminology, either with reference to the summaries or elsewhere in his writings. We shall return to Athanasius' attitude to the logic of relation when we come to look at his positive use of the argument from the correlativity of the Father and Son to characterize the Father–Son relation.

The prominence given to the correlativity of Father and Son in the summaries of Arian thought gives added weight to the suggestion that the wording and order of the opening article of the summaries represent Athanasius' deductions from Arius' christology, and not the thought of Arius himself. Having rejected the argument from relations as applicable to the Father–Son relation, Arius would hardly have been likely to have used its logic to diminish God's fatherhood. It would have made no sense to him, whereas for Athanasius it makes frighteningly good sense.

Given the leading position that Athanasius accords the issue of fatherhood in the credal summaries, the reader might well be surprised to discover that this is not reflected in the order in which he subsequently goes on to deal with the credal articles. In ἑνὸς σώματος he does not take up the claim that God was not eternally Father at all[16] and in *Contra Arianos* I. 11 he begins his refutation of the Arian position by quoting the slogan 'there was [a time] when the Son was not'.[17] Although he then makes the point that God's nature is eternal and says that God has always been the Father of the Son,[18] he does so only very briefly before turning his

---

[14] *Categories* 7ᵇ15, quoted above p. 131.
[15] Quoted above, p. 133.
[16] Pointed out by Stead, 'Athanasius' Earliest Written Work', p. 83.
[17] *CA* I. 11, 33B.
[18] Ibid.

attention to a lengthy discussion of the introductory slogan. *Contra Arianos* is organized around the three slogans concerning the Son, not the credal formula of *Contra Arianos* I. 5–6.

Athanasius' most sustained discussions of the fatherhood of God occur in *Contra Arianos* I. 14–29 and 30–4 where he replies to criticisms of his vision of God which he attributes to the Arians. In the course of his lengthy treatment of the generation of the Son, he deals in I. 14–29 with the claim that by arguing for the equality of the Son with the Father, he effectively teaches that the Son is the Father's brother. In I. 30–4 he responds to the charge that teaching the eternal generation of the Son is tantamount to teaching that there are two unoriginate entities. The arguments of both passages reflect the influence of the Origenian trinitarian model which Athanasius recasts in post-Methodian terms. In both passages Athanasius contends that the fundamental statement to be made about the nature of God is that God is Father. The latter passage will be considered first.

In *Contra Arianos* I. 30, Athanasius replies to the question whether, on his understanding of the eternal generation of the Son, there is 'one ingenerate (*ἀγέννητον*) or two', a question which he attributes to the Arians.[19] As we have seen, the Arians were particularly concerned that the eternal generation of the Son jeopardized the concept of an ingenerate first principle. Athanasius replies, not by addressing the philosophical issue of what constitutes unoriginateness, but by looking at the question as a question concerning the uniqueness of the Father–Son relation and the priority of Father as the name for God.[20] He lays the groundwork for his argument with an analysis of the meaning and significance of the word 'unoriginate' for trinitarian thought.

After stating what he considers to be the point of their question—if one replies that the unoriginate is one, then it necessarily follows that the Son is 'one of the originate' (*τῶν γενητῶν*)[21]—Athanasius points out that the word 'unoriginate' is not found in

---

[19] *CA* I. 30, 73A. This is the only time in the discussion that Athanasius uses *ἀγέννητος* rather than *ἀγένητος* of God.

[20] There are parallel discussions in *De Decretis* 28–31 and *De Synodis* 46–7.

[21] *CA* I. 30, 73A–B.

Scripture, but that it has its provenance among the Greeks.[22] If Asterius' definition, 'that which is not made, but is eternal',[23] is to be accepted, then the Son must be regarded as unoriginate, since he has been eternally with the Father and did not come into existence from nothing.[24] If the definition 'existing but not begotten from anyone or having a father of his own' is accepted, then only the Father can be called 'unoriginate'.[25] But these are not the only ways in which the relation of God to other existents is to be construed. Athanasius introduces another possibility: the Son is an offspring (γέννημα), begotten by the Father.[26] Between the originate and the unoriginate there can of course be no likeness, but there is a likeness between the one who is begotten and the one who begets.[27] Athanasius goes on to maintain that only if the Son is considered to be the Father's offspring, rather than a thing originated, can God's character as creator be maintained.

Athanasius has altered the basis of the discussion in a way which allows him to advance the claim that it is more appropriate to call God Father than to call him unoriginate. God is to be regarded first through his relation with the Son. Athanasius posits two distinct orders in the logic of relations: Father and Son are correlatives, and unoriginate and originate are correlatives. These two orders correspond to the two orders of reality, the divine and the created. The Arians are guilty of failing to recognize the existence of the two orders of relations.

Athanasius sets up the contrast between the two orders of relations in language that echoes that of Origen. Like Origen (perhaps in imitation of him), he makes a distinction between God as Father and God as Almighty and Lord; but he uses the Origenian contrast for his own ends. Because the Son is the means whereby God exercises his power and mastery over all things, and because the Son also exercises that power, it is not with respect to the Son that God is Lord and Almighty but with respect to the

---

[22] *CA* I. 30, 73B.
[23] 76A.
[24] 76A–B.
[25] 76B.
[26] 76B–C.
[27] 76C.

things that are originate.[28] He succinctly states his version of the contrast in a passage in *Contra Arianos* I. 33:

And just as 'unoriginated' is indicated with reference to originated things, so also 'Father' is indicative of the Son. The one who names God 'maker', 'fashioner', and 'unoriginate' sees and discovers (βλέπει καὶ καταλαμβάνει) the creatures and originated things, while the one who calls God 'Father' immediately (εὐθὺς) knows and contemplates (νοεῖ καὶ θεωρεῖ) the Son.[29]

The language of Origen's presentation of the argument from relations has been recast in the language of a post-Methodian conception of God and the world. The contrast between Father and Lord gives way to the contrast of Father and unoriginate, and the contrast between Son and servant gives way to that of Son and the originate. In this context, the language of servanthood completely disappears.[30] What might be described as Origen's attempt to capture the distinction between the Father–Son relation and the Almighty–creation relation by characterizing the distinction in terms of the temper of the relationships has been absorbed into an ontological description of the distinction.

Athanasius' argument takes for granted the logic of the category of relation, and he appears to be treating the two orders of relations as parallel instances of correlativity. However, this is not the case. We shall return below to the problem of how Athanasius distinguishes between the application of the argument from relation to the Father–Son relation and its application to the unoriginate and originate relation.

Athanasius' construction of the two kinds of relations assumes the doctrine of creation from nothing, an assumption found with Origen only in relation to the physical creation. And it further assumes that the Son shares fully in the exercise of the Father's activities, an assumption that presupposes that the Son also shares in the divine being. Origen, as we have seen, edges towards the idea that the Son has a full share of the exercise of the Father's

---

[28] *CA* I. 33, 80A–81A.
[29] 80B.
[30] Though as we shall see, it continues to play a soteriological role.

powers, but he does not support this with a concept of shared being. Both Origen and Athanasius think that the Father–Son relation is metaphysically prior to and source of the existence of all other things. Just as it is because of the Father–Son relation that there can be an Almighty-governed relation in Origen's scheme, so also with Athanasius it is because of the Father–Son relation that there can be an unoriginate–originate relation. But, again, in Athanasius' theology this is based on a doctrine of creation and shared divine being that is not found with Origen.

Athanasius argues that the cause of the Arian inversion of the order of priority of the terms Father and unoriginate in the doctrine of God is a faulty theological epistemology. The reason why the Arians fail to grasp that God is first to be characterized as Father is that, like the Greeks, they fail to recognize the existence of the Son.[31] (Athanasius nowhere acknowledges that the Greeks call God Father.) Their knowledge of God is acquired through their observation of the natural order, which is to say, originate things, rather than through the Son. Consequently, it is inevitable that their conception of God is inadequate. Athanasius makes it clear in *Contra Gentes* and *De Incarnatione* that for fallen man such an epistemology results in an idolatrous understanding of God.

The correct epistemological alternative is 'to signify God from the Son'. This provides an epistemological specificity which, according to Athanasius, is missing from the Arian doctrine of God:'

It is more pious and more accurate to signify God from the Son and call him 'Father', than to name him from his works only and call him 'unoriginate'. For the latter title, as I have said, does nothing more than signify all the works, individually and collectively, which have come to be at the will of God through the Word; but the title Father has its significance and bearing only from the Son.[32]

The force of the argument is not entirely clear. Athanasius appears to be suggesting that the correlativity of the terms Father and Son is single in its focus and gives a precise indication of the nature of

[31] *CA* I. 33, 81A.
[32] *CA* I. 34, 81A–B.

God, while unoriginate and originate give a diffuse and uncertain indication. The term unoriginate leads the mind to many ideas; the term Father is simple, more accurate, and only implies the Son.[33] Athanasius assumes that the singleness of focus which he attributes to the term Father corresponds to the simplicity of God's nature. But the importance of the term Father is not just that it is single in focus. It is also more complete in that it incorporates the works made through the Son, whereas the title unoriginate has no reference to the Son.[34] Certainly Athanasius regards Father as epistemologically more secure.

Having distinguished between the two orders of relations, Athanasius sets in place the cornerstone of his argument for the priority of the word Father in the doctrine of God: Father is the word used of God in the Bible. While the word Father is scriptural, the word unoriginate is not and therefore it is 'suspect'.[35] As we have seen, Athanasius regards the Bible as the authoritative text for thinking about the divine being because it speaks more distinctly and with greater exactitude about the things of God than do non-biblical sources. Here he makes the grounds for the Bible's authority more specific: we may be confident that the word Father has primacy because it is the word used by the Son to refer to God, and, what is more, he does not call him unoriginate:

And 'unoriginate' is a word of the Greeks, who do not know the Son; but 'Father' has been acknowledged and granted by our Lord. For he, knowing whose son he was, said, 'I am in the Father, and the Father is in me' [John 14: 11], and 'He that has seen me, has seen the Father' [John 14: 9], and 'I and the Father are one' [John 10: 30]. But nowhere is he found to call the Father 'unoriginate'.[36]

Athanasius feels no need to justify this claim to authority; for him it is self-evident that the Son's testimony is definitive.[37]

---

[33] 81B.
[34] *CA* I. 33, 81A.
[35] *CA* I. 34, 81B.
[36] *CA* I. 34, 81B–C.
[37] Athanasius' use of the example of the Son's addressing God as Father is different from Origen's. Athanasius is not concerned to appeal to the Son's usage as a means of establishing that the incarnation brings to man a knowledge of God as

Fatherhood, for Athanasius, is the divine attribute in relation to which all other attributions must be made. Fatherhood orders those attributes and makes their significance for the divine nature intelligible. He is happy to allow a place for unoriginateness in the description of God. It signifies that God has no prior cause.[38] But its place is necessarily subordinate to fatherhood and can only be given its proper weight in relation to fatherhood. There can be no orthodox speculation about the nature of God that does not take the two terms Father and Son as its starting-point, and which is not in harmony with these two central metaphors. All thought about the nature of God ultimately is to be about the Father–Son relation; that relation is theology's beginning and its end.

Athanasius seals his argument for the pre-eminence of the word Father by adducing the evidence of the spiritual tradition and practice of the church. Not only does the Son describe God as his Father; he also enjoins us to do the same. Thus, when the Son 'teaches us to pray, he does not say, "When you pray, say, O God unoriginate", but rather, "When you pray, say, Our Father, which art in heaven"'.[39] In a similar way, with respect to the baptismal formula, the 'summary of our faith', the Son does not instruct us to be baptized 'in the name of unoriginate and originate, nor in the name of creator and creature, but in the name of Father, Son, and Holy Spirit'.[40] Athanasius immediately goes on to point out that our salvation depends on the fact that God is called 'Father' and not 'unoriginate', for only as we are baptized in the name of the Father are we who have been creatures enabled to become sons, and so to call God 'Father'.

Athanasius cites the examples of Jesus calling God 'Father', and his injunction to us to do the same, simply as evidence that in the Bible God is referred to as Father and not as unoriginate. Except for the brief reference to the soteriological significance of the

Father which is unique. The focus of discussion has changed from determining how it is that we may *know* that God is Father to determining the significance of fatherhood as an attribute of the divine being.

[38] *CA* I. 33, 80B.
[39] *CA* I. 34, 81C.
[40] 84A.

baptismal formula, he does not elaborate on them. Nevertheless, the damning implications are clear. In Athanasius' view, Arian theology creates an improper perception of God which cuts across the heart of true Christian spirituality, prayer, and worship, and it flies in the face of a specific injunction given by the Lord to his church. In failing to recognize the priority of the word Father in describing God, and in giving a disproportionate importance to the word unoriginate, the Arians fail to give adequate 'reverence' and 'honour'[41] to God. Moreover, the Arian emphasis on God as unoriginate vitiates a correct understanding of the way in which God expresses himself as man's saviour. Athanasius thinks that the Arians' religious sensibility is essentially sub-Christian. Notwithstanding the fact that he places the fatherhood of God as the first article in his summaries of Arian belief, his negative assessment of the consequences of Arianism for Christian piety reflects an awareness that in their writings the Arians were disinclined to refer to God as Father, and that they referred often to God as unoriginate.

Athanasius' most explicit and formally developed statement of the relation of the attribute of fatherhood to the being of God occurs in a short passage in *De Decretis* 22, and he makes a similar statement in *De Synodis* 34–5. The statement is part of his defence of the use of the language of 'being' in the creed of Nicaea. He argues that like the word God, the word Father signifies the essence of God. He acknowledges as a commonplace of theological reflection that it is not possible to comprehend the essence of God.[42] Nevertheless, the biblical titles Father, God, and Lord[43]

---

[41] *CA* I. 33, 80B–C.

[42] Opitz 18. 30–31.

[43] In *De Decretis* 22, Athanasius places 'Lord' alongside 'Father' and 'God', perhaps because it is found in Exodus 3: 14–15; in *De Synodis* 35, 'Almighty' (παντοκράτωρ, Deut. 6: 4) replaces 'Lord' (Opitz 262. 12). In the immediate context of the discussion in *De Decretis* 22, he refers to the Son as 'Lord' (Opitz 18. 27), and in his list of titles shared by the Father and the Son, which he gives in *De Synodis* 49, 'Lord' and 'Almighty' figure prominently (Opitz 273. 11–274. 8). Father, he says, is the only title that is not shared by the Son (Opitz 273. 11–13). Athanasius is not arguing that the biblical title Father is unique in the *fact* that it refers to the essence of God, though clearly for him it is unique in its *priority* of reference.

give us nothing other than a genuine intimation of the nature of God's being; they do not refer to something accidental[44] or external[45] to his essence: 'If God be simple, as he is, it follows that in naming him Father, we are not saying something about God, but signifying his essence itself.' (εἰ δὲ ἁπλοῦν τί ἐστιν ὁ θεός, ὥσπερ οὖν καὶ ἔστι, δηλονότι λέγοντες τὸν θεὸν καὶ ὀνομάζοντες τὸν πατέρα οὐδέν τι ὡς περὶ αὐτὸν ὀνομάζομεν, ἀλλ' αὐτὴν τὴν οὐσίαν αὐτοῦ σημαίνομεν.)[46] He cites Exodus 3: 14 and 15 'I am he who is' (ἐγώ εἰμι ὁ ὤν), and 'I am the Lord God', as evidence of their use in the Bible.[47] He explains that we may have confidence in the capacity of these titles for two reasons: because the divine being simply is, and because the titles are those used of God in the Bible.[48] The former reason presupposes that what is correctly said of God must be said of his essence. Underlying the latter is the unstated assumption that however metaphorical they may be, the divine titles of the Bible are correct. They have a real relation to the being of God, and thus are able to convey a knowledge of God as he truly is (by implication, the *sine qua non* for Athanasius of theological discourse). Fatherhood then is part of what Athanasius thinks makes God who he is.[49]

In *Contra Arianos* I. 14 Athanasius makes clear the significance of his thinking about the fatherhood of God in relation to the third-man argument of the Alexandrian tradition. He begins with the supposed Arian charge that 'if there never was when the Son

---

[44] Opitz 18. 21.

[45] Opitz 18. 22.

[46] Opitz 18. 28–30

[47] Opitz 18. 33. The Exodus passage is cited because it is proof that God simply *is*, and because, both for that statement and for the title 'Lord', it is evidence that the descriptions of God that are recorded in the Bible are given by God himself. As we have seen, both of these reasons are also important in Origen's use of the passage. For him, however, Exodus 3: 14–15 primarily identifies God as the source of being, and, though he associates the title ὁ ὤν with the title Father, and tends to think of the two titles in the same way, he does not use the passage to argue specifically that fatherhood belongs to the being of God. Unlike Origen, Athanasius does not support his theory of (biblical) language with philosophical speculation. Athanasius, of course, is unable to find evidence in the Bible of God calling himself Father.

[48] Opitz 18. 28–31.

[49] And so, consequently, is sonship.

was not, but he is eternal and coexists with the Father, you say he is no longer Son but brother of the Father'.[50] There is no independent textual evidence to confirm that the early Arians actually made the charge, though Eusebius of Caesarea's question of 'how the Father is Father and the Son is Son', if the Father and Son have their existence together and the Father is not prior to the Son,[51] assumes that if the Son is co-eternal with the Father, the distinguishing characteristics of sonship and fatherhood are eliminated. Whether or not Eusebius reached the conclusion that this effectively makes them brothers, it is a reasonable and readily comprehensible deduction from the supposition of the Son's coeternity with the Father, on the assumption that coeternal first principles must share in the same attributes. While Athanasius seems to relish the opportunity to refute the supposed charge, it is unlikely that he would have fabricated it; to have done so would have served no obvious polemical purpose. The charge strikes at the very heart of his theology by claiming that rather than protecting the divine status of the Son, his doctrine of God both denies the individual identities of Father and Son, and destroys their divine status by reducing them both to the condition of derived beings.

Athanasius correctly recognizes that the Arians assume that his position founders on the third-man argument—the supposition that both the Father and the Son are to be considered as coeternal, and thus as brothers, presupposes the existence of a third pre-existing origin for both—though he gives no indication that he recognized it as a formal argument. He does not answer by addressing the metaphysical issues involved directly (elsewhere he attempts to).[52] Instead, he answers with an argument based on the occurrence in Christian tradition of the two words Father and Son.

---

[50] 40C.

[51] *U.* 3, 4. 4–5.

[52] In *De Synodis* 51 (Opitz 274. 35–275. 26), Athanasius, in defence of his use of the concept of coessentiality to describe the relation of the Father to the Son, gives an account of the structure of the philosophical argument involved in the charge that he teaches that the Father and Son are brothers, and he attempts to reply in a more analytical manner than he does in *CA* I. He argues that since an offspring is coessential with its progenitor, a coessential relation does not necessarily mean that the participants in that relation must share all of the same attributes.

Like Origen before him, Athanasius assumes that the meaning of the names themselves protects the distinct identities of the Father and the Son. In *Contra Arianos* III. 4, defending himself against the charge of Sabellianism, he says that the Father and the Son are two 'because the Father is Father and not Son, and the Son is Son and not Father'.[53] Here in *Contra Arianos* I. 14, he argues that if he had not identified the Son by using the word Son, but had simply identified him as being *with* the Father, without having named him, then the Arian charge would have had some validity. But inherent to the terms Father and Son is the idea of their relation to each other arising from the generation of the latter from the former:

For the Father and the Son were not generated from some pre-existing origin (ἀρχῆς προϋπαρχούσης), that they may be regarded as brothers. But the Father is the origin (ἀρχή) and begetter of the Son; and the Father is Father and not born son of any; and the Son is Son and not brother.[54]

Nothing pre-exists the Father and the Son, and the identity of the Father as Father and of the Son as Son and the order of their relation are given and incontrovertible in the very use of the names. They are the irreducible and defining first terms of the Christian doctrine of God.

Within this relation, the word Father carries a particular significance. In itself it specifically signifies that God is the self-existent first principle, the source and cause of all things, beyond which there can be nothing else. This is Athanasius' answer to the problem of the third-man argument: the idea that God is Father cuts off the infinite regress. The description of God as Father tells us that God is the source of all existence, and it tells us that he is so *because* he is Father of the Son. The Father's οὐσία is the ἀρχή of the Son. Rejecting the idea that coessential realities presuppose the existence of a pre-existing third in *De Synodis* 45, Athanasius writes that 'the Father's being was the origin and root and fountain of the Son'.[55] In *Contra Arianos* III. 28, he rejects the claim that he

---

[53] 328C.
[54] *CA* I. 14, 41A–B.
[55] Opitz 270. 7–8.

teaches that there are two eternals by arguing that the Son, as Son by nature, co-exists in the eternity of the Father.[56] The fatherhood of God signifies that the Father is the fount of divinity, and just as there is one divine οὐσία and one θεότης of the Trinity, so there is one ἀρχή of creation.[57] The Son then is not a first principle co-ordinate with the Father; rather, the Son is eternally dependent on the being of the Father and integral to the expression of that being as the source of all existence.

But Athanasius' assertion of the irreducibility of the terms Father and Son does not simply rely on the fact that they are the given terms of Christian tradition. Further Arian criticism constrained him to explain the manner in which the two attributes which they signify exist in the divine being. The certainty of the two terms is guaranteed by the fact that in the divine being the two attributes which they identify are perfectly expressed, permanent, and unchanging.

In *Contra Arianos* I. 21, Athanasius reports that the Arians argue that if the Son is offspring and image of the Father and like him in all things, then he must be like the Father even in that characteristic which makes the Father Father, that is, in the capacity to beget. The Son must become a father in his turn, and his son a father in his turn, and so on *ad infinitum*.[58] Athanasius responds to the charge by distinguishing between divine and human generation on the basis of his distinction between the

---

[56] 384B.

[57] E. Meijering, 'Athanasius on the Father as the Origin of the Son', *NAKG* 55 (1974), repr. in his *God, Being, History: Studies in Patristic Philosophy* (Oxford, 1975), p. 96, adds ἀρχή to Harnack's list of Athanasius' synonyms for divinity. He gives the list as θεότης, ουσία, ὑπόστασις, ἰδιότης τῆς οὐσίας, and οἰκειότης τῆς οὐσίας (ὑποστάσεως).

[58] 56B–C. Athanasius deals with a similar challenge in the *Letters to Serapion* I. 15–16 (*PG* 26, 565C–569B) and IV. 3–6 (*PG* 26, 640C–648A), where he reports the charge that if the Holy Spirit is divine then he is either a brother of the Son or the Father is his grandfather. He perceives the charge to be an issue of the fixedness of the identity of the three and asserts simply and starkly the principle that because they are the given words of scriptural and liturgical tradition Father, Son, and Holy Spirit are necessarily and exclusively the terms within which thinking about God must be conducted. He also uses the same argument which he employs here in *Contra Arianos*, that in the divine being the attributes of fatherhood and sonship are perfectly expressed, permanent, and unchanging.

realms of divine and created reality. His response contains several echoes of Origen's argument for the eternal generation of the Son. Like Origen, he links the eternity of God's fatherhood with the divine attributes of immutability and perfection. But his argument is more complex than Origen's. With it he lays the basis for the development of the thesis that all of the attributes ascribable to the divine nature are perfectly and fully realized in that divine nature.

According to Athanasius, the points of difference between divine and human generation turn on the contrast between the impassibility and eternal immutability of God, on the one hand, and the corresponding opposites in man, on the other. Man, because of the imperfection of his creaturely nature, begets in time, whereas the Father begets the Son eternally.[59] He asks, in words similar to those of Origen, 'What is there to hinder God from always being Father of the Son?'[60] Because God is impassible and simple, he begets impassibly and eternally.[61] In human experience, a son's existence is not simultaneous with his father's because man's 'transitive nature' means that he begets passibly. In human succession, the father was once a son, and the son becomes a father. In man, therefore, fatherhood and sonship do not 'properly' (κυρίως) exist, since they do not stay in their respective 'characters'.[62] But, says Athanasius, this is not so in the godhead:

With respect to the godhead alone is the Father properly (κυρίως) father

[59] *CA* I. 14, 41B.

[60] *CA* I. 27, 68B. Unlike Origen, Athanasius does not use this as part of a 'willing/able' form of argument.

[61] *CA* I. 28, 69A. As with earlier Christian writers, the analogy between God and mind plays an important role in Athanasius' theory of the eternal generation of the Son, though he has no recourse to the idea of the Son's generation as an act of will from the mind. Taking care to ensure that both Son and Word are understood to be scriptural titles, Athanasius uses the title Word as a commentary on that of Son in order to confirm that the divine generation is incorporeal. The title Son signifies 'the natural and true offspring of [the Father's] essence', whereas, lest anyone should think of this divine generation in a human sense, the titles Word, Wisdom, and Radiance signify 'that the generation was impassible, and eternal and worthy of God' (69B). With man, words are not the product of affection or a part of the mind. Even less is this the case with God (69C). Athanasius tends to use the relation of the mind and word to establish the coeternity of the Father and the Son, and the relation of father and son to establish their coessentiality.

[62] *CA* I. 21, 56C.

and the Son properly (κυρίως) son, and in them and them only, is it the case that the Father is always Father and the Son always Son.[63]

Human fathers and sons do not fully realize what it is to be father and to be son. Because man is a creature and inherently unstable, his experience of each condition is transitory and so imperfect. But what is true of God must be true of him perfectly and permanently, for he is eternally perfect and immutable. God is 'eternally Father, and the character of Father is not adventitious to him, lest he be thought mutable'.[64] Because they are characteristics which are true of God, as Scripture testifies, fatherhood and sonship are fully and properly realized in the godhead.

The attributes of fatherhood and sonship, contingently express-ed in human nature, are essentially expressed in the divine nature. Athanasius sums up the basic principle of his theological metho-dology in a passage in *Contra Arianos* I. 23, where he maintains that just as it is immediately obvious to a person when he first hears about God that God's being is not the same as man's, so also it is plain that God does not beget as man, but as God:

For God does not make man his pattern. Rather we men, because God properly and alone truly is Father of his Son, have also been called fathers of our own children; for 'of him is every father (πατριά) in heaven and on earth named' [Eph. 3: 15].[65]

This is the first time among the authors considered in this study that Ephesians 3: 15 has been cited in connection with the fatherhood of God. Athanasius seizes on the verse as proof of the correctness of his approach to the discussion of the fatherhood of God and the Father–Son relation. He has found a statement with which he can confirm his methodological principle and which carries with it the authority of Scripture. Created reality reflects divine reality, which is its causal exemplar. In Athanasius' theolo-gical perception, if we are to see the full and primary expression of reality, we must look to its expression in God. If we are to think and speak correctly about the human experience of the father–son

[63] 57A.
[64] *CA* I. 28, 72A.
[65] 60B–C.

relation, our terms and concepts must be ordered by the perfection of their expression in God, an expression that we may know through the systematic reading of their revelation in the Bible. In the order of being, the divine is primary, the human secondary.

The fact that Athanasius uses Ephesians 3: 15 as a proof-text for his methodological principle reflects the extent to which Arian questions had forced the issue of the fatherhood of God and the generation of the Son to be dealt with in a more self-conscious and systematic manner than previously had been the case. Origen too, as we have seen in the fragment from the *Commentary on Genesis*, distinguished between God as Father and human fathers, on the grounds that God, unlike human fathers, did not become Father, and he also sought to distinguish the Son's generation from human generation. But the series of questions that Athanasius attributes to the Arians, questions which could well have been put to Origen (and perhaps were), now systematically posed in response to the Alexandrian stress on the coeternity of Father and Son and the relation of nature between them, necessitated a systematic response which made a methodological principle of the distinction between divine and human fatherhood. For Athanasius, the interpretation of the metaphor of Father is controlled by its context of reference. It could thus be employed with its core meaning intact. The designation Father thus signifies that God is generative by nature without compromising the divine attributes of eternity and immutability. Indeed, the idea of divine immutability, protected with Origen by the positing of the eternity of God's fatherhood, is with Athanasius made integral to the perfect expression of fatherhood, and by implication, all other divine attributes. He has no doubt that God is Father. God must therefore define what fatherhood is.

But if Athanasius is concerned to emphasize the relation between divine immutability and the eternal correlativity of the Father and the Son, he is equally concerned to reject the conclusion that the same relation holds between divine immutability and the Maker and his works. In *Contra Arianos* I. 29, immediately following his statement that fatherhood cannot be considered adventitious to God because he is immutable, Athanasius reports that the Arians claim that the logic of this proposition must also hold for God's attribute as Maker. If God is eternally Maker, then it necessarily follows that creation too is eternal.

The structure of this Arian extrapolation resembles that of Origen's argument for the eternal existence of the rational creatures recast in post-Methodian terms: if the immutability of God is to be protected, then just as God can never have begun to be Father, so also he must never have begun to be Almighty. It may be that the Arians hoped to embarrass Athanasius by obliquely associating his argument for the eternity of God's fatherhood with the (possibly) discredited one of Origen. But whether or not this was their intention, the supposed extrapolation corresponds to genuine Arian fears about the implications for the doctrine of God of the use in the Origenian–Alexandrian tradition of the category of relation. By extending the argument from the Son to things made, the Arians (of Athanasius' presentation) succeed in exposing the apparent flaw in the Athanasian argument. Athanasius' assertion of the eternal correlativity of Father and Son seemingly allows the readmission into Christian theology of the Platonic belief in the existence of an eternal reality alongside God.

Athanasius appears to have appreciated the point of the Arian counter-argument, but he does not respond specifically to Arius' dismissal of the relevance of the argument from relation. His attitude to the argument from correlativity is much like that of his attitude to cosmological arguments; he is interested in its theological rather than its philosophical significance. More pointedly, unlike Alexander and Arius, Athanasius makes no use of the technical philosophical language of the argument. His thought about the Father–Son relation is so deeply imbued with the logic of the argument from correlativity that he appears not to recognize it *as* an argument. He has absorbed the very point that Arius rejected: that the argument presupposes a relation of being. Unlike Arius, he thinks that this is exactly what has to be grasped in trinitarian theology.

Having recognized the force of the Arian counter-argument, Athanasius accordingly answers it in *Contra Arianos* I. 29 with a clear statement of his fundamental theological beliefs. He places his reply at the same juncture in his explanation of eternal fatherhood as Origen had placed his argument for the eternal existence of rational souls in his account, but he responds to it on his own very different terms.[66] He makes a distinction, set out within the parameters of his doctrine of creation *ex nihilo*, between the two types of relation, that of Father and Son and that of Maker and thing made. He affirms the divine freedom, but it is a freedom that expresses the divine nature. This distinction corresponds to the one he makes in *Contra Arianos* I. 33 between Father and Son and unoriginate and originate. In the later section he is concerned primarily with knowing and naming God as Father; here he is concerned with the metaphysical grounds for assigning a unique place in the godhead to the attribute of eternal fatherhood, and the Father–Son relation. The distinction turns on the difference between being and will.

According to Athanasius, the two types of relation are not similar. Although there is a correlativity of sorts between the maker and the thing made, it is not the same kind as that of father and son:

A work is external (ἔξωθεν) to the one who makes it, as has been said, but the Son is the proper offspring of the being (ἴδιον τῆς οὐσίας γέννημα). Thus it is not necessary that a work should always exist, for the workman works when he will (βούλεται); the offspring is not subject to will (βουλήσει), but is proper to the being (τῆς οὐσίας ἐστὶν ἰδιότης). One may be a maker, and may be so called, even if the works do not exist, but he would not be called father, nor would he be a father, unless a son existed.[67]

As we have seen, Athanasius fully accepts the underlying assumption of the argument from the logic of relation, which the Arians found intolerable, namely that the relation between two correlative entities must be a relation of being. He assumes a linguistic

---

[66] Athanasius proceeds to treat the untenable conclusion that the works are eternal as if it were the *Arian* position—an example of the rhetorical method which Christopher Stead, 'Rhetorical Method in Athanasius', *VC* 30 (1976), 121–37, repr. in his *Substance and Illusion in the Christian Fathers*, pp. 133–4, calls *reductio retorta*. Athanasius is inclined to regard such a conclusion as the kind of absurdity that necessarily follows from the Arian failure to make the fundamental distinction between the Son and creatures.

[67] *CA* I. 29, 72B.

correlativity between the maker and the thing made: they are a corresponding pair of words, but because the relation is one of will, the correlativity is not ontological. The existence of the attribute of maker does not of necessity entail the existence of the things made. Indeed, they are made from nothing. The relation of father and son is of a different order; it is a relation of being. The existence of the one necessarily entails the existence of the other. Accordingly, Athanasius can say in *Contra Arianos* III. 6 that 'calling God a Maker in no way also declares the things which have come to be, for a Maker is before his works. But when we call God Father, we signify at once (εὐθύς) with the Father the Son's existence.'[68] In the godhead Father and Son exist simultaneously and eternally with each other.

This distinction between the two types of relation Athanasius thinks is attested by common human experience. The relation a man has as father with a son is qualitatively different from the relation he has as builder of a house. A father does not have a son as something 'external or as foreign' to himself. Rather, he is 'from' a father, 'proper to his essence and his exact image', whereas a house is created from nothing, from 'without', and so is a possession which can be passed from one to another.[69] The begetting of the son is 'by nature',[70] and there is therefore an indelible natural continuity between father and son which cannot exist between the maker and the thing made, because the latter is a relation of will. God's act of creation, because it is an act which is external to him and dependent on his will, is free and does not bring about a change in God. The distinction between will and being, which underlies the contrast between father and maker, is further set out in *Contra Arianos* III. 59–67, a passage of critical importance for Athanasius' conception of the fatherhood of God. We will return to that passage, after comparing the place that Athanasius assigns to the attribute of divine goodness in his doctrines of God and of creation with the place that Origen gives it.

[68] 333A.
[69] *CA* I. 26, 65B–68A.
[70] *CA* I. 27, 68A.

Like Origen, Athanasius links the eternity of the fatherhood of God not only with the attribute of immutability but also with the attribute of goodness, and he assigns it a role in his understanding of the act of creation. But in both contexts he says comparatively little about it.[71] He refers to God's goodness in the context of establishing the eternity of the fatherhood of God at the end of *Contra Arianos* I. 28. His phrase is reminiscent both of Origen's statement about the goodness of God and the fatherhood of God in the fragment from the *Commentary on Genesis* and in *De Principiis* 2. 9, and of Alexander's in ἡ φίλαρχος.[72] The sentence, quoted above,[73] in which Athanasius writes that God is 'eternally Father, and the character of Father is not adventitious to him, lest he be thought mutable', continues, 'for if it be good that he be Father, but has not always been Father, then good has not always been in him'.[74] Though the statement is similar to those of Origen and Alexander in its association of fatherhood with goodness, it is different from them both in that it does not make the link by referring directly to the Son. Origen and Alexander identified the existence of the Son as the good thing that God could not be without, and both used it directly to argue (for different reasons) for the eternal generation of the Son. Athanasius, by contrast, makes the attribute of fatherhood itself the good thing which God must never have been without, and does not make immediate reference to the generation of the Son. The supposition that it is a good thing that God is Father is assumed to be true. To deny the eternity of God's fatherhood is to deny the eternity of his goodness, which in turn is a denial of his immutability. Athanasius is not directly concerned with the attribute of goodness. Rather, he uses the idea of God's goodness to reinforce the argument from immutability. The fact that it is fatherhood *per se* which is the good thing is again evidence that Athanasius had a more deliberate sense than his Alexandrian predecessors that fatherhood had a

---

[71] The idea of the divine goodness, however, does play an important illustrative role in the argument of *CA* III. 59–67, as will be seen below.

[72] As we have seen above, pp. 132–3, Alexander's statement may have been dependent on Origen's.

[73] See p. 177.

[74] 72A.

place among the divine attributes which can be formally identified and analysed.

Gone also from Athanasius' statement of the association of fatherhood with goodness is the reference to the perfection of the Father which is found in both Origen and Alexander. Athanasius does mention perfection at the end of the next section, *Contra Arianos* I. 29, but he uses it of the being of God, rather than his fatherhood, and does not directly connect it with his goodness: to say that the offspring of the Father is not eternal is to disparage the perfection of the Father's being.[75] He appears to have adopted the Alexandrian phrase associating fatherhood and goodness as little more than a useful tag and develops the idea in his own way.

For both Origen and Athanasius it is a fundamental premise that the well-spring of God's act of creation is his eternally expressed attribute of goodness. But the goodness of God requires much less attention in Athanasius' explanation of the act of creation than it did in Origen's. Having introduced the idea of the divine goodness at the end of *Contra Arianos* I. 28, he takes up the theme again in *Contra Arianos* I. 29 in the course of his reply to the charge that the logic of his argument for the eternity of God's fatherhood leads to the eternity of creation. For Origen, writing against Marcionite denials of the goodness of the God of the Old Testament, it is of especial importance that it be recognized that God never began to be good. Thus it is necessary that the objects of that goodness be eternal. The structure of his argument is parallel to that of the argument for the eternal existence of the maker and things made. But Athanasius is untroubled by denials of the goodness of God; if the Arians put the argument to him with respect to the divine goodness as they had with respect to God as maker, he does not record it.

In Athanasius' view, God is not dependent on the eternal existence of things external to himself in order to realize his eternal goodness. He does not explain in *Contra Arianos* I. 29 why this is so. But as we shall see when we turn to *Contra Arianos* III. 59–67 below, it is clear that for him the reason that God does not need an eternal recipient of his goodness in order to be eternally good is

[75] *CA* I. 11, 33B.

that the divine goodness is eternally and fully expressed within the relation of Father and Son as love. Realized first in the relation of the Father and the Son, *this* form of divine goodness is effected in the divine act of creation by the Word,[76] who eternally shares in the Father's being and goodness. What determines the point at which God creates is God's foreknowledge of what will be good for the things that are to be created;[77] the act of creation is not an arbitrary act of the divine will. Athanasius compares it with the incarnation: although God was capable by *fiat* of saving man at any time, he fitted the time of salvation to the good of man and the whole of creation.[78] God's will to create is an expression of his being, a being which is characterized by goodness and providential care.

Athanasius' fullest account of his conviction that the fundamental way in which God's being is to be understood is as a relation of Father to Son, a relation in which love is both given and received, occurs in *Contra Arianos* III. 59–67. The parameters of the discussion are set by the dilemma posed by Athanasius' Arian opponents: if the Father does not beget the Son 'by will' (βουλήσει), then he must beget him 'by necessity' (ἀνάγκῃ),[79] and God is not free. But Athanasius rejects this antithesis, advancing the counter-charge that his opponents have failed to understand the terms within which it is appropriate to speak of God's being and action.[80] It makes no sense, he writes, to think of God deciding to be what he is.[81] God does not decide to be good; nevertheless he is consciously and intentionally good, and is not constrained to be so from without.[82] And if it is true that 'the Father is eternally good by nature (φύσει)', it is equally true that 'he is eternally generative (γεννητικὸς) by nature (φύσει)'.[83] Atha-

---

[76] *CA* I. 11, 33B.

[77] *CA* I. 29, 72C.

[78] Ibid. In *CA* II. 68–70, there is a longer account of how the incarnation demonstrates that God's activity towards his creation is not based on an arbitrary act of will.

[79] 453A–B.

[80] 453B–C.

[81] 456A–B.

[82] 453C–456A.

[83] 464B.

nasius implies that, as with goodness, God does not decide to be Father of the Son, yet he is so consciously and intentionally, and is not constrained to be so from without.[84] The Father takes 'pleasure' ($εὐδοκία$) in the Son whom he has begotten 'by nature'. This for Athanasius is summed up in the words of the Father at the baptism of Jesus: 'This is my Son, in whom I am well pleased' (Mk. 1: 11).[85]

Athanasius is not attempting to eliminate the idea of will from the divine nature.[86] Rather, he is attempting to find an understanding of the divine will which is suitable to a nature where being and act are one. The human model of choosing, which follows a sequence of understanding, reflection, and action which takes place over time, cannot then be applied to God, for God does not act by calling on a habit from moment to moment.[87] To think that it can is to fall prey to the error of Valentinus and Ptolemy for whom God must first generate the principle of thought before he can act.[88] Citing Proverbs 8: 14 'I have counsel and sound wisdom, I have insight, I have strength',[89] Athanasius maintains that the Scriptures make it clear that the Word is the understanding and purpose of the Father. He is the Father's 'living will' ($ζῶσα$ $βουλή$).[90] To say then that the Son exists as a result of an act of will is nonsensical. There is no understanding and will in the Father antecedent to the Son—he alludes to the line in the *Thalia* about

[84] 461C–464A.
[85] 461B.
[86] For a discussion of the place of will in the theology of Arius and Athanasius, see Christopher Stead, 'The Freedom of the Will and the Arian Controversy', in *Platonismus und Christentum*, 245–57; repr. in his *Substance and Illusion in the Christian Fathers*. See also E. Meijering, 'The Doctrine of the Will and of the Trinity in the Orations of Gregory of Nazianzus', *NedThT* 27 (1973), 224–34, repr. in his *God, Being, History*. Stead, 'The Freedom of the Will', pp. 255–6, argues that Athanasius' comments on the nature and action of God are not entirely consistent.
[87] 460B; Williams, *Arius*, p. 229.
[88] 448C–449A.
[89] 457A. He also cites Isaiah 9: 6 and Psalm 73: 23–4 (457A–B).
[90] 457A, repeated frequently in *CA* III: 64, 457B; 67, 464C. The adjective 'living' presumably signifies that the Father's will has hypostatic existence, but it also signifies that the Son is effective as the divine agent of creation. See *CA* II. 2, 149B–152B.

Wisdom coming into existence through Wisdom[91]—since the Son is the Father's conscious, purposeful act. Athanasius refuses to separate the divine will from the divine being in the Father's generation of the Son. As naturally generative, 'what [the Father] does in producing the Son is the enactment of what he is; and as his acts are not temporal and episodic, he always and necessarily "does" what he is—by the necessity of his own being, not by any intrusive compulsion.'[92] Over against the Arians, Athanasius is able to assert that the generation of the Son is both free and natural.

The climax of the discussion in *Contra Arianos* III. 59–67 (indeed, of the whole of the work) is the description of the distinctive quality of the divine act of being as that of the eternal love of the Father for the Son and of the Son for the Father. This is the first time among the authors considered in this study that the characteristic and determinative quality of the relation of Father and Son is identified as that of love. He introduces the idea with the text of John 5: 20 'The Father loves the Son and shows him all things'.[93] He writes, 'Let the Son be willed (θελέσθω) and loved (φιλείσθω) by the Father';[94] with that same will, the Son 'loves (ἀγαπᾷ), wills (θέλει), and honours (τιμᾷ) the Father'.[95] There is nothing intermediate between Father and Son: 'the Son is the Father's all, and nothing was in the Father before the Son'.[96] The giving and receiving of love within the divine being is reciprocal and complete and exists for its own sake. It can be so because the Son, eternally begotten of the Father, shares in, and is expressive of, the divine act of being, which is itself a 'generative love that is eternally generative *of* love'.[97]

It is this conception of the being of God as an act of eternal giving and responding that allows Athanasius to distinguish the relation of the Father and the Son decisively from that of God and

---

[91] 461A, 464C–465A; *De Synodis* 15 (Opitz 243. 5).
[92] Williams, *Arius*, p. 229.
[93] 461C.
[94] Ibid.
[95] 464A.
[96] 465A.
[97] Williams, *Arius*, p. 241.

the created order. The eternal generativeness of the divine being is actively and fully expressed first in the giving and responding of Father and Son. And by implication, the divine being in all of its attributes is based on and expressive of the eternal activity of the common love of Father and Son. Thus the Father is not dependent on the existence of things external to himself to be who he is. It is from this very relation of Father and Son that the capacity and the will to create arise. Only by recognizing that the divine nature is inherently generative is it possible to account for the existence of creation at all. This, says Athanasius, is what his opponents fail to do. If the Son is not a Son and is called a work, then God should not be called 'Father', but 'Maker' and 'Creator'. Being thus without 'generative nature' (γεννητικῆς φύσεως), he will be unable to create.[98] 'For if the divine being is not fruitful itself, but barren, as they maintain, like a light that does not lighten and a dry fount, are they not ashamed to speak of his possessing creative energy?'[99] Athanasius identifies the creative energy as the Son, who is not 'external' to the Father, but 'proper' to him.[100] The divine act of bringing things into existence from nothing can only be conceived if fatherhood is understood to be the primary attribute of the divine being. For Athanasius, the fatherhood of God is the ground of reality.

[98] *CA* II. 2, 149B.
[99] 149C.
[100] 152A.

10

Father and Son

IN Athanasius' theology, the reciprocal relation of eternal knowledge and love that exists between the Father and the Son is the basis not only of the divine act of creation but also of the divine act of salvation. Because of the Father's love for the Son, he first creates through the Son and then responds in compassion to the need of mankind through the incarnation of the Son. The Son's ability to save turns on the fact that the Son shares in the Father's being, in his life, and in his attributes. In Athanasius' view the Arian conception of the Son as creature, however special, has disastrous consequences for salvation. To suggest that the Son is anything less than divine in the same sense as the Father is to nullify the Son's ability to save and thus to make inexplicable the Christian life. God must be directly involved in the work of salvation: the work of Christ must be the work of God. Only thus can the Christian experience of transformation and freedom, prayer and worship be accounted for and sustained.

For Athanasius the Son's sharing in the Father's being is signified by the fact that he is *begotten* from the Father: the concept of generation entails the idea that there is a community of nature between the begetter and the one begotten. The Bible, in its use of the words Father and Son to identify the Father and the Son, and in the pattern of its use of generative language, provides authoritative evidence that the Son is begotten from the Father, and Athanasius devotes much of *Contra Arianos* to providing an alternative to the Arian reading of the biblical language of begetting and making.

Repeatedly throughout *Contra Arianos* Athanasius employs a range of set phrases, sometimes singly, often in various combinations with each other, as virtually synonymous shorthand indicators of the Son's unique status and his distinction from the creatures. These include descriptions of the Son as 'offspring of the Father', 'true Son', 'of the same being as the Father', 'of one nature', 'Son by nature', 'proper to the being of the Father'. He frequently places these in opposition to 'having been made', 'participation by grace', 'son by adoption', 'foreign to the Father's essence', 'external to the Father'. He seldom attempts to give precise definitions of what he means by such phrases; nor does he attempt to investigate their technical philosophical sense. Among the key aspects of his thought for interpreting his sense of these phrases are his attitude to the use of the ideas of participation and ἴδιος in the characterization of the Son's relation to the Father.

Athanasius formulates his conception of participation in *Contra Arianos* in reaction to Arius' apparent abandonment of the traditional understanding of the concept. Before turning to the analysis of his attitude to participation, it will be helpful to attempt to establish Arius' view of it. For this, we must rely mainly on what Athanasius accuses Arius of saying about it. At the end of his summary of Arian beliefs in *Contra Arianos* I. 5–6, Athanasius attributes to Arius a number of statements about the Son's relation to the Father which indicate that Athanasius thought that there were two opposed senses of participation. The first, the strong sense, links participation with being. He reports that Arius says that 'the beings of the Father and the Son and the Holy Spirit are separate in nature, and estranged, and disconnected, and alien, and without participation of each other (καὶ ὅτι μεμερισμέναι τῇ φύσει, καὶ ἀπεξενωμέναι καὶ ἀπεσχοινισμέναι, καὶ ἀλλότριοι, καὶ ἀμέτοχοί ἐστιν ἀλλήλων αἱ οὐσίαι)', and that 'the Son is distinct by himself and in no respect participant in the Father' (διῃρημένον δὲ εἶναι καθ᾽ ἑαυτόν, καὶ ἀμέτοχον κατὰ πάντα τοῦ πατρὸς τὸν υἱὸν).[1] The second, the weak sense, links participation with will. Athanasius alleges that Arius teaches that the 'Word is not true (ἀληθινός) God. Even if he is said to be true God, he is not true God; but by participation of grace (μετοχῇ χάριτος), he, like all others, is called God only in name (ὀνόματι μόνον).'[2] These attributions may be

---

[1] 21D–24B.
[2] 24A.

paraphrases of propositions from the *Thalia* of *De Synodis* 15, lines 8 and 9 of which read: 'He [the Son] possesses nothing proper (ἴδιον) to God, in the real sense of propriety (καθ' ὑπόστασιν ἰδιότητος). For he is not equal to God, nor yet of the same substance (ὁμοούσιος).'[3] Further on, the *Thalia* reads: the 'subsistences' (ὑποστάσεις) of the Trinity 'are not mixed (ἀνεπίμικτοι) with each other',[4] and 'the Father is foreign to the Son in being (ξένος τοῦ υἱοῦ κατ' οὐσίαν)'.[5] Eusebius of Nicomedia explicitly rejects the idea that the Son's relation to the Father is one of participation of being, saying that the Son does not participate (μετέχω) in any way in the nature of the ingenerate.[6]

But if Athanasius' reports can be trusted, it would seem that Arius may on occasion have used μετοχή in its weakest sense to describe the way in which the Son participates by grace in the divine attributes of reason, wisdom, and goodness.[7] This participation in the eternal Word and Wisdom allows him to be correctly designated Word and Wisdom, and for this reason also he is called Son;[8] if he is called God, it is because he participates in divine grace.[9] Although Athanasius attempts to force the Arians to admit that if the Son's attributes do not belong to him by nature, they must have come to him at a particular point in time, as the result of his own moral achievement, Williams suggests that it is more likely that Arius thought the Son shared in the attributes because he was their direct product and reflected what they are like in a meaningful way.[10] Lorenz concludes that the Arian Son's participation in

---

[3] Opitz 242. 15–16.
[4] Opitz 242. 24.
[5] Opitz 242. 27.
[6] *U.* 8, 16. 3–4.
[7] Following Williams, 'The Logic of Arianism', pp. 73–7.
[8] *CA* I. 5, 21B. Accordingly, Athanasius can claim that Arius teaches the existence of two Words. Stead, 'The *Thalia* of Arius and the Testimony of Athanasius', *JTS* NS 29 (1978), p. 33, and 'Rhetorical Method', pp. 132–3, points out that this was a common charge in patristic debates. Further references are set out in the tables in Rudolf Lorenz, *Arius judaizans? Untersuchungen zur dogmengeschichtlichen Einordnung des Arius* (Göttingen, 1980), pp. 40–1 and 188–9.
[9] See the quotation above, p. 189, from *CA I.* 6, 24B.
[10] 'The Logic of Arianism', p. 74.

the Father is κατὰ συμβεβηκός.[11] Williams agrees, but cautions that it is not that the Father and Son are two substances which accidentally correspond to each other in the possession of certain non-necessary features. He points out that for Arius God is Word and Wisdom intrinsically, not contingently. By contrast, to be rational and wise cannot be part of the essential definition of the Son.[12]

For Athanasius, however, the Arian understanding of participation is inadequate. He thinks that it is tantamount to ascribing the divine titles to the Son 'improperly' (καταχρηστικῶς),[13] in a transferred sense, which he regards as equivalent to saying that the Son has them only 'notionally' (κατ' ἐπίνοιαν),[14] or 'nominally' (ὀνόματι).[15] It is thus only a metaphor to call the Son wise. Such words do not convey anything about the essence of that to which they refer. In the Athanasian interpretation of Arius, the divine attributes are only fully and properly possessed by God; the Son does not possess them as his own; they are not proper to him. But according to Athanasius' doctrines of God and salvation, if the divine being is to be understood as a relation of reciprocal love, and if the Son is to reveal the Father as he truly is, and thus to save, the Son must possess the divine attributes in exactly the same sense as the Father and not metaphorically.

Athanasius' own attitude to the concept of participation appears at first glance to be ambivalent. Early in *Contra Arianos* he counters the Arian understanding of the idea of participation with his own. In his only discussion of the strong sense of participation, in *Contra Arianos* I. 15, he argues that the Arian belief that the Son is 'called Son and God and Wisdom only by participation' follows from their assertion that the Son 'was begotten from nothing' and 'was not before his generation'. To say that the Son is called God by participation is to place him in the same relation to God as the creatures. It means that the Son participates in

[11] *Arius judaizans*, p. 59.
[12] 'The Logic of Arianism', p. 74.
[13] *U.* 4b, 7. 23.
[14] *CA* I. 9, 29C.
[15] 29B.

something other than the Father himself, something 'external' (ἔξωθεν) to the Father. But, Athanasius argues, the Father says, 'This is my beloved Son' (Matt. 3: 17), and the Son describes God as his 'own Father' (Jn. 5: 18), which proves that the Son participates not in something external to the Father, but in his being.[16] The Son participates 'wholly' in the Father, and 'to say that God is wholly (ὅλως) partaken is the same as saying that God begets'.[17] Participation, applied to the Son's relation to the Father in the strong sense, is synonymous with the idea of generation. There is no gap: the Son is not second to the Father,[18] and there is nothing between the Father and the Son.[19]

It is this strong 'whole' participation which allows the Son to grant participation by grace to those who are creatures by nature.[20] In *De Decretis* 9 and 10, Athanasius makes it clear that salvation cannot be brought about through a hierarchical chain. If the Son were an intermediate reality, he would separate us from the Father as much as uniting us to him. If the Son participates in the Father in the same way in which we participate in the Son, then the Son would not be able to impart the Father to us.[21] In *De Synodis* 51, he explains that such an understanding of participation would mean that the Son could not deify us, since he too would be in need of deification.[22] Rather, we participate in the Son and so participate in the Father.[23]

This distinction between a strong and a weak sense of participation corresponds to Athanasius' division of reality into the divine and creaturely realms, the unoriginate and the originate. It is unlikely that his understanding of participation reflects in any direct way the influence of the developments in third-century thought that may underlie Arius' rejection of the strong sense of the term. But the division that he posits between the two realms of

---

[16] *CA* I. 15, 44A–C.
[17] *CA* I. 16, 45A.
[18] *CA* I. 15, 44C.
[19] Ibid.
[20] *CA* I. 16, 45A.
[21] Opitz 8. 33–9. 12.
[22] Opitz 274. 25–33.
[23] *CA* I. 16, 45A.

being means that, like Arius, he is unable to accept a realist-vertical sense of participation, such as that of Origen, in which οὐσία is transmitted from higher to lower, and in which the Son as image, though having a continuity of being with the Father, is less than the Father as prototype. For Athanasius, the image must possess all of the attributes of the one whose image he is, unless he is image in 'name only'.[24] But Athanasius also rejects any lateral sense of participation in which Father and Son are seen as co-ordinates and belonging to one genus, for, as we have seen, the identity of God as Father, and thus source of the Son, rules this out.[25]

But having established early on in *Contra Arianos* I a sense of participation that he considered acceptable as a description of the relation of Son to Father, Athanasius does not subsequently use it. The idea of participation as 'whole' drops out of *Contra Arianos* and subsequent writings, and references to participation are restricted to the idea of participation by grace. Why this should have been so is not entirely clear, but the effect is to bring the issue into sharper focus. Athanasius may have felt that to use the idea of participation in two senses would be to run the risk of obscuring the clarity and force of his charge that the Arians were wrong in their application of participation by grace to the Son. He had other ways of positively describing what he considered to be the ortho-dox understanding of the Son's relation to the Father, ways which he may have thought were less potentially ambiguous. One of these was ἴδιος.

Athanasius uses the word ἴδιος with startling frequency through-out *Contra Arianos* to describe the Son's relation to the Father. Its frequency is startling not only because there are only two other known instances of its use for this purpose among his Alexandrian predecessors, but also because, notwithstanding its comparative novelty, he apparently does not feel the need either to defend or to explain his introduction of it as a critical term in trinitarian thought. We must look to its occurrence in the Bible, the (brief)

---

[24] *CA* I. 21, 56A. Williams, *Arius*, p. 225, notes that Arius avoids the word 'image' in his credal professions.
[25] See the discussion above, pp. 174–5.

history of its interpretation in the Alexandrian tradition, and its place in the Arian controversy to help determine what Athanasius intended the word to tell us about the Son's relation to the Father.

The word ἴδιος is used of the Father and Son twice in the New Testament: in John 5: 18 'This was why the Jews sought all the more to kill him, because he not only broke the sabbath but also called God his own Father (πατέρα ἴδιον), making himself equal to God', and in Romans 8: 32 'He who did not spare his own Son (τοῦ ἰδίου υἱοῦ), but gave him up for us all, will he also not give us all things with him.'[26] Origen cited both these verses, but not for the purpose of commenting on the status of the Son, and he made no reference to the occurrence of ἴδιος in them.[27] Dionysius of Alexandria may have used it. In *De Sententia Dionysii* 4, Athanasius appears to acknowledge that there is a letter in which Dionysius wrote 'that the Son of God is a creature and made, and not proper to him by nature, but is alien in being to the Father' (ποίημα καὶ γενητὸν εἶναι τὸν υἱὸν τοῦ θεοῦ μήτε δὲ φύσει ἴδιον, ἀλλὰ ξένον κατ' οὐσίαν αὐτὸν εἶναι τοῦ πατρός),[28] though this could possibly be an Athanasian paraphrase.

In ἡ φίλαρχος, as we have seen,[29] Alexander employs ἰδίου υἱοῦ from Romans 8: 32 once, as part of his argument for the eternal correlativity of the Father and the Son,[30] and gives a fairly precise indication of what he means by it. In the context of Romans 8: 32 the phrase may be suggestive of the contrast between the only-begotten Son and sons by adoption.[31] Certainly Alexander thinks

---

[26] The statement by Williams, 'The Logic of Arianism', pp. 62–3 n.34, that 'ὁ ἴδιος Υἱός is *common enough* [my italics] in the New Testament in an entirely untechnical sense', a view which he attributes to Christopher Stead and endorses, is misleading. Though the sense of the expression may be 'common enough'—τὸν ἑαυτοῦ υἱόν in Romans 8: 3, e.g., might be compared with ἴδιος in Romans 8: 32—ἴδιος is actually used of the Father and Son only in John 5: 18 and Romans 8: 32.

[27] John 5: 18 in *Com. Jn.* XX. 35. 313, and Romans 8: 32 in *C. Cel.* VIII. 42.

[28] Opitz, 48, 20–1, referred to above, p. 122.

[29] Above, pp. 136–7.

[30] The argument runs from *U.* 14, 23. 28 to 25. 7.

[31] C. E. B. Cranfield, *A Critical and Exegetical Commentary on the Epistle to the Romans*, i (The International Critical Commentary on the Holy Scriptures of the Old and New Testaments: Edinburgh, 1975), p. 436. Paul refers to adoption as sons

of it in this way. As I pointed out earlier, he uses the phrase to distinguish between us, who are not God's own (ἴδιος), and the Son, who is. He appears to think of ἴδιος as a synonym for γνήσιος, and he contrasts them both with adoption.

Williams argues that Arius reacted against the description of the Son as 'proper to the Father's being', which, he thinks, was current in Alexander's circle. He says that early in the Arian controversy Arius is depicted as rejecting the phrase *expressis verbis*.[32] In *Contra Arianos* I. 9 (and elsewhere on a few occasions[33]), Athanasius appears to allege that the Arians deny that the Son is 'proper to the Father's essence'. In *Contra Arianos* I. 9 he attributes to Arius the proposition that '[The Son] is not from the Father, but he as others has come into existence out of nothing; he is not ἴδιος to the Father's being for he is a creature and a work'.[34]

But since there is no independent evidence that Arius rejected the phrase, it is difficult to assess how much weight to give to Athanasius' allegation, and, in any case, it is not clear that it is the word ἴδιος which is the specific object of Athanasius' complaint. The inclusion of the word in the proposition may simply reflect Athanasius' natural usage; it may not have been of concern to Arius. Nevertheless, Williams suggests that it is possible to develop a picture of how Arius thought about the phrase.[35] He observes that in his list of propositions supposedly drawn from the *Thalia* in *Contra Arianos* I. 5 Athanasius attributes to Arius the idea that the Son is not that Wisdom which is proper to God and coexists with him (τὴν ἰδίαν καὶ συνυπάρχουσαν τῷ θεῷ), nor is he God's eternal and proper δύναμις.[36] This indicates that Arius regarded the divine properties as eternal and impersonal. To say that the Son is ἴδιος to the Father is to reduce the Son to an impersonal quality. Williams concludes that Arius is 'quite clear

in Romans 8: 22, and the thought expressed in Romans 8: 32 is similar to that of John 3: 16.

[32] 'The Logic of Arianism', pp. 58–9.
[33] e.g. *CA* I. 15 and *De Synodis* 52.
[34] 29B.
[35] 'The Logic of Arianism', pp. 58–62. What follows is a summary of his argument.
[36] 'The Logic of Arianism', p. 59.

about the meaning of ἴδιος: it relates only to a quality predicated of a substance'.[37]

Williams conjectures that behind this lies third-century Aristotelian and Porphyrian logic. In the *Isagoge*, ἴδιος is defined as a word that cannot be used of a substance in its own right. If Athanasius' reproduction of Dionysius' letter is literal, it is possible that something of such a sense of ἴδιος may have been known in Alexandria in the third century. According to Williams' reconstruction, in Arius' view to say that the Son is 'proper to the Father's essence' would be to deny his independent existence and embrace Sabellianism. In the Alexandrian tradition from Origen onwards, as we have seen, the Son was understood to exist καθ' ὑπόστασιν. The Son himself is an οὐσία, a proper subject of predication, and irreducible to being part of the definition of another subject. Williams concludes:

The Son therefore has his own properties, his own essential characteristics, which for Arius must logically be other than the essential characteristics of the (essentially eternal) Father. Hence Arius can say that the Son cannot possess the Father's attributes as essentially proper to him, being 'entirely unlike the Father's substance and *property*':[38] what makes the Son what he is cannot be what makes the Father what he is, and thus he cannot by nature or inalienability possess any of the essential and defining properties of the Father.[39]

If Williams' reconstruction of Arius' rejection of the idea that the Son is 'proper to the Father's essence' is correct, it reflects Arius' general attitude to the idea of substantial identity and participation between the Father and the Son. If the Son is to be considered to have independent existence, and not to be a rival ingenerate first principle to the Father, he must be related to God by will and not by being.

When we turn to Athanasius, we find a very different picture from that proposed by Williams for Arius. As has already been suggested, the phrase 'proper to the Father's being', and variants

---

[37] 'The Logic of Arianism', p. 59.

[38] Footnoted by Williams 'The Logic of Arianism', p. 61 n.30, as *Thalia* (*ap.* Athanasius, *CA* I. 6).

[39] 'The Logic of Arianism', p. 61.

of it, play an essential if unspecified role in his thinking about the status of the Son.[40] It has a particularly important place in his conception of how the Son shares in the divine attributes of the Father. He uses ἴδιος in three contexts: to describe the Son's relation to the Father; to describe the relation of the body to the Word in the incarnation; and to describe the relation of attributes to their subject.

Unlike his predecessor Alexander, Athanasius makes no mention of a biblical source for his idea that the Son is proper to the Father. He does not quote Romans 8: 32, the verse used by Alexander, in *Contra Arianos*; and although he quotes John 5: 18 certainly twice, once in *Contra Arianos* II. 12[41] and once in II. 73,[42] and probably a third time, in *Contra Arianos* I. 15 in the course of his discussion of participation,[43] he makes no comment on the occurrence of ἴδιος in the verse. The fact that he quotes John 5: 18 shows that he was aware that there was biblical authority for the use of ἴδιος in relation to the Father and Son, yet he feels no apparent need to call attention to this. He seems simply to have absorbed Romans 8: 32 and Alexander's interpretation of it into his thought—he often uses ἴδιος in conjunction with the idea of sonship by nature and in contrast with the idea of adoptive sonship—without any concern about uncertainty of meaning. It is therefore unlikely that he regarded the phrase 'proper to the Father's being' as a particular point of controversy with the Arians, whatever Arius may have thought about the term.[44]

Athanasius commonly refers to the Son as 'proper to the Father's being', a phrase which he uses sometimes by itself and sometimes together with such phrases as 'from the Father's being' or 'one in nature' with the Father. He writes that 'the Son is

---

[40] He was later to extend this to include the Holy Spirit. In *Letters to Serapion* I. 25 he describes the Spirit as not a creature but 'proper to the Son's being' (*PG* 26, 588C); and in IV. 4 he says that the Spirit is not a creature but is 'proper' to the Son and to God (*PG* 26, 641C).

[41] 172C.

[42] 301C.

[43] 44C, referred to above, pp. 191–2.

[44] Such a conclusion creates difficulties for Williams' attempt to demonstrate that the word was of especial concern to Arius, but it also leaves unanswered the question of why Athanasius should have used it so extensively.

different in kind and different in essence from things originate, and on the contrary is proper to the Father's essence and one in nature with it (τῆς τοῦ πατρὸς οὐσίας ἴδιος καὶ ὁμοφυής)',[45] or that 'the Word is Son of God, by nature proper to his essence, and is from him and in him'.[46] More simply, just as he can write that the Son is 'of the Father', so also he can write that the Son is 'proper to the Father'.[47] He can use ἴδιος to signify the unique status of the sonship of the Son: 'the Father shows him to be his own proper and only Son when he says "Thou art my Son" (Ps. 2: 7) and "This is my beloved Son in whom I am well pleased"' (Matt. 3: 17).[48] In the course of his discussion of participation in *Contra Arianos* I. 15 and 16, the description of the Son as ἴδιος to the Father occurs several times. The Son is 'proper offspring of the Father's being';[49] 'what is from the being of the Father, and proper to him, is entirely the Son'.[50] This latter phrase he immediately follows with the statement 'for to say that God is wholly partaken is the same as saying that God begets'.[51]

It is perhaps worthwhile adding that very occasionally Athanasius uses ἴδιος to describe the Father's relation to the Son, rather than the Son's to the Father. In *Contra Arianos* II. 59, he writes that the 'term "Father" is proper to the Son, and not to the term "creature", but the term "Son" is proper to the Father';[52] and in *Contra Arianos* I. 19, as part of his explanation of the Son's co-eternity with the Father, he says that the Son is proper to the being of the Father and that 'the Father is proper to the Son'.[53] In both instances he uses the word reciprocally of Father and Son as a way of stressing their correlativity. It is noticeable in the second example that while the Son is said to be proper to the Father's being, the Father is *not* said to be proper to the Son's being. It is

[45] *CA* I. 58, 133B.
[46] *CA* II. 31, 212B.
[47] *CA* II. 22, 192C–D.
[48] *CA* II. 23, 196A.
[49] *CA* I. 15, 44A.
[50] *CA* I. 16, 44D–45A.
[51] 45A.
[52] 273B.
[53] 52C–D.

likely that the rarity of the description of the Father as proper to the Son reflects a fear on the part of Athanasius that such a usage might compromise his basic supposition that the Father is the source of the Son.

The examples set out above suggest that Athanasius thought of the word ἴδιος both as a shorthand indicator of the idea of the Son's (unique) generation from the being of the Father, and as a way to make more emphatic other phrases which express the same idea. This impression is confirmed by what Athanasius contrasts it with. He often places phrases describing the Son as ἴδιος to the Father over against descriptions of created things as 'external' (ἔξωθεν) to the Father (which, as we have seen, he also did with the strong sense of participation),[54] and as 'foreign' (ξένος) to him, a word used in the *Thalia* to characterize the Father's being in relation to the Son,[55] and sometimes over against 'alien' (ἀλλότριος), also a word used in the *Thalia*, possibly to describe the Holy Spirit's relation to the Father and the Son.[56] All four of these words occur in a passage from *Contra Arianos* I. 20. Responding to a statement of the Arian denial of the eternity of the Son, he asks:

When was God without what is proper (ἰδίου) to him? Or how can one consider what is proper (ἰδίου) as foreign (ξένου) and alien in essence (ἀλλοτριοουσίου)? For other things, such as are originate, do not have likeness according to essence with their maker, but are external (ἔξωθεν) to him, made by the Word in his grace and will, and thus are capable of ceasing to be again, if their maker should wish it; for this is the nature of originate things.[57]

In *Contra Arianos* I. 26, he maintains that the idea of generation implies 'the natural and the proper', in contrast to the 'alien' and 'external'.[58]

But this is not the only sense of ἴδιος conveyed by the contrast

---

[54] Above, pp. 191-2.
[55] *De Synodis*, Opitz 242. 27.
[56] Opitz 243. 4. The meaning of line 22 of the *Thalia*, in which the word occurs, is uncertain. Williams, *Arius*, p. 102 and n.42, thinks that there may have been a line or lines following line 22 which dealt with the Spirit.
[57] 53A.
[58] *CA* I. 26, 65B-C.

between 'proper' and 'external' in Athanasius' thinking. This is evident from his discussions of the relation between the Word and the body in the incarnation. The contrast between 'proper' and 'external' is central to Athanasius' explanation of the unique quality of the relation that holds between the Word and the body which makes the incarnation the effective means of salvation. He describes the body as the Word's 'own' (ἴδιον).[59] The Word was not 'external' (ἐκτός) to the body,[60] nor was the flesh 'external' (ἔξωθεν) to the Word.[61] Rather, the affections of the body became 'proper' (ἴδια) to the Word,[62] and thereby we become 'proper' (ἴδιοι) to the Word, and may have a share in eternal life.[63] Otherwise, as was the case with Adam, grace would have been 'from without' (ἔξωθεν) and thus ineffective.[64] Because the relation between the Word and the flesh in the incarnation is characterized by ἴδιος, our salvation is made secure. What ἴδιος used in this context suggests is a closeness between the Word and the body which makes this relation salvific. This sense of closeness is also apparent in Athanasius' use of ἴδιος to describe the Father–Son relation.[65]

As well as using ἴδιος to describe the relation between Son and Father and Word and body, Athanasius also uses it to describe the characteristic attributes of things. This he does in a non-technical manner, and there is no hint that he has been influenced by the third-century philosophical discussion of the word. He writes in the *Letters to Serapion*, for instance, that omnipotence[66] and unalterability[67] are things that are 'proper' to God, and in *De Incarnatione* that invisibility is 'proper' to God.[68] In *Contra*

---

[59] *CA* III. 32, 392B.
[60] 389C.
[61] Ibid.
[62] 392B.
[63] *CA* III. 33, 393C.
[64] *CA* II. 68, 292C–293A.
[65] The occurrence of ἴδιος in both the trinitarian and incarnational contexts creates a loose correlation between the two natures of the incarnation and the two 'persons' of the Trinity in Athanasius' soteriology.
[66] *Letters to Serapion* II. 5, 616C.
[67] Ibid.
[68] *DI* 32.

Arianos he writes that it is 'proper' to creatures not to exist before they come to be.[69] Ignorance is 'proper' to man, whereas the Son knows all things.[70] Affections are 'proper' to the nature of man,[71] but the Word is impassible by nature.[72] But it is clear that such a meaning is not what he intends when he uses ἴδιος to describe the Son's relation to the Father. There is no evidence in *Contra Arianos* that Athanasius was worried by the possibility that by describing the Son as ἴδιος to the Father's being, he was reducing the Son to the level of an impersonal predicate, and promulgating a Sabellian doctrine. This is made abundantly clear in his use of ἴδιος in the early sections of *Contra Arianos* III.

The discussion of *Contra Arianos* III. 1–6 is important not only for Athanasius' understanding of ἴδιος, but also for his conception of the Son's divinity and effectiveness as saviour. In the discussion, he replies to the supposed Arian ridicule of the implications of his theology for the interpretation of John 14: 10 'I am in the Father and the Father in me', and in *Contra Arianos* III. 4 he takes up the issue of Sabellianism. Throughout these early sections of *Contra Arianos* III he continues to use ἴδιος to characterize the Son's relation to the Father without feeling the need to defend his use of it against the charge of Sabellianism. Indeed, in *Contra Arianos* III. 5 Athanasius appears to play on the two senses of the word—the 'impersonal' usage of the word as a description of the characteristic attributes of things, and the Father–Son usage—to underscore the idea that the Son possesses the divine attributes in the same way as the Father. Athanasius' attitude to ἴδιος is a serious reason against finding the origins of its fourth-century use in third-century philosophy as Williams is inclined to do.

In *Contra Arianos* III. 1 and 2, Athanasius rejects several incorrect interpretations of the preposition 'in' as it is used in John 14: 10. The preposition, he explains, is not to be interpreted in a material sense, nor in a spatial sense, since neither category is appropriate to the nature of God's being; neither is it to be thought

---

[69] *CA* II. 22, 193B.
[70] *CA* III. 46, 420C.
[71] *CA* III. 33, 393B.
[72] *CA* III. 34, 396A.

of in terms of participation by grace.[73] Rather, the correct understanding of the preposition in the verse is one that is consistent with God's being as incorporeal and as generative. He writes that 'the Son is in (ἐν) the Father . . . because the whole being of the Son is proper (ἴδιον) to the Father's being'.[74] The 'form' (εἶδος) and 'divinity' (θεότης) of the Father is the 'being' (τὸ εἶναι) of the Son.[75] John 14: 10, taken in conjunction with John 10: 30 'I and the Father are one', shows that there is an 'identity' (ταὐτότης) of divinity and a 'unity' (ἑνότης) of being between the Father and the Son.[76]

Athanasius goes on to address the question of whether or not his interpretation of the two texts is Sabellian. He deals with it briefly, his cursory treatment suggesting that he thought such a possibility absurd. His answer consists of two simple points. He asserts that the Father and the Son are two 'because the Father is Father and not Son, and the Son is Son and not Father'.[77] Here, as in his discussion of the priority of calling God 'Father', and in his rejection of the idea that Father and Son should be regarded as brothers, Athanasius assumes it is self-evident that the occurrence in Christian tradition of the words Father and Son in themselves demonstrates the existence of two irreducible subsistent realities. Origen, much more fearful of Sabellianism than Athanasius, made, as we have seen, a similar point, though he attempted to develop it into an argument, something which Athanasius does not pause to do.[78] Athanasius supplements this first point with a second not made by Origen: an offspring is other than its father.[79] Again Athanasius assumes that the language of Father and Son, and its inherent generative sense, testify to the independent subsistence of the Son and do not require further explication. But

---

[73] *CA* III. 1, 321B–324C.

[74] *CA* III. 3, 328A. Athanasius does not suggest ἔνδοθεν as an alternative to ἔξωθεν, perhaps because that would have appeared Sabellian.

[75] 328B.

[76] 328C.

[77] *CA* III. 4, 328C.

[78] Above, p. 70.

[79] 328C. The same point had been made by Justin Martyr, *Dialogue* 129. 4.

even here, in the midst of his defence against Sabellianism, Athanasius' main concern is to continue to emphasize the divine status of the Son as offspring from the Father.[80] After each of the two points, he hastens to ensure he has not allowed any room for (Arian) misconceptions. Although the Father is Father and the Son is Son, 'the nature is one',[81] and although as offspring the Son is other, 'still he is the same as God'.[82]

This assertion of the identity and unity of the being of Father and Son is the springboard for a strong declaration of the unity of Father and Son in their attributes and in revelation, a declaration in which ἴδιος is central. Because the godhead of Father and Son is one, Athanasius argues, all things that can be said of the Father can also be said of the Son, excepting only that the Father is said to be Father. He continues:

And on hearing the things of the Father (τὰ τοῦ πατρός) spoken of the Son, we shall thereby see the Father in the Son; and we shall contemplate the Son in the Father when these things said of the Son (τὰ λεγόμενα ἐφ᾽ υἱοῦ ταῦτα) are said of the Father also. And why are the things of the Father (τὰ τοῦ πατρός) said of the Son, except that the Son is an offspring from him? And why are the things of the Son proper to the Father (τὰ τοῦ υἱοῦ ἴδιά ἐστι τοῦ πατρὸς), except again because the Son is the proper (ἴδιον) offspring of his being? And the Son, being the proper (ἴδιον) offspring of the Father's being, reasonably says that the things of the Father (τὰ τοῦ πατρός) are his own (ἑαυτοῦ) also.[83]

In this passage ἴδιος is used to characterize both the relation of being that exists between the Son and the Father and the impersonal attributes that make a thing what it is. Having established to his satisfaction in the preceding section that the Son is a subsisting entity, and not simply an impersonal predicate of the Father, he has no hesitation in making the Son the subject of the attributes of the Father. The fact that he is proper to the Father's being in no

---

[80] In later writings Athanasius is more inclined to emphasize the distinction of hypostases within the godhead, for instance in *Tom. ad Ant.* 5–6 (*PG* 26, 800C–804A) and *Letters to Serapion* I. 28 (*PG* 26, 593C–596C).

[81] 328C.

[82] Ibid.

[83] *CA* III. 5, 329B–C.

way signifies for Athanasius that the Son is not himself a self-determining agent. The Son possesses the divine attributes (things) in the same way as the Father possesses them, because he is the 'proper offspring' of the Father's being. He possesses them not in a transferred sense, but fully and properly, since they do not 'accrue to his being by grace or participation, but because the being of the Son is itself the proper offspring of the Father's being'.[84] And it is also because the Son is the 'proper offspring' of the Father's being that his attributes can be said to be 'proper to the Father', that is, can be said to be the characteristic properties, fatherhood excepted, that make the Father what he is. This is one of the few occasions in *Contra Arianos* where Athanasius uses the 'impersonal' sense of ἴδιος with respect to the Father, or of the divine nature. Although he might well have used it to ascribe the 'things of the Father' to the Father and the 'same things said of the Son' to the Son throughout the passage, he uses it in this way only once. If he was clearly aware of the distinction between the two senses of the word, the fact that he is prepared to use the 'impersonal' sense with respect to the Father at all suggests that for him the distinction does not finally hold in the godhead. There is no distinction between who the Father and Son are, and what they are. In any case, his use of the two senses of ἴδιος serves to emphasize not only the closeness in being by which the Son is related to the Father, but also that the possession of the attributes is reciprocal: those things that can be said of the Son are those things that make the Father who and what he is.

In sum, Athanasius brings together the two senses of ἴδιος to heighten the closeness and intimacy of the Father–Son relation, the one sense deriving perhaps from general philosophical considerations, and the other from the Bible. On the one hand, the word serves to stress that the Son is as closely related to the Father as attributes are to their subject, while, on the other hand, it serves to stress that as Son and agent, the Son is more than an attribute, but is equally with the Father a subject of their common attributes.

Athanasius links his understanding of the incarnation as revelation directly to his understanding of the Father–Son relation as a

[84] *CA* III. 6, 333A.

community of natures. The identity and unity of godhead, and the consequent reciprocal possession of attributes, Athanasius argues, is what is signified not only by John 14: 10 'I and the Father are one' and John 10: 38 'the Father is in me and I am in the Father', but also by John 14: 9 'He that has seen me has seen the Father'.[85] The Son is able to reveal the Father because through his sharing in the Father's being and attributes he in himself makes immediately manifest who the Father is, what he is truly like. In contrast to Origen there is with Athanasius no concept of a progression to a knowledge of God by means of an ascent from the apprehension of the body of Christ to the apprehension of the incarnate Word and finally to the eternal Word. To know the incarnate Son is immediately to know the Father, 'for the Father's godhead is contemplated ($\theta\varepsilon\omega\rho\varepsilon\tilde{\iota}\tau\alpha\iota$) in the Son',[86] and, conversely, 'the Son is in and contemplated in the divinity of the Father'.[87] There is no epistemological gap between knowing the Son and knowing the Father because there is no gap between the being of the Father and the Son. Furthermore, according to Athanasius, 2 Corinthians 5: 19 'God was in Christ reconciling the world unto himself' testifies to the fact that the Son was able to redeem the created order because, through his sharing in the Father's being and attributes, the Son's works are also the works of the Father.[88] This identity and inseparability of the being and acts of Son and Father also has direct implications for our faith and devotion: they too have one recipient. To believe in the Son is to believe in what is 'proper to the Father's essence', and so to believe in one God,[89] and as there is one divinity, the worship that is 'paid to the Father in and through the Son' is one worship.[90]

But the ideas of communion of *οὐσία* between Father and Son and the divinity of the Son are fundamental for Athanasius not only because they establish the Son's ability to save. They also form the basis of his understanding of the tenor of the eternal

[85] *CA* III. 5, 329C–332A.
[86] 332A.
[87] *CA* III. 6, 332C.
[88] Ibid.
[89] 333A–B.
[90] 333B.

relationship within the godhead between the Father and the Son, and his understanding of that relation as the source of creation and of redemption. As we have already seen in the discussion of the fatherhood of God and the Father's inherent generativeness,[91] Athanasius in *Contra Arianos* III. 66 characterizes the relationship between Father and Son as that of an eternal giving and receiving of love, a relationship within which, by implication, the divine attributes are fully expressed. This is complemented in his thought by the ideas that the Father and the Son know each other fully, and that the Father and the Son have a mutual delight in each other.

In apparent reaction against Arius' affirmation in the *Thalia* of the absolute unknowability of the Father and the Son's ignorance of him, Athanasius allows no possibility that the Son's knowledge of the Father is less than the Father's knowledge of himself, as Williams has suggested was Origen's belief.[92] Originate things, Athanasius explains, can neither see nor know the Father, since he surpasses all sight and all knowledge. But the Son has declared that 'No one knows the Father except the Son'; therefore the Word is different from all originate things, for he alone knows and sees the Father.[93] There can be 'nothing greater or more perfect' than the Son's knowledge of the Father.[94] Such a knowledge is possible only because the Son shares fully in the divine nature: the Son alone knows the Father, for he alone is proper to the Father.[95] The Son's ability to reveal the Father is dependent on this comprehensive knowledge.

Athanasius frequently describes the relation of Father and Son as one characterized by delight, referring several times in *Contra Arianos*[96] to Proverbs 8: 30 'I was by him, daily his delight, rejoicing always before him'. Like Origen and Alexander, he argues that Proverbs 8: 30 shows that the Son has eternal existence, since it is inconceivable that the Father's self-expression should not be eternal. He asks, 'When then was it when the Father

---

[91] Above, pp. 184–6.
[92] *Arius*, pp. 139–40, referred to above pp. 42–3.
[93] *CA* II. 22, 193A–B.
[94] *CA* III. 46, 421B.
[95] *CA* II. 22, 193B.
[96] e.g. at *CA* I. 20, I. 38, II. 56, and II. 82.

did not rejoice?', and he answers, 'but if he ever rejoiced, he was ever in whom he rejoiced.'[97] The Father is able to rejoice in the Son only if the Son is perfect (τέλειος)[98] and does not need to be promoted to divine status. But in several ways Athanasius makes more of the theme than his two Alexandrian predecessors. In words similar to those he uses to describe the love between the Father and the Son, he takes Proverbs 8: 30 to signify that the delight that the Father has in the Son is the same joy as that with which the Son rejoices in the Father.[99] Their delight in each other is fully reciprocal and complete. This in turn 'again proves that the Son is not foreign, but proper to the Father's being';[100] their mutual delight is grounded in, and an expression of, the communion of nature that exists between them. Athanasius goes on to spell out, as he did not do in his discussion of the Father and Son's mutual love, what the implications of this are for the distinction between the Father–Son relation and the relation of the Father and Son with creation. Stating explicitly a theme that had only been implicit in Origen's thought, Athanasius uses the idea of mutual delight to make it plain that the Father–Son relation does not exist for the sake of anything other than itself. He notes that Proverbs 8: 31 goes on to say that on finishing the world the Father also had delight in the sons of men. But this he reckons is consistent with the preceding verse. Creation does not add to the Father's delight: the Father's delight in creation is the same delight as that which he has in the Son, for it is the fact that the creation is made after his own image, the Son, which is the cause of his rejoicing in it.[101] Earlier, in *Contra Arianos* II. 31, arguing against the supposed Arian claim that the Word was brought into existence in order to create, he maintains that had God decided not to create, the Word nevertheless would have been 'with God and the Father in him'.[102] Creation does not need to exist for the divine life to be what it is.

[97] *CA* II. 82, 320C.
[98] *CA* I. 38, 92A.
[99] *CA* II. 82, 320B.
[100] Ibid.
[101] 320C.
[102] *CA* II. 31, 212B.

For Athanasius, this reciprocal delight is possible because the Father and the Son share in the same nature and possess the same attributes. Thus the Son's relation to the Father cannot be one of participation; the Son cannot have come into being through an impersonal divine attribute of wisdom, word, or son. There can be no gap in being between the Father and the recipient of those attributes that make the Father what he is, a nature that is inherently one of giving and responding in love. The Son cannot be 'external' to God and intermediate between God and the world, if God is to be God. The Father, perfect in nature, can only fully express his nature in love and joy with a subject, equally perfect, who is able perfectly to return that love and joy. The Father delights in seeing himself in his own image, and, conversely, the Son rejoices in seeing himself in the Father.[103] As Athanasius conceives of it, the divine life consists in a plurality and mutuality in which there is an eternal richness of intentional enjoyment and love arising from God's generative nature as Father. This enables the Father and the Son to act freely to bring a creation into being which is reflective of the nature of the divine life but distinct from it.

This eternal relation of love and delight is the cause not only of the act of creation, but also of the act of redemption, which two acts Athanasius closely links. He frequently refers specifically to the Father's love for mankind, and to the Son's, as the cause of the incarnation, and sometimes also of creation. He does not directly identify the love that is the love of the Father for the Son and the Son for the Father as that love which brings about creation and redemption, but the idea is not far from his mind. Creation, the incarnation, and the love of God are brought together in *Contra Arianos* II. 64, where he writes of the creation of originate things that

they could not have endured [the Son's] nature, which is the unadulterated splendour of the Father, unless by virtue of that love for mankind which he shares with the Father (εἰ μὴ φιλανθρωπίᾳ πατρικῇ) he had helped them by coming down to their level and so used his power to bring them into existence. And then again it was by the Word coming down to our

---

[103] *CA* II. 82, 320C.

level a second time that the creation itself also was made a son through
him. And so he became, as Scripture says, first born of creation in every
respect—first in creating and then in being brought into the world for the
sake of all.[104]

A few lines later, he remarks that because of Adam's fall, 'the
Word of God, who loves man, puts on him created flesh at the
Father's will'.[105] The love which the Son has for mankind and
which impels his acts of creation and redemption is the same love
which the Father has for mankind and which the Son shares.

There is another element which fits into Athanasius' picture of
the relation of the divine being to creation and redemption: the
Father's intention to save is eternal and reflects his eternal nature.
Because of the Father's love for mankind[106] and his eternal
goodness,[107] the redemption of mankind, the appearing of grace to
us in the incarnation, was prepared for us in the Son, by whom the
Father also created us, before the world began.[108] This, Athanasius thinks, is attested by Paul in the words of Ephesians 1: 3–5:
'Blessed be the God and Father of our Lord Jesus Christ, who has
blessed us in Christ Jesus with every spiritual blessing in the
heavenly places, even as he chose us in him before the foundation
of the world, that we should be holy and blameless before him in
love, having destined us to be his sons through Jesus Christ.'[109]
Thus for Athanasius the whole of the divine nature, and its
expression towards the created economy, is contained in the
eternal relation of the Father and the Son. Were the Son not
eternally begotten and so divine, he could not save. Were the
divine being not eternally expressed as the love of Father and Son,
there could be neither a world nor its salvation.

Athanasius supports his claim for the divine status of the Son by
appealing to the witness of the Scriptures. He argues that when
they are read correctly, and not as the Arians read them, the
Scriptures attest that the Son is eternally begotten from the Father.

---

[104] *CA* II. 64, 284A–B.
[105] *CA* II. 65, 285A.
[106] *CA* II. 75, 305B–C.
[107] *CA* II. 77, 309B–C.
[108] *CA* II. 75, 305B–308B.
[109] 308A–B.

Of critical importance for his argument is the distinction he posits in biblical language between 'begetting' and 'making' as they were applied to the Father's production of the Son. Much of the three Orations of *Contra Arianos* is taken up with his attempt to develop, and to apply to the relevant texts, a hermeneutical procedure that would ensure that the language of begetting would be interpreted as referring to the eternal Son, while that of making would be interpreted as referring to the incarnate Son.

The interpretation of texts was a critical issue early in the Arian controversy. It is probable that the texts over which the disagreement between Alexander and Arius first focused were Psalm 45: 7–8, Proverbs 8: 22–5, Isaiah 1: 2, and a number of New Testament texts.[110] The evidence for Arius' attitude to the biblical terminology of begetting and making, however, is limited. He does not engage in an exegetical analysis of the two types of language in either of his two letters, or in his and Euzoius' confession, or in the *Thalia* extracts of *De Synodis*. One of Athanasius' earliest and often repeated charges against Arius is that he taught that the Son was *made (ποιέω)* by the Father. In ἑνὸς σώματος, for instance, Athanasius writes that 'the God who exists has made him who did not exist [to exist] out of nothing'.[111] As Stead notes, there is no primary evidence for this, but he thinks that it is probable that Arius did use the word ποιέω, in view of Hebrews 3: 2 and the precedent set by Dionysius of Alexandria, but without sharply opposing it to γεννάω, as Athanasius did.[112] In the *Thalia* of *De Synodis* both τεχνοποιέω[113] and γεννάω[114] are used to describe the generation of the Son, though the non-committal terms ὑπάρχω[115] and ὑφίστημι[116] are also used.

---

[110] So Williams, *Arius*, pp. 108–9. Williams suggests a list of 'plausible' additional candidates from among those mentioned by Athanasius, which includes Phil. 2: 9–10, Heb. 1: 4 and 3: 1–2, Acts 2: 36, and Rom. 8: 29, as well, possibly, as the Gospel texts of *CA* III.

[111] ὁ . . . ὢν θεὸς τὸν μὴ ὄντα ἐκ τοῦ μὴ ὄντος πεποίηκε. *U.* 4b, 7. 20.

[112] 'Athanasius' Earliest Written Work', pp. 87–8.

[113] Opitz 242. 15. For a comment on the correct translation of the word, see below p. 228, n. 35.

[114] Opitz 243. 9 and 21.

[115] Opitz 243. 1, 3, and 5.

[116] Opitz 243. 12.

Proverbs 8: 22–5 was of particular importance in the controversy. It included (in the Septuagint) both a making verb, κτίζω,
and a begetting verb, γεννάω. In his letter to Eusebius of
Nicomedia, Arius appears to be alluding to the Proverbs passage
in his list of synonyms for the Father's generation of the Son. He
begins the list with γεννηθῇ, followed in sequence by κτισθῇ, ὁρισθῇ,
and θεμελιωθῇ.[117] Three of these occur in Proverbs 8: 22–5 in the
sequence: ἔκτισεν (8: 22), ἐθεμελίωσεν (8: 23), and γεννᾷ (8: 25).
(The verb ὁρίζω occurs in Romans 1: 4.) According to Williams,
this re-ordering 'suggest[s] very clearly' that γεννάω, 'though a
metaphor, is the primary metaphor' for Arius.[118] But, not surprisingly, it seems not to have made such a distinct impression on
Athanasius. This re-ordering of the verbs is the closest we get to a
commentary on Proverbs 8: 22–5 in Arius' writings.

Elsewhere, in his credal letter to Alexander, Arius cites and
briefly comments on three ambiguous scriptural texts: 'from him'
(Rom. 11: 36), 'from the womb' (Ps. 110: 3), and 'I came from the
Father and have come' (Jn. 8: 42). His rejection of any interpretation of them that would suggest that the Son was a 'consubstantial'
portion of God, or an 'emanation' from God,[119] gives an indication
of the hermeneutical limits within which his exegesis of the
generative language of the Bible would probably have proceeded.

Eusebius of Nicomedia, however, in his letter to Paulinus, does
provide us with a clear example of an Arian exegesis of the biblical
language of begetting in his discussion of the correct way to
interpret the Proverbs passage. Quoting the relevant phrases from
Proverbs 8: 22–5 (without re-ordering the sequence in which they
occur in the passage), Eusebius argues that because the Son is
described as created (κτίζω) and founded (θεμελιόω), as well as
begotten (γεννάω), in his οὐσία, he cannot be said to be 'from
[God]', since what is of the ingenerate cannot be created or
founded.[120] For Eusebius, the occurrence in the same passage of
other words alongside 'begot' to describe God's production of the

---

[117] U. 1, 3. 3.
[118] 'Quest of the Historical Thalia', p. 31 n.51.
[119] U. 6, 17. 13–20.
[120] U. 8, 16. 8–15.

Son serves to make relative the importance of 'begot' as a description: it is only one among others. Since these other words cannot be taken to indicate a unique relation between the being of the Son and the being of God, neither can 'begot'.

Lest there be any lingering thought that this word must indicate *something* peculiar to the Son's relation to the Father that is not true of other beings created by God's will, Eusebius seals his argument by going on to point out that Scripture does not use 'begotten' exclusively of the Son, but also of things that are entirely unlike God in nature. In support of this claim, he cites three texts: Isaiah 1: 2 'Sons have I begotten (ἐγέννησα) and brought up, but they have rebelled against me'; Deuteronomy 32: 18 'You have rejected the God who begot (γεννήσαντα) you'; and Job 38: 28 'Who has begotten (τετοκώς) the drops of dew?'. These he thinks demonstrate that the word γεννάω in the Scriptures means nothing more than that the generation of everything which has come into being has come into being by God's will.[121]

Athanasius undertakes a detailed commentary on three of the four texts referred to by Eusebius of Nicomedia: Proverbs 8: 22–5, Deuteronomy 32: 18, and Isaiah 1: 2. But before turning to an analysis of his interpretation of the texts, we need to begin with a brief examination of his exegetical methodology. Although the passages of exegesis in Athanasius' writings are often extensive, repetitious, and seemingly convoluted, it is nevertheless possible to identify a number of basic elements in his exegetical procedure. Three of the most helpful for understanding his treatment of generative language are the application of the principle that there is a 'double account' of the Son in the Bible which corresponds to the rule of faith; the application of the principle that reality is prior to words, and not words to reality; and the application of grammatical analysis. While he does not work out the relationship in his hermeneutics between the three elements, and employs them in a less than consistent and thoroughgoing manner, they loosely complement each other in his attempt to develop an exegetical reply to the Arians which would protect the divine

[121] *U.* 8, 16. 15–17. 5.

nature of the Son. He assumes throughout his exegetical writings that the application of these elements in his methodology is to be guided by the rule of faith. Without this guidance it is not possible to come to the correct interpretation of the texts.[122] The first two of the three elements will be outlined first and then his detailed commentary on the three biblical texts will be examined, showing how he applies all three in practice.

As we have already seen with reference to the first element, Athanasius thinks that there exists a correspondence between the scope of the Christian faith and the 'scope and character' of the Scriptures.[123] This 'scope and character' of the Bible 'contains a double account of the Saviour: that he was eternally God, and is the Son, being the Father's Word and Radiance and Wisdom; and that afterwards for us he took flesh from a virgin, Mary bearer of God, and became man.'[124] The double account is found through-out the Bible.[125] In order to determine on which side of the account a text belongs, the exegete asks three questions: to what time does the text refer, to what person, and to what purpose?[126] We shall return to the application of this element after an extended discussion of the second.

Athanasius states the second principle of his exegetical method, namely that reality is prior to words, and not words to reality, at the beginning of *Contra Arianos* II, after setting out the argument for regarding the Son as Son and not a work, on the grounds that the Son is the living will of an inherently generative divine Father. He then uses the principle to demonstrate how even those scriptural texts in which the occurrence of both begetting and making language is contrary to (his) expectations can be reconciled with the rule of faith. Covering both of Eusebius of Nicomedia's points, he argues that the words 'begot' and 'made' are not always used in the Bible to convey their primary meaning: the Son can be said to have been made, and, conversely, creatures can be said to

---

[122] See the comments on his introduction to the Proverbs commentary, below, p. 217.
[123] Above, pp. 156–7.
[124] *CA* III. 29, 385A.
[125] Ibid.
[126] *CA* I. 54, 124B.

have been begotten, without the Son's true nature being compromised. In both cases, the words are being used in a secondary sense. Consequently, the begetting language of Scripture has not been made relative.

In *Contra Arianos* II. 3, Athanasius discusses the problem of a making word being ascribed to the Son in Scripture with reference to the use in Hebrews 3: 2 of the verb ποιέω to describe the relation of the Son to God, 'He was faithful to him who made (τῷ ποιήσαντι) him', rather than the seemingly more appropriate verb γεννάω, which, Athanasius remarks, would have given the reading 'to him who begot (τῷ γεννήσαντι) him'.[127] He explains, however, that

it does not matter what word is used in such instances, so long as what he [the Son] is according to nature is confessed. For words do not diminish his nature; but, rather, that nature draws to itself those words and changes them. For words are not prior to essences (οὐσιῶν), but essences are first and words are second to them.[128]

For Athanasius the implications of this for the biblical language of begetting and making are plain:

Therefore also when the essence is a work or creature, then the words 'He made', and 'He became', and 'He created', are both used of it properly (κυρίως) and designate the work. But when the essence is an offspring and a Son, then 'He made', and 'He became', and 'He created' no longer properly (κυρίως) belong to it, nor designate a work.[129]

In confirmation he notes the common practice of fathers calling their sons servants, and their servants sons, a practice for which he finds evidence in the Bible. Bathsheba calls Solomon 'your servant' when speaking to David, and so does Nathan.[130] But we nevertheless account Solomon a 'natural and genuine' (φύσει καὶ γνήσιον) son of David.[131] Parents also use of their sons the words: 'made'—as for instance Hezekiah does (Isa. 38: 19, LXX)—and

---

[127] 152B.
[128] 152C.
[129] Ibid.
[130] 153A.
[131] *CA* II. 4, 153B.

'created' and 'become', without denying their nature.[132] Accordingly, when we hear it said of the Son that 'He was faithful to him who made him' (Heb. 3: 2), and the Son says of himself 'The Lord created me' (Prov. 8: 22), and 'I am your servant and the Son of your handmaiden' (Ps. 116: 16), we are not misled, but we continue correctly to acknowledge that he is the 'natural and genuine' Son of the Father.[133] The rule of faith is the assumed framework which is governing Athanasius' application of this second principle; it provides us with the necessary prior knowledge that the Son who may be described as 'made' in any given text is in fact the Son by nature.

Athanasius' converse point, that creatures can be *said* to be begotten without compromising the Son's unique nature as begotten, follows the same logic. The biblical language of begetting (as it applies to God and man) always properly refers to the Son alone. Generally, when the Scriptures wish to signify a son, they use the word 'begot'.[134] But what Athanasius means by 'son' is ultimately *the* Son. For while what is 'begotten' may be said to have 'become' or to have been 'made',

things originate, being created things, cannot be called begotten, except in so far as after their participation in the begotten Son they are also said to have been begotten, by no means because of their own nature, but because of their participation of the Son in the Spirit.[135]

The creature is creature by nature and always remains so; its status as 'begotten' comes through its participation in the 'begottenness' of the Son, who alone is properly begotten Son, Son by nature. The language of begetting in the Bible, according to Athanasius, though used of creatures, is only so used in a secondary, transferred sense, and the language of making is used of the pre-existent Son in a secondary, transferred sense.

---

[132] 156A–B.
[133] 153B–C.
[134] *CA* II. 59, 272B.
[135] *CA* I. 56, 129B: τὰ δὲ γενητὰ ἀδύνατον, δημιουργήματα ὄντα, λέγεσθαι γεννητά, εἰ μὴ ἄρα, μετὰ ταῦτα μετασχόντα τοῦ γεννητοῦ υἱοῦ, γεγεννῆσθαι καὶ αὐτὰ λέγονται· οὔτι γε διὰ τὴν ἰδίαν φύσιν, ἀλλὰ διὰ τὴν μετουσίαν τοῦ υἱοῦ ἐν τῷ πνεύματι.

Athanasius' commentary on two phrases from Hebrews 1: 1–4 in *Contra Arianos* I. 55 and 56 provides an example of how he applies the first two elements of his exegetical method together in the interpretation of a single biblical passage. The phrases are: 'In many and various ways God spoke of old to our fathers by the prophets; but in these last days he has spoken to us by a Son' (1: 1–2); and 'when he had by himself made purification for our sins, he sat down on the right hand of the Majesty on high, having become (γενόμενος) as much superior to angels as the name he has obtained is more excellent than theirs' (1: 3–4).[136] He begins the passage of commentary by stating the necessity of asking the three questions,[137] but he then proceeds to answer only one of them directly: the two phrases refer to the *time* of the economy.[138] Having established the time, he appears to assume that the other two questions do not need explicitly to be put to the text.

He goes on to address the problem of how to account for the occurrence of 'become' in Hebrews 1: 4. Surprisingly, he does not attribute 'become' to the ascension of the human nature of the incarnate Word, an argument he exploits when explaining the statement of Philippians 2: 9 that God has 'highly exalted' Christ.[139] Instead, he employs what seems to be the question of the *person* in combination with the second principle to interpret the word. He charges the Arians, who use the presence of the word 'become' to show that the Son is originate, with having failed to note the significance of the fact that the word Son occurs throughout the passage. The Son, it seems, is the *person* to whom the text refers. He maintains that the presence in the passage of the word Son is proof that the Son is not originate.[140] The word Son, conceived in Athanasius' theology as conveying in itself the idea of a relation of nature between the Father and Son, here controls the exegesis of the word 'become'. Son, in effect, functions as a theological shorthand for Athanasius, signifying the essence of the

---

[136] *CA* I. 55, 125B–C. The words 'by himself', δι' ἑαυτοῦ, occur in the Bezae NT manuscript, and are cited by Origen and Chrysostom, among others.

[137] 125B.

[138] 125C.

[139] *CA* I. 41, 96C.

[140] *CA* I. 56, 129A.

rule of faith. The word Son is the core biblical image in relation to which all other descriptions of the Son are to be interpreted. But having made this point about the person of the text, he appears to feel that he is still left with the eternal Son as the subject of the verb 'become'. His solution is to apply the second principle: that which is *properly* described as 'begotten' (established here in the word 'Son') may be *said* to have 'become', or to have been 'made'.[141]

But although Athanasius takes considerable care in the opening sections of *Contra Arianos* II to establish that even when the making language of Scripture is applied to the 'very Word',[142] it does not compromise the status of the Son as eternally begotten, and applies this principle to Hebrews 1: 1–4 and 3: 2, he predominantly uses the first principle in his exegesis, and seldom resorts to the second. It is hardly ever necessary for him in practice to apply making language to the eternal Son even in the secondary sense, since there is always another subject, the human nature of the incarnate Word, to which this language properly applies.

Of the three texts referred to by Eusebius of Nicomedia on which Athanasius comments, Proverbs 8: 22–5, Deuteronomy 32: 18, and Isaiah 1: 2, he gives most attention to the first, the discussion of which runs from *Contra Arianos* II. 18 to II. 82. Interwoven into the discussion are lengthy treatments of other texts, including Deuteronomy 32: 18. It is necessary, he says in *Contra Arianos* II. 18, to examine the passage from Proverbs because the Arians make much of it everywhere and many who are ignorant of the Christian faith give the Arian teachings credence.[143] In sections 18 to 43 he sets out the theological context for the exegesis of the passage—in effect, the rule of faith—in the course of which he reviews the purported Arian presentation of the Son as a creature and establishes that the Son is not a creature. This truth, he declares in section 44, must be clearly understood prior to the reading of Proverbs if misinterpretations of the passage are to avoided.[144]

---

[141] 129B.
[142] *CA* II. 11, 168C–169A.
[143] 185B.
[144] 184C; *CA* II. 44, 240C.

Athanasius begins his examination of the text of Proverbs 8: 22–5 by remarking on the type of literature that Proverbs is, one whose meanings are hidden in the text. Particular care therefore must be taken to determine the 'person' of the text, so that 'with reverence' one may arrive at its correct sense.[145] In this instance he does not point out the necessity of asking the other two questions. He follows this with a tissue of what he regards as confirmatory and complementary arguments, held together by the 'double account'. He argues that the phrase 'The Lord created me a beginning of his ways, for his works' refers to the economy of the incarnation of the Word in human flesh and the redemptive purposes accomplished through it, and not to the essence of the Son's divinity.[146] He justifies this claim on the grounds that the one who is speaking concerning himself in this text of Proverbs is the Wisdom of God, who as Creator can distinguish himself from creatures.[147] Wisdom presumably is that which Athanasius understands to be the *person* of the text, though he does not explicitly make the identification.

Among the arguments that he employs in support of this use of the double account is one which illustrates the third element of his hermeneutical procedure: the use of grammatical analysis. He argues that the occurrence of *two* verbs, 'created' and 'begot', in Proverbs 8: 22–5, and the sequence in which they occur, are both significant. He maintains that had the two words meant the same thing, a belief which he attributes to the Arians, there would have been no need to add the second. Furthermore, because the verb 'begot' comes after the verb 'created',[148] it has adversative force and its meaning takes priority over that of 'created'. This sequential pattern he also identifies in the scriptural passage in which Deuteronomy 32: 18 occurs, which will be discussed below; in Malachi 2: 10 'Has not one God created us? Have we not all one Father?',[149] a text which is not referred to in the extant writings of

---

[145] *CA* II. 44, 240D.
[146] *CA* II. 45, 241C.
[147] *CA* II. 44, 241A–B.
[148] *CA* II. 60, 273C–276B.
[149] *CA* II. 59, 273A–B.

his Arian opponents; and in John 1: 12–13, where 'begotten' follows 'become'.[150]

He finds further support for his contention that in Proverbs 8: 22–5 'begot' has priority over 'created' in the presence of the particle δέ in 8. 25 πρὸ δὲ πάντων βουνῶν γεννᾷ με, which is the only occurrence of the particle in the four verses of the passage. (It is not answering a preceding μέν.) Although the Migne text of the passage in which he makes the point, *Contra Arianos* II. 60,[151] is muddled, the sense of it is clear enough: he is assuming that δέ has the adversative force of a stressed 'but'.[152] He concludes accordingly that Proverbs 8: 22–5 demonstrates that offspring and creature are not 'by nature' the same thing and that the Word is not a creature 'by nature and in his essence'.[153]

Deuteronomy 32: 18 is discussed in *Contra Arianos* II. 58 and 59. Again, Athanasius accuses the Arians of failing to make the distinction between offspring and creature, this time by conflating 'begot' and 'made', in their interpretation of the Deuteronomy text; and again, he makes similar grammatical points to those which he made about the Proverbs passage. He begins by looking back to Deuteronomy 32: 6 'Is not he your Father who acquired (ἐκτήσατο) you, who made (ἐποίησεν) you, and created (ἔκτισεν) you?'. He maintains that the addition of the verb 'begot' in Deuteronomy 32: 18 'You have rejected the God who begot (γεννήσαντα) you' shows that 'begot' carries a different meaning from 'made', and moreover takes precedence over 'made' because it follows 'made' in the text.[154] (In this passage, there is no particle to help him in his argument.)

Having established that the two words have a different meaning,

---

[150] 272B–273A.

[151] *PG* 26, 273C–276B.

[152] Manlio Simonetti, *Studi sull'arianesimo* (Rome, 1965), p. 60, describes this as a 'procedimento tanto sottile quanto arbitrario'. However, Nigel Wilson of Lincoln College, Oxford, in a private conversation, while recognizing that little is known about the changes in use of the particles that took place after the Classical period, has suggested that Athanasius' understanding of the significance of the particle δέ might well have been in accord with the grammatical assumptions of his contemporaries.

[153] 276A.

[154] *CA* II. 58, 269C.

indicating different natures, 'begot' taking precedence over 'made', Athanasius is still left with the task of replying to the specific point that Eusebius of Nicomedia had made about this text, and about Isaiah 1: 2 and Job 38: 28: the verb 'begot' is used in Deuteronomy 32: 18 of something other than the Son and so is not indicative of a unique relation of being between Son and Father. Athanasius applies his second exegetical principle to this verse. He explains that the word 'begot' demonstrates the loving-kindness that God exercised towards men after he had created them as creatures; this loving-kindness is the Father's adoption of us through the Son.[155] He asserts that 'the term "begot" is here as elsewhere expressive of a son', and cites Isaiah 1: 2 'Sons have I begotten (ἐγέννησα) and brought up' and John 1: 12 and 13 as other instances.[156] But he is careful to ensure that it be understood that this sonship is ours only in a transferred sense. We remain creatures and are accounted sons only by virtue of the presence in us of the one who is Son by nature: 'the Father calls them sons in whomever he sees his own Son, and says, "I begot".'[157] In Athanasius' view, a Eusebian attempt to make relative the biblical language of begetting *cannot* be valid since all instances of such language, whatever initial impression they may give, properly refer to the Son and the Father.

Athanasius seems not to have attempted to explain how on the basis of this interpretative premise the occurrence of τετοκώς in Job 38: 28, Eusebius' third example where 'begetting' language apparently designates something other than the Son, could be seen properly to refer to the Son and not to drops of dew. He may have felt that since the text used τετοκώς rather than γεννάω, it was not incumbent upon him to provide an explanation.

Athanasius' use of Isaiah 1: 2 demonstrates how the Alexandrian tradition of interpretation could affect his perception of a controversial text. As we have seen, both Origen and Alexander comment on the verse in the course of their discussions of

---

[155] Athanasius' lack of clarity about the time at which we become sons will be discussed below, pp. 231 ff., with reference to his soteriology.

[156] *CA* II. 59, 272C.

[157] 273B.

sonship.[158] Athanasius cites it not only in *Contra Arianos* II. 59, but also in *Contra Arianos* II. 37, *De Decretis* 10, and *Festal Letter* 10. 5. His inclusion of the verse in the discussion of Deuteronomy 32: 18 in *Contra Arianos* II. 58 and 59 suggests that he had understood the point the Arians were making about the text more clearly than his predecessor Alexander, and that he had been more successful in adapting the Origenian use of the text to the new theological context. But even so, his sense of the text retains the hallmarks of the Alexandrian tradition.

In *Contra Arianos* II. 59, a few lines after quoting the first phrase of the verse as an illustration that the word 'begot' is expressive of a son in biblical usage, he refers to the following phrase, 'but they have rebelled against me', in order to demonstrate the inconstancy of man's recognition of God as Father and the necessity of receiving the Son by nature, if we are to become sons of God.[159] The text naturally lends itself to such a use, and, as we have seen, both Origen and Alexander had used it as evidence of the contrast between the two types of sonship. Origen had linked Isaiah 1: 2 with Deuteronomy 32: 6 and 18, in conjunction with Deuteronomy 32: 20 (not referred to by Athanasius), and with Malachi 1: 6 as well (not referred to by Athanasius), in his argument to show that there was no 'firm and unchangeable affirmation of sonship in the Old Testament'.[160] Alexander did not refer to either the Deuteronomy or the Malachi texts.

In *Contra Arianos* II. 37 Athanasius includes Isaiah 1: 2 in his response to the Arian misreading of Philippians 2: 9–10 and Psalm 45: 7. Alexander had also linked Isaiah 1: 2 with Psalm 45: 7. The context of the discussion in *Contra Arianos* II. 37, like that of Alexander's letter, is the question of whether or not the Son is mutable, and Athanasius interprets it in much the same way as Alexander had, though with greater elaboration. He sees it as evidence that we are not sons by nature but that we become sons through participation in the Son, a participation which we may lose

---

[158] Alexander's interpretation of Isa. 1: 2 is compared with Origen's above, pp. 136–8.
[159] 273A.
[160] See above, p. 108.

and have restored. He uses the text to comment more on our status than on that of the Son and does not refer to the occurrence of γεννάω in the text. In *De Decretis* 10 Athanasius again uses Isaiah 1: 2 to comment on our status,[161] and in *Festal Letter* 10. 5 he cites the verse to make the historical point that the Jews were unfaithful.[162] In neither instance does he refer to γεννάω.

Although the evidence of Athanasius' interpretation of Isaiah 1: 2 is not extensive, it suggests that the interpretation of the text and its role in theological discussion had acquired a fixed place within the Alexandrian exegetical tradition, a tradition which stemmed from Origen. While Athanasius grasped the significance of the Arian citation of Isaiah 1: 2 for the argument about the generative language of the Bible, working within the Alexandrian tradition, he nevertheless largely ignored Eusebius of Nicodemia's use of it.

---

[161] *De Decretis* 10, Opitz 9. 6–19.
[162] *NPNF*, IV. 529–30.

11

Adoption, Salvation, and the Life of Unity

THE idea of sonship is central to Athanasius' soteriology. As Son of God by nature who becomes Son of Man, and bestows upon us the Holy Spirit, the Son enables us to become sons of the Father by adoption. By taking on flesh, the Son is able to manifest the divine life in a way in which we in our fallen condition are able to apprehend it; by making the sinfulness and corruptibility of the human condition his own, he is able to perfect us. Adopted by the Father, we are transformed; we are given a true knowledge of the Father, purity of life, and freedom from the fear of death. Athanasius stresses that our perfected life is to be lived out in the context of the church. The hallmark of that common life is to be its unity. The model for that unity is the unity of the Father–Son relation. Through the incarnation, the Father, Son, and Holy Spirit give grace to us so that as adopted sons and members of the worshipping community, we may share in the divine life that is the relation that is Father and Son.

The idea of sonship by adoption runs as a leitmotif throughout *Contra Arianos*. Athanasius does not give an ordered account of his soteriology in the work, and his theological anthropology is largely assumed. Nevertheless, he says enough in the course of the work to make it possible with the aid of *Contra Gentes* and *De Incarnatione* to build up a reasonably clear picture of the anthropology that informs it.[1]

---

[1] For a survey of Athanasius' anthropology and its relation to his Christology, see J. Roldanus, *Le Christ et l'homme dans la théologie d'Athanase d'Alexandrie: Étude de la conjonction de sa conception de l'homme avec sa Christologie* (Studies in the History of Christian Thought 4: Leiden, 1968).

Human nature, according to Athanasius, was created 'with a capacity for perfection and with a destiny to correspond with such capacity'.[2] As originate, it lacks immortality and incorruptibility; through the grace of its maker it is maintained in existence.[3] In *De Incarnatione* 3 Athanasius identifies this grace as the grace of having been made in the image of the Word. This 'grace of the image' ($\dot{\eta}$ $\varkappa\alpha\tau$' $\varepsilon\dot{\iota}\varkappa\acute{o}\nu\alpha$ $\chi\acute{\alpha}\varrho\iota\varsigma$)[4] made it possible for man 'to remain in felicity and live the true life in paradise' and to have the 'promise of immortality in heaven';[5] it allowed man before the Fall to know the Word and, through him, to know the Father.[6]

Because of Adam's disobedience, a disobedience in which we all participate,[7] the protection and promise of the grace of the image is lost. We become subject to the penalty of the law, judgement, death, and corruption.[8] We lose our conception of God and form idolatrous conceptions instead.[9] Athanasius depicts the condition of fallen man as one in which we are permanently and 'insatiably' directed towards sinning, a condition from which we are unable to free ourselves;[10] it is a condition characterized by the fear of death.[11]

Athanasius argues that we can only be redeemed from this condition through a saviour who is both fully God and fully man. On the one hand, creature cannot save creature;[12] the Son cannot

---

[2] Archibald Robertson, 'Prolegomena', *NPNF* iv, p. lxxi.

[3] *CA* I. 58, 133A.

[4] *DI* 12.

[5] *DI* 3.

[6] *DI* 12. For a recent discussion of Athanasius' understanding of the knowledge of God in *CG* and *DI*, see Christopher Stead, 'Knowledge of God in Eusebius and Athanasius', in R. Van Den Broek, T. Baarda, and J. Mansfeld (eds.), *Knowledge of God in the Graeco-Roman World*, Études Préliminaires aux Religions Orientales dans l'Empire Romain 112: Leiden, 1988), pp. 229–42. Stead argues that Andrew Louth's thesis, put forward in his article 'The Concept of the Soul in Athanasius' *Contra Gentes–De Incarnatione*', in *Studia Patristica* 13 = *TU* 116, pp. 227–31, that there is a sharp contrast between *CG* and *DI* in the account they give of the Fall of man, and in the assumptions they make about our knowledge of God, is overstated.

[7] *CA* I. 51, 117B–C.

[8] *DI* 4.

[9] *DI* 11–12.

[10] *CA* II. 68, 292C–293A.

[11] *CA* II. 67, 289B.

[12] *CA* II. 41, 233B.

create in us what would need to be created in him.[13] God alone can decisively break into the continuities of our world and 'renew the first creation'.[14] Only the Son who created in the beginning can give us renewed life;[15] only the one who passed judgement on us at the Fall can reverse that judgement;[16] only the one who fully knows God can make him known.[17]

On the other hand, the Son can also only do these things effectively if his identification with human need is complete. The human condition must be transformed from within. Athanasius maintains that, although it was possible for God to have revoked the penalty of the law simply by speaking, this would not have been of any 'advantage' (τὸ λυσιτελοῦν) to mankind.[18] It would not have been fitted to our actual spiritual need; it would not have broken our predisposition to sin; and, consequently, it would have necessitated continual acts of pardon. Having learned to transgress, we would have been in a worse position than Adam, since

if he had been seduced by the serpent, there would again have been the need for God to command and undo the curse, and so the need would have been endless, and men would have remained no less under guilt, slaves to sin. Always sinning, they would always have been in need of pardon, and never have become free.[19]

With such an inadequate giving of grace, grace would have remained 'external' (ἔξωθεν) to man, as it had been for Adam in paradise.[20] But accommodating himself to man's need in the incarnation, the Father creates a union of grace with the body of his Son, and thus grace is no longer from outside.[21] By taking on the human condition, the Son makes our infirmities his own, and is able to overcome them: Christ's flesh is representative of our flesh.[22] The incarnation is the objective guarantee of our salvation.

[13] *CA* II. 69, 293A.
[14] *CA* II. 65, 285B.
[15] *CA* II. 70, 296A.
[16] *CA* II. 67, 289C–292A.
[17] *CA* II. 22, 192D–193B.
[18] *CA* II. 68, 292A.
[19] 292C–293A.
[20] 292C.
[21] Ibid.
[22] *CA* II. 69, 293A–296A.

The gifts which the Word receives as man are contained in him, so that in contrast to the grace given to Adam, the grace given at the incarnation may be 'certain and enduring'.[23] Athanasius neatly sums up the two aspects of the Son's work of salvation in what he describes as a paradox: as Son of God, the Son bestows grace; as Son of Man, he receives it.[24]

Athanasius frequently uses the term divinization to describe this process of salvation.[25] For instance, he writes that 'as the Lord, putting on the body, became man, so also we are divinized (θεοποιούμεθα) by the Word, having been taken to him through the flesh, and henceforth inherit eternal life'.[26] The concept of divinization includes not only the idea of the bestowal of incorruptibility but also the idea of communion with God.[27] Through our divinization in the body of Christ, we are exalted and brought into the presence of God. It signifies that the destiny to which we are summoned through the incarnation is one that is not given immediately in our creation: 'Mankind then is perfected in [the Son], and restored as it was made in the beginning, and with a much higher grace. For, being raised from the dead, we no longer fear death, but reign eternally with Christ in the heavens.'[28] Divinization, however, does not entail the dehominization of mankind; man remains man and does not become God. We shall return to this last point below when the idea of sonship by adoption is discussed.

It is not, however, the incarnation of the Son alone that Athanasius thinks brings about our salvation; the Holy Spirit also has a central role, a role integrally bound up with the incarnation. The Holy Spirit is 'poured out' upon mankind by the Son, an outpouring that takes place with the incarnation.[29] Through the

---

[23] *CA* III. 38, 405B; see also *CA* I. 45, 105A; II. 70, 296B. The theme of the permanence of the benefits brought through the incarnation recurs throughout *Contra Arianos*. See below, pp. 238 and 247–8.

[24] *CA* I. 45, 105A–B.

[25] For a more detailed discussion of the place of divinization in Athanasius' theology see Roldanus, *Le Christ et l'homme*, pp. 166–70.

[26] *CA* III. 34, 397B.

[27] *CA* I. 39–42, 92C–100B.

[28] *CA* II. 67, 289B.

[29] *CA* II. 18, 184B.

incarnation, we are given the 'indwelling and intimacy (ἐνοίκησιν καὶ οἰκειότητα) of the Spirit'.[30] The particular point at which this takes place is the baptism of Jesus. When the Spirit descended upon Jesus in the Jordan, it was the eternal Son who gave it, but it is more than the Son's human nature that received it; we too, who are in the Son by virtue of his bearing our body, were made recipients of the Spirit and thus are sanctified.[31] It is through participation in the Spirit that we are enabled individually to appropriate that which has been done for mankind, representatively and conclusively, by the Son's assumption of our condition. In *Contra Arianos* I. 9, he explains that we may be called gods (Ps. 82: 6) only because we participate in the Word through the Spirit.[32] Elsewhere, as we shall see, he refers to our participation in the Spirit as the means by which we become sons and by which we become one with the Father and Son.[33]

The idea of sonship by adoption is integral to this general pattern of Athanasius' soteriology. Indeed, the transformation from the status of creature only to that of son by adoption also is one of the principal ways in which Athanasius conceives of salvation. Sonship by adoption signals our participation in the divine love of the Father for the Son and the Son for the Father; this participation is effected by the Son by nature, who is set in direct contrast with sons by adoption. Included in his understanding of adoption is the idea that through it we come to a knowledge of God as Father. Although his thinking about sonship in *Contra Arianos* is orientated to the task of proving that the Son is begotten from the Father, is Son by nature and not by adoption, and he gives rather less attention to the positive role that adoption plays as a soteriological category, the concept of sonship by adoption nevertheless figures significantly in the work.

We have already looked at the background in Alexandrian theology to the use of the ideas of Son by nature and sons by adoption. Origen had given the contrast between the two types of

---

[30] *CA* I. 46, 108B.
[31] The whole of *CA* I. 46–50, 105B–117B is relevant.
[32] *CA* I. 9, 29A.
[33] *CA* III. 19, 364B; III. 24, 373B–C.

sonship an important place in his writings, as had Alexander in the letter to his namesake.[34] There is, however, no evidence other than that contained in the allegations of Athanasius that the Arians had employed either idea of sonship, and Athanasius had considerable incentive to attribute a straightforward apotheosis christology to the Arians.[35]

Athanasius himself does not use either idea in *Contra Gentes* or *De Incarnatione* (though he does use the idea of participation by grace);[36] neither does he use it in ἑνὸς σώματος. By contrast, throughout *Contra Arianos* he uses the two ideas repeatedly, both paired and separately. He seems not to have felt the need to support his references to either by citing the relevant biblical texts. Only once, in *Contra Arianos* II. 75, does he certainly quote a text, Ephesians 1: 3–5, where the word 'adoption' is used. Although the idea of adoption as sons is important to the argument in the section, he does not draw particular attention to the fact of its occurrence in the text.[37] He quotes Galatians 4. 6 once, possibly twice, in *Contra Arianos* II. 59.[38] In *De Decretis* 31, he again quotes Galatians 4: 6, this time as a commentary on the baptismal formula.[39] He occasionally quotes part-verses that refer to sonship. For instance, he quotes the phrases 'sons of God' and 'children of God' from Romans 8: 19 and 20 in *Contra Arianos* II. 63.[40] It is probable that Athanasius was assuming that the biblical

[34] Origen, above, pp. 91–2 and p. 99; Alexander, above, pp. 136–7.

[35] Williams, *Arius*, p. 286 n.40, and Stuart Hall, 'Review of R. Gregg and D. Groh, *Early Arianism: A View of Salvation* (London, 1981) in *King's Theological Review* 5 (1982), 28, are surely correct in arguing that the second line of the couplet from the *Thalia*—ἀρχὴν τὸν υἱὸν ἔθηκε τῶν γενητῶν ὁ ἄναρχος/καὶ ἤνεγκεν εἰς υἱὸν ἑαυτῷ τόνδε τεκνοποιήσας (*U*. 3, 242. 14–15)—should not be translated with Gregg and Groh as 'he (God) advanced him as a Son to himself by adoption' (*Early Arianism*, pp. 23, 56, 73, 96). Williams, *Arius*, p. 102, translates it as 'And, having fathered such a one, he bore him as a son for himself'. Although the early Arians may well have been motivated partly by soteriological concerns, Gregg and Groh's use of Athanasius as a guide to Arian thought on the issue is unsatisfactory.

[36] *DI* 5. The idea of participation also is used to characterize the relation of man to the Logos in *DI* 6 and in *CG* 46, where it is set in contrast with the Word's relation to the Father.

[37] *CA* II. 75–7, 305B–312B.

[38] 273A–B.

[39] Opitz 27. 31–3.

[40] 281B.

provenance of the phrase 'sons by adoption' was obvious to his
readers, perhaps because the idea was well established in the
theological tradition, and that its use did not need to be defended.
He does not specifically defend the use of the idea of Son by nature
either, though he plainly saw it as an idea that was synonymous
with the ideas of begottenness and being 'proper to the Father's
being'. The idea is not found in the Bible, but it too was part of the
tradition.

Athanasius' first reference to the idea of adoption occurs early
in *Contra Arianos*. Following his summary of Arian beliefs in I. 9,
he sets out what he considers to be the possible alternative
statements that can be made about the Son. The idea of adoption
is included in the list. He asks whether it is fitting to say of the Son:

he was, or he was not; eternal, or before he came to be; eternal, or from
this and from then; true (ἀληθινόν), or by adoption (θέσει) and participation (μετοχῇ) and according to aspect (κατ᾽ ἐπίνοιαν); to call him one of the
originate things, or to unite him to the Father; to consider him to be unlike
the Father in being, or to be like and proper to him; a creature or the one
through whom creatures came to be.[41]

Here, 'adoption' is placed in direct contrast with 'true', and in
parallel with the ideas of 'from participation' and 'according to
aspect'. Adoption is a concept which pertains to originate reality,
to the creatures, not to the Son. Earlier in I. 9, he had described
the Son as 'true (ἀληθινός) Son of the Father by nature (φύσει) and
genuine (γνήσιος), proper to his essence'.[42]

Athanasius succinctly states the transition in our status, from
creature to adopted son, which marks our salvation, in *Contra
Arianos* II. 59: 'From the beginning we are creatures by nature and
God is our creator through the Word, but afterwards we are made
sons (υἱοποιούμεθα) and henceforth God the creator becomes our
Father also.'[43] Like Origen, he can describe this transition as a
movement from servanthood to sonship. As originate things, 'we
are servants by nature' (δοῦλοι κατὰ φύσιν ὄντες), and accordingly

[41] *CA* I. 9, 29C–32A.
[42] 28D.
[43] 273B.

we address the Father as Lord, for in relation to us 'he is Lord by nature'.[44] This transition has a mirror image in the transition of the Son from his eternal to his incarnate existence: 'For God, being his Father by nature, afterwards becomes both his creator and maker when the Word puts on the flesh, which was created and made, and becomes man.'[45] When the Son becomes incarnate, he who alone calls him 'Father' because he is 'proper' to God calls him 'Lord' out of love for man.[46] It is axiomatic for Athanasius that the former transition is possible only because of the latter: it is the Son's assumption of humanity that allows us to become sons by adoption and so to be able to address God as Father. This description of the inverse relation between the shift in the status of the Son as he moves towards man, and in man's as he moves towards God, corresponds to the general chiastic pattern of Athanasius' presentation of the process of salvation, a pattern typified by his statement in *De Incarnatione* 54 that 'God became man, that man might become God'. We now need to look in detail at the way in which Athanasius thinks about this transformation: how and when it is brought about, what it consists in, and what effect it has on our ongoing experience of the life of faith.

Our adoption arises from the eternal relation of the Father and the Son, and their love for mankind. Quoting Ephesians 1: 3–5,[47] Athanasius argues that because of God's love for us, this adoption was predestined in God's Word prior to creation.[48] The Son by nature is able to bring us into adoptive sonship because of his eternal nature as God's creative Word and Wisdom. Just as the Son can re-create fallen existence because he is the one who first created it, and just as he is able to lift the judgement of the law from us because he first imposed it, so also he is the 'offspring from the Father, in whom the whole creation is created and adopted into sonship'.[49] He saves us from the 'bondage of corruption' and

---

[44] *CA* II. 51, 253C.
[45] *CA* II. 61, 276C.
[46] *CA* II. 50-1, 252B–256A.
[47] Referred to above, p. 209.
[48] *CA* II. 75–6, 305B–309B.
[49] *CA* III. 9, 340C.

'brings adoption and deliverance', and, with them, 'freedom'.[50] It was God's eternal purpose that the Son should 'through the flesh take on himself all that inheritance of judgement that lay against us', so that henceforth we would be 'made sons in him'.[51]

Athanasius generally maintains that we are given the grace of sonship, as with all the benefits of our redemption, specifically through the incarnation (though there is some ambiguity in his thinking about this, as we shall see). Following his quotation of Ephesians 1: 3–5 in *Contra Arianos* II. 75, which he places in conjunction with 2 Timothy 1: 8–10 God 'saved us and called us with a holy calling, not in virtue of our works but in virtue of his own purpose and the grace which he gave us in Christ Jesus ages ago, and now has manifested through the appearing of our Saviour Christ Jesus, who abolished death, and brought life to light',[52] Athanasius explains in section 76 that we receive the adoption as sons, prepared for us before the 'foundation of the world' (Eph. 1: 4), 'afterwards in time' through the incarnation: the grace of adoption 'has reached us' by being 'stored in Christ'. He then goes on to link our adoption with the life referred to in the passage from 2 Timothy: we shall become capable of eternal life and live in Christ.[53] He regards the idea of the Son being our brother, expressed in the biblical description of the Son as 'first-born among many brethren' (Rom. 8: 29), as signifying the identification that the Son makes with us and our condition through the incarnation.[54] He summarizes his view of the incarnation of the Son and our adoption as sons in a characteristically concise statement in *Contra Arianos* I. 38, where he says that the Son 'has made us sons with the Father and divinized men by himself becoming man'.[55] Here, as elsewhere, as we shall see, he associates the idea of sonship with divinization as the goal of our redemption.

There is, however, an element of ambiguity in Athanasius'

---

[50] *CA* II. 72, 300C.
[51] *CA* II. 76, 308B–C.
[52] *CA* II. 75, 308A–B.
[53] *CA* II. 76, 308B–309B.
[54] *CA* II. 61, 276C–277C.
[55] *CA* I. 38, 92B.

thinking about how exclusive the giving of the grace of sonship and the knowledge of God as Father is to the incarnation. He does not explicitly address the question of how the incarnation and the pre-incarnational activity of the Word are related to the adoption of sons. But there are a few passages in his writings which suggest that he thought that adoption took place before the incarnation. In his comments on Isaiah 1: 2 in *Contra Arianos* I. 37, he gives the appearance at least of attributing adoptive sonship to people in the Old Testament. The threefold pattern which he presents in I. 37 of those to whom Isaiah 1: 2 refers as having been given the grace of sonship, then having had it taken away because of 'alteration', and finally having had it restored following repentance, loosely corresponds to the general pattern of his soteriology, in which man, having been given the 'grace of the image'[56] following his creation, loses it at the Fall, and subsequently regains it through the incarnation. But it is unlikely that he intends this description to refer to man's actual historical development from creation. It seems more likely that he intends it to be a timeless statement of the inconstant nature of the sonship of mankind.

It is similarly unlikely that in *Contra Arianos* II. 58 and 59 he intends Deuteronomy 32: 6–18 to be taken in a historical way either.[57] Roldanus, however, argues to the contrary. He thinks that our adoption is attributed in the passage specifically to the incarnation. He contends that ὕστερον, in the statement from II. 59 that God 'later' becomes Father of those for whom he is Creator, which he translates 'plus tard', refers to the incarnation, on the grounds that Athanasius goes on to attribute this change to the Holy Spirit, and we know that Athanasius thought that the Holy Spirit comes to us through the incarnation and our acceptance of the Word.[58] But this can hardly be conclusive proof, and it raises the further question of whether or not Athanasius absolutely restricted the bestowal of the Holy Spirit to the New Testament period. We shall see in a moment that there is evidence he did not.

If Athanasius' comments on Isaiah 1: 2 and Deuteronomy 32:

---

[56] See above, p. 224.
[57] *CA* II. 58–9, 269B–273C.
[58] Roldanus, *Le Christ et l'homme*, pp. 144–5.

6–18 are inconclusive, his comments on Psalm 82: 1 'God stands in the assembly of the gods' in *Contra Arianos* I. 39 are rather more definite.[59] He acknowledges that the verse shows that 'God called the ancient peoples sons' and 'gods', and implies that the Arians have been using such evidence to show that there were those who were called sons and gods before the Son, and that therefore the Son was not always Son, but only later was named Son as a reward for virtue. This Old Testament phenomenon of adoption and divinization he attributes to the action of the pre-existing Word: 'all that are called both sons and gods, whether in heaven or on earth, were adopted and divinized through the Word.'[60] Presumably, Athanasius thought of this action as having taken place prior to the incarnation and that it was not just retrospective, but his reference to 'heaven and earth' again suggests that he did not think of this in strictly historical terms. He does not go on to take the issue up; his concern in this and the surrounding passages is to prove that the Son was not promoted to his status, but was eternally and unalterably Son of God. Elsewhere when he refers to texts where people are called sons and gods in the Old Testament, he does not mention the provenance of the texts and treats them ahistorically, in order to make the point that, in contrast to the Son, man's sonship and divinization are by grace and participation.[61]

This uncertainty about the uniqueness of the incarnation is not restricted to Athanasius' understanding of sonship, but it is true also of the overall pattern of his doctrine of the incarnation and salvation. It is an uncertainty he shares with Origen. In *Contra Arianos* I. 48, as part of his proof of the continuity of the Son's divine status prior to the incarnation, he says that the Son gave the Holy Spirit to the saints before the incarnation, as well as to the

---

[59] 92C–93A.

[60] 93A.

[61] *CA* I. 9, 29A; and possibly *CA* III. 19, 361C–364B, and *CA* III. 25, 376B–C. In *Contra Arianos* I. 9, Athanasius quotes Psalm 82: 6 'I say, "You are gods"', setting the nature of this divinity in contrast with the Son's. That this text should appear in Athanasius' opening credal reply to the Arians suggests that it was a text that the Arians were using against Alexander and his circle, or that Athanasius feared that they might use it.

disciples after it. The Son gave the Spirit to Moses and the seventy, and it was through the Word that 'David prayed to the Father, saying "Take not thy Holy Spirit from me" [Ps. 51: 11]'.[62] Although this is a rare example, it shows that on occasion Athanasius was willing to suggest that the giving of the Spirit is not specific to the Son's assumption of flesh. In *Contra Arianos* III. 31, he remarks that the Son came to 'each of the saints of old' and 'sanctified those who received him correctly',[63] and it is the Spirit, according to Athanasius, who sanctifies. In a few places he makes remarks similar to those of Origen that might be taken to mean that he thinks the incarnation brings a quantitative, rather than a qualitative, change: because of the incarnation, redemption and the benefits of the Holy Spirit come to all and not just a few, as had been the case before the incarnation. But he does not put the few and the many in direct tension with each other, and it is not clear that this is the significance he intends.[64]

There is, however, a passage in *Contra Arianos* III. 33 that goes some way to suggesting a solution to the uncertainty about Athanasius' perception of how soteriologically definitive the incarnation is. In the course of explaining why the Word had to take the properties of the body as his own, Athanasius says that though many had been made 'holy and clean from all sin' (prior to the incarnation)[65] without the incarnation we still would have remained 'mortal and corruptible'. In support of this claim he cites Romans 5: 14 ἐβασίλευσεν ὁ θάνατος ἀπὸ Ἀδὰμ μέχρι Μωϋσέως καὶ ἐπὶ τοὺς μὴ ἁμαρτήσαντας ἐπὶ τῷ ὁμοιώματι τῆς παραβάσεως Ἀδάμ, which is translated in the RSV as 'death reigned from Adam to Moses, even over those whose sins were not like the transgression of Adam', but which Athanasius seems to have taken as 'even over those who *had not sinned* in the pattern of Adam's transgression'.[66] When this statement is brought into conjunction with the

---

[62] 112A–113A.

[63] 388C.

[64] 388C–389A; I. 48, 112 A–B.

[65] Jeremiah is cited as an example on the grounds that he was consecrated from the womb (Jer. 1: 5), and John the Baptist because, while still in the womb, he leapt for joy at hearing Mary's voice.

[66] 393A–B.

idea, which we have already seen, that only by the divine taking on the human body could grace cease to be external and be able to transform man's propensity to continue to sin, Athanasius may be implying that although there may have been those in history who were sinless, this condition could not become permanent, except through the incarnation.

If this line of thought is applied to the condition of adoptive sonship, it would mean that sonship and the knowledge of God as Father, while experienced by a few prior to the incarnation, only became a permanent and general experience after the incarnation. But it must be said that Athanasius does not make this application. Indeed, it would be an exaggeration to say that he had given the problem of pre-incarnational sonship much thought at all. In any case, the explanation he gives in *Contra Arianos* III. 33 runs the distinct risk of creating a division between the ontological and moral conditions of fallen and redeemed humanity, which would undermine Athanasius' general picture of the incapacity of fallen human nature and the centrality of the incarnation to salvation. He has not thought the problem through, and in *Contra Arianos* III. 33, as in II. 39 where he deals with the 'sons and gods' of the period before the incarnation, he gives the distinct impression of arguing on an *ad hoc* basis, finding an immediate solution to the immediate problem, without looking at its consequences for his doctrine of salvation as a whole.

If we are to take *Contra Arianos* II. 39 to indicate that there were some before the incarnation who were made sons, we must go on to ask whether or not in principle this means that Adam before the Fall also was an adopted son, whether the 'grace of the image' of the Word included adoption. Athanasius nowhere says this was the case. As we have already seen, there is no reference to the idea of adoption as sons in *De Incarnatione*. Furthermore, in *Contra Arianos* II. 75 and 76, he argues that our adoption as sons and divinization was prepared in the eternal purposes of the Father in anticipation of the Fall and that this grace, stored in Christ, reached us through his assumption of our flesh. His focus is not on man before the Fall, but on us as remade in Christ through Christ's identification with our condition in the incarnation. He predominantly thinks of the transition from creaturehood to sonship by adoption in conjunction with the salvific benefits brought by the Son through his incarnation, death, and resurrection: divinization and adoption represent the destiny won for us by the Son of God becoming Son of Man.

If it is God who, in his eternal purposes and (mainly) through the incarnation, makes the status of adopted son a *possibility* into which we may enter, it is also God who *enables* us to do so. He does this by granting to mankind the Holy Spirit. The presence of the Holy Spirit enables us to apprehend the sonship given to us by the Son by nature and make it effective in our lives. Athanasius' most concerted statement in *Contra Arianos* of how we enter into our adoption occurs in II. 59 in the course of his commentary on Deuteronomy 30: 18, and there he includes comments on the role of the Spirit. After pointing out that the order of the verbs 'become' and 'begotten' in John 1: 12–13 indicates that there is a transformation in our status from creature to adopted son, Athanasius goes on to consider how this transformation takes place. Because of God's love for mankind, God 'according to grace later becomes Father' (πατὴρ κατὰ χάριν ὕστερον γίνεται) also of those to whom previously he has been 'Maker' (ποιητής) only. He becomes their Father, Athanasius explains—

whenever men, his creatures, receive into their hearts, as the Apostle says, 'the Spirit of his Son, crying Abba, Father' [Gal. 4: 6]. And these are they, who, receiving the Word, gained power from him to become sons of God [Jn. 1: 12]; for [men] cannot otherwise become sons, being by nature creatures, unless they were to receive the Spirit of the natural and true Son. Therefore, in order that this might happen, 'the Word became flesh', that he might make man capable of divinity.[67]

A few lines later, he says that it is the Word in us through whom we cry 'Abba, Father'.[68] It is the reception of the Holy Spirit into our hearts that enables us to call God 'Father', to become God's children; because we are creatures, becoming sons is not something we can do for ourselves. This reception, Athanasius implies, is concurrent with our reception of the Word. The Word's ability

[67] 273A.
[68] 273B.

to confer upon us the adoption-bestowing Spirit is a function of the Son's status as the 'natural and true Son'. Again, he associates sonship and divinization.

For Athanasius, the particular vehicle through which we each receive the Spirit and enter into the status of adopted sons is baptism. As we have seen, Athanasius believes that the Spirit was bestowed upon mankind at Jesus' baptism in the Jordan. He does not go on to make a connection between Jesus' baptism as the vehicle for the giving of the Spirit and our baptism as the vehicle of our individual reception of the Spirit. In the discussion of Christ's baptism in *Contra Arianos* I. 46–9, his attention is focused primarily on its implications for the divine status of the Son and not on its implications for our initiation into the Christian faith. Nevertheless, he believes that it is through our individual baptism that we enter into the benefits won for us representatively in the Son, and this includes our sonship.

Baptism marks the transition from our condition of death in Adam to that of life in Christ. We are granted a new beginning. Athanasius writes in *Contra Arianos* III. 33 that

just as we are all from the earth and die in Adam, so being born anew from above by water and Spirit, in the Christ we are all made alive, the flesh being no longer earthly, but henceforth being adopted as word ($\lambda o\gamma\omega\theta\epsilon i\sigma\eta\varsigma$), through God's Word, who became flesh for us.[69]

Here, exceptionally, he stretches the concept of adoption to encompass our re-created relation to the Son as Word, and by using $\lambda o\gamma\omega\theta\epsilon i\sigma\eta\varsigma$ he heightens the contrast between earthly flesh and living flesh. In *De Decretis* 31, Athanasius makes explicit the relation between our baptism, the reception of the Holy Spirit, and our adoption as sons. We shall return to this passage below.

But while Athanasius is convinced that our transformation in *status* from that of creature to that of son by adoption is a saving transformation, he takes considerable care to ensure that it is understood that our sonship is distinct from that of the Son and will always remain so. We remain in our *condition* of creaturehood even when we are made sons by adoption. We are creatures by

[69] 396A.

nature and sons by the grace of adoption; the latter does not nullify the former. 'Grace' is the means whereby those who do not have a relation of being with the Father, namely the creatures, come to participate in the Father,[70] but we still remain creatures by nature. He explains in *Contra Arianos* I. 37 that those who are called sons, having 'received the Spirit by participation', remain 'themselves something other than the gift itself'. Because, unlike the Son, we are not sons by nature, our status as sons can change: we are given it, and, if we alter, the Holy Spirit will be taken away and we shall be 'disinherited' (ἀποκηρύσσω); through repentance we will be given it again.[71]

Athanasius argues that the verb order in Deuteronomy 30: 6–18, 'bought' succeeded by 'begot', in Proverbs 8: 22–5, and in John 1: 12–13, serves to ensure that when those who 'from the beginning' were creatures are said to have been begotten according to grace as sons, they might know that 'men are still no less than before works according to nature'.[72] If we are called sons, it is because of the Son in us and if we address God as Father, it is because of the Son in us.[73] Commenting on Malachi 2: 10, he says that the prophet

first put 'created', then 'Father', to show, like the other writers, that from the beginning we are creatures by nature, and God is our creator through the Word; but afterwards we are made sons, and henceforth God the creator becomes our Father also. Therefore 'Father' is proper to the Son; and not 'creature', but 'Son' is proper to the Father. Accordingly, this passage also proves that we are not sons by nature, but the Son who is in us; and again that God is not our Father by nature, but of the Word in us, in whom and through whom we 'cry Abba, Father'. And so in a similar way, the Father calls them sons in whomsoever he sees his own son and says 'I begot', since 'to beget' signifies a son, but 'to make' is indicative of works.[74]

The begetting language of Scripture is reserved for the Son; there

---

[70] *CA* I. 9, 29B.
[71] 89A–B.
[72] *CA* II. 59, 273C.
[73] Discussed above, p. 215.
[74] *CA* II. 59, 273B–C.

is to be no blurring of the sonship of the Son and that of man. Our divinization does not involve our dehominization.

As we have seen, Origen too had been concerned to maintain the distinction between God and man in his status as adopted son. He explained that while the words of John 1: 12–13 testify to the fact that we may become sons, they do not mean that we are transformed into God's nature (φύσις).[75] This distinction is based on the difference between the two types of sonship, the one by nature and the other by adoption. However, unlike Athanasius, Origen did not use the idea of *creaturehood* to describe our initial condition, and to distinguish our sonship from that of the Son. Writing prior to the post-Methodian acceptance of a clear division between Creator and created, he thought of our pre-adoption status, as well as that to which we move, mainly in psychological and relational terms. We move from servitude and fear to sonship and love. As we shall see shortly, Athanasius also thinks in these terms, but he is concerned primarily to secure the place of the Son on the divine side of the Methodian division of reality, and he works mainly with concepts and a theological vocabulary that stress the ontological parameters within which the transformation of man's status takes place.

For Athanasius, our sonship, unlike that of the Son by nature, is not part of the definition of what we are; it is a quality that we have only in a transferred sense. The language of adoptive sonship does not tell us about the essence of that to which it refers. But although this is the logical implication of how Athanasius thinks about such sonship, he does not draw this out. His interest lies primarily in protecting the Son against the possibility that the Son's sonship might be thought only to be conferred upon him, rather than being that which makes him what he is, that the Son too might be regarded as adopted as son by grace because of moral achievement, rather than as eternally son by nature. He has no desire to dwell on the comparative inferiority of our status as redeemed. Rather, he is convinced that the new status we are granted, the characteristic of sonship that we exhibit, is a reality, made possible for us by the Son and the Holy Spirit and integral to our salvation.

---

[75] Fr. 73 of the *Homilies on Luke*, discussed above, p. 99.

He believes that the Son and the Holy Spirit are truly in us, and that our knowledge and experience of God as Father is fundamentally determined by our adoption.

The wording of his comments about baptism in the passage from *De Decretis* 31 gives a remarkable demonstration of the strength of his feelings about this. There, in the context of his discussion of the superiority of the word 'Father' to the word 'unoriginate' as a name for God, he joins the baptismal injunction of Matthew 28: 19 with Galatians 4: 6. The Son taught us to say 'Our Father who art in heaven', and he

instructed us to be baptized not in the name of unoriginate, and originate, nor in the name of Creator and creature, but in the name of Father, Son, and Holy Spirit. For being thus initiated, we too are truly made sons (οὕτως γὰρ τελειούμενοι υἱοποιούμεθα καὶ ἡμεῖς ἀληθῶς), and saying the name of Father, we acknowledge also from that name the Word in the Father.

Athanasius goes on to explain that our ability to call God 'Father' is due to the presence of the Word, and, concurrently, the Spirit, within us. The Son wills that we should call his Father our Father; he bore our body and came to be in us; and the 'Spirit of the Word in us names through us his own Father as ours, which is the Apostle's meaning when he says, "God has sent the Spirit of his Son into our hearts, crying, Abba, Father" (Gal. 4: 6)'.[76] It is not surprising that Athanasius should so strongly stress the necessity for baptism, the vehicle of grace and consecration, the vehicle of our adoption, to be administered and received, not simply with the correct words, but also with the correct understanding and the correct faith that follows from such understanding.[77] The baptismal formula, and its place in the church's tradition, is not only important for Athanasius as evidence of the divinity of the Son.

But this passage speaks of more than the centrality of baptism in our entry into sonship. It also makes a startling claim about the radical nature of the change which we undergo as a result of our

---

[76] *De Decretis* 31, Opitz 27. 9–33. In the parallel passage in *CA* I. 32–3 Athanasius does not make reference to the Galatians text.

[77] *CA* II. 41–3, 233A–240C. The correct understanding and belief is that the divinity of the Son is the same as that of the Father.

adoption. He says that in our baptisms 'we too are truly made sons' (*υἱοποιούμεθα καὶ ἡμεῖς ἀληθῶς*) and call God 'Father'. Lest this give rise to a confusion of our status with that of the Son, he immediately goes on to specify that we should not 'on that account measure ourselves with the Son according to nature'. But given his manifest anxiety to ensure that his words are not misunderstood, it is all the more extraordinary that he should have risked using *ἀληθῶς* to describe the making of our sonship at all. The word 'true' (*ἀληθινός*), witnessed in the passage from *Contra Arianos* I. 9 quoted above[78] and often elsewhere, is one of the key words in his defence of the divine status of the Son. It signals that the Son, unlike all others, is *properly* called Son, and does not have the title simply by participation and ascription; it signals that the Son's sonship is not by grace and adoption. That he should use such a word, however cautiously, of those who are adopted as sons through baptism is an index of how important it was for him to be able to affirm the reality of that sonship, even if it is an adoptive sonship, secondary to that of the Son. For Athanasius we truly do participate in the Son and we truly share through the grace of the Holy Spirit in his sonship.

As we have already observed, Athanasius posits a transformation in our knowledge of God concurrent with our transformation from servant to son: to be saved is to come to a knowledge of God as Father. As originate things, 'we are servants by nature' (*δοῦλοι κατὰ φύσιν ὄντες*), and accordingly we address the Father as Lord, for in relation to us 'he is Lord by nature'. Only by receiving the Spirit from the Son can we come to have the 'confidence' (*θάρσος*) to call God 'Father'.[79] But compared to Origen, Athanasius gives little attention to this point.

The belief that the divine being is a relation of Father and Son, however, not only is the basis for our transformation in status to adopted sons; the Father–Son relation is also the model for how as adopted sons we are to live the Christian life. His vision of the Christian life so guided is dynamic and spiritually perceptive. In *Contra Arianos* III. 17–25 he gives an extensive account of how our

[78] p. 229.
[79] *CA* II. 51, 253C.

transformation into sons is reflected in the spiritual and moral fabric of our lives. The account comes in his response to the supposed Arian charge that the Athanasian conception of the *Son's* relation to God leads to an untenable conception of *our* relation to God. Athanasius reports that the Arians conclude on the basis of Christ's prayer that his disciples might be one as he and the Father are one (Jn. 17. 11 and 20–23) that if the Son is 'proper and like the Father's being', it 'follows either that we too are proper to the Father's being, or that he [the Son] is foreign to it, as we are foreign to it.' He replies that his opponents fail to appreciate that our sonship is by grace, whereas the true Son is Son by nature.[80] Although the succeeding discussion is orientated towards maintaining the distinction between the two types of relation, much of it is taken up by the positive exploration of what our relation to God looks like when it is transformed by redemptive grace. He has much to say about the nature of the Christian life and the Christian community.

He uses the manner in which we are instructed to be virtuous and the manner in which we become sons to illustrate what the Gospel of John means when it says 'that they may be one as we are one'. He explains that the injunctions 'Be merciful, even as your Father is merciful' (Lk. 6: 36), and 'You must be perfect, as your heavenly Father is perfect' (Matt. 5: 48), pertain not to our being, but to our moral actions. We are not intended to become God's equal and to become benefactors by nature. Rather, we are to imitate God's beneficent acts, imparting to others the mercy that has come to us through the grace of God. Similarly, he concludes that it is by the imitation of the Son, through the grace which comes to us in our participation in the Holy Spirit, that we become sons. Although he does not elaborate on our sonship and precisely what it is about the Son, the imitation of which brings sonship, the context suggests that it is the Son's oneness with the Father that is to be our model.[81]

Correspondingly, it is by the imitation of the oneness in being of the Father and the Son that we become 'one in them'. This oneness

---

[80] *CA* III. 17, 357A–360A.
[81] *CA* III. 19, 361B–364B.

in the Father and the Son, which we are to express, Athanasius takes as applying to how we are to live the Christian life as members of the community of the faithful. In *Contra Arianos* III. 20, he explains that we are to become 'one with each other in disposition (διάθεσις), having as our copy the Son's natural unity with the Father'.[82] We are to become 'one in the Father and Son, in mind and harmony of spirit'.[83] Just as when the Son said, 'Learn from me, for I am gentle and lowly in heart' (Matt. 11: 29), he meant not that we should become equal to him, 'but that looking towards him, we might remain meek continually', so also with respect to our oneness with each other we should take the Son as our pattern, in order that our attitude to each other might be 'true and firm and indissoluble'.[84]

The Son, then, in his unity with the Father, is the model for how the Christian community is to live. But he is more than the model for this life; he is also the means. As with the themes of redemption and of adoption, here too in relation to the community's oneness, Athanasius makes it clear that our ability to imitate the oneness of the Son with the Father is only possible because of the Son's identification with our condition in the incarnation. He states this in a long and telling passage in *Contra Arianos* III. 23, where, in imitation of Jesus' prayer in John 17, he imagines the Son to say to the Father:

If I had not come and borne their body, none of them would have been perfected, but all would have remained corruptible. So then, work in them, Father; and as you have given me this [body] to bear, give to them your Spirit, in order that they too might become one and be perfected in me. For their perfecting shows the sojourn (ἐπιδημίαν) to have been of your Word; and the world, seeing them perfect and borne by God, will fully believe that you sent me and that I sojourned. From whence would be their perfecting, if I, your Word, having taken their body, had not become man and perfected the work which you gave me, Father? And the work is perfected because men, having been redeemed from sin, no longer remain dead, but also having been divinized, have in each other, by

---

[82] 365A.
[83] *CA* III. 23, 372A.
[84] *CA* III. 20, 365B.

looking at us, the bond of love (τὸν σύνδεσμον τῆς ἀγάπης).[85]

In this passage Athanasius brings together the ontological and the spiritual dimensions of the salvation brought by the Father's giving of the Son in the incarnation. We are perfected by the Son bearing our body, and are no longer subject to the corruption of death. The Holy Spirit is given to us in order that we might become one and so that we might be perfected.

The statement about love in the last line of the quotation is an echo of the phrase from Ephesians 4: 2–3, 'forbearing one another in love (ἀγάπῃ), eager to maintain the unity of the Spirit in the bond (συνδέσμῳ) of peace', and the phrase from Colossians 3: 14, 'put on love (ἀγάπην), which binds everything together in perfect harmony (σύνδεσμος τῆς τελειότητος)'. Both phrases occur in the context of descriptions about the attitude Christians are to have to one another. The Ephesians passage continues in a manner consistent with Athanasius' theme: 'There is one body and one Spirit, just as you were called to the one hope that belongs to our call, one Lord, one faith, one baptism, one God and Father of us all, who is above all and through all and in all' (Eph. 4: 4–6). As we have seen, Athanasius thinks of the life of death and corruption as one of fear. Here he characterizes the life that is free from death, the life of the divinized, as one of love. This love is realized in the relationships which are fostered in the community of the faithful, through the inspiration of the relation of the Father and the Son. Our divinization through the incarnation allows us to give love to one another; the unity of the Father–Son relation shows us how.

In his description of the relation between our love for one another and the Father–Son relation, Athanasius comes close to identifying the love of the redeemed with the eternal love of Father and Son. The fact that he does not do so may spring from a fear that such an identification would blur the distinction between the two relations and so compromise the unique nature of the Son's relation to the Father. When he quotes John 17: 20–3 in *Contra Arianos* III. 17, he omits the last phrase, given in italics here, from the second half of verse 23: 'so they may become

[85] 372B–C.

perfectly one, so that the world may know that thou hast sent me *and hast loved them even as thou hast loved me'*.

The long quotation cited above from III. 23 makes it clear that Athanasius saw the activity of the Holy Spirit as integral to our perfecting. What is not clear from the passage is how he thought of the relation between the perfecting of the community brought by the incarnation of the Son and that accomplished by the Spirit. In the following two sections, III. 24 and 25, however, he goes on to comment on the Holy Spirit and its place in our relationship with God. Anticipating an Arian interpretation of the idea that we are in God and God in us, Athanasius says that 1 John 4: 13 'we abide in [God] and he in us, because he has given us of his own Spirit', tells us how the preposition 'in' is to be understood. We are in the Father, not as the Son is in the Father by nature, but by participation in the Spirit. The Spirit, given by the Son, acts as the bridge between the Father and Son and the believer. Without the Spirit, Athanasius explains, 'we are foreign (ξένοι) and distant (μακράν) from God, and by participation in the Spirit we are united with the godhead (συναπτόμεθα τῇ θεότητι)'.[86] Earlier, in *Contra Arianos* I. 46, Athanasius had referred to the 'indwelling and intimacy' (ἐνοίκησιν καὶ οἰκειότητα) of the Spirit.[87] Our being in the Father 'is not ours, but is the Spirit's, who is in us and abides in us'.[88] It is because of the 'grace of the Spirit' that we may become one as the Father and Son are one: 'For what the Word has according to nature . . . he wishes to be given to us through the Spirit irrevocably.' This is attested by the words of Paul: 'Who shall separate us from the love of Christ?' (Rom. 8: 35), and 'the gifts of God and the grace[89] of his calling are irrevocable' (Rom. 11: 29).[90] As we have seen, the theme of the permanence of the benefits brought by the incarnation recurs throughout *Contra Arianos*.[91]

Thus for Athanasius, the Holy Spirit's role in the perfecting of

---

[86] *CA* III. 24, 373B–C.
[87] 108B.
[88] *CA* III. 24, 373B–C.
[89] The words ἡ χάρις do not appear in the principal NT manuscripts.
[90] *CA* III. 25, 376B.
[91] Above, p. 226, and n.23, and see below, pp. 247–8.

man is to draw us into the relation of the Father and the Son. But more than that, although he nowhere says so explicitly, he seems to think of this perfecting as a taking forward of the perfection effected for man in the incarnation into the present spiritual and moral experience of the individual believer. Although his comments on the Christian life in III. 24–5 are brief, they are adequate to give us at least a sense of how Athanasius thought about the dynamics of the relationship between the believer and the Holy Spirit, which the latter's 'indwelling and intimacy' bring about. He says that we 'maintain' (φυλάττομεν) the indwelling of the Holy Spirit by 'confession', namely, the confession that 'Jesus is the Son of God' (1 Jn. 4: 15).[92] We come to be in the Father by participation in the Spirit and 'improvement of conduct'.[93] Earlier, in III. 20, he writes of us 'learning' by imitation.[94] In the *Festal Letters* Athanasius frequently comments on the Christian life, stressing the necessity of a correct understanding of the faith and the life of Christian virtue. In *Letter* X. 2, for instance, he remarks on the need to bring the church together in harmony and the bond of peace in terms similar to those he uses in *Contra Arianos* III. 23.[95] In *Letter* X. 11 he enjoins the believers to prepare themselves for the Easter feast by confessing their sins, and they are to 'keep the feast' in conversation and moral conduct.[96] Elsewhere in *Contra Arianos*, Athanasius refers to those of us who have a correct understanding of the Son as those 'who love Christ and are Christ-bearing' (φιλόχριστοι καὶ χριστοφόροι).[97] Though he does not develop this, it implies that he thought that our Christian life also involved loving the Son and being filled with a sense of his presence.

These comments suggest that for Athanasius our perfecting entails a correct understanding of the doctrine of the Son and an active moral and spiritual participation in the process of our

---

[92] *CA* III. 24, 373C.

[93] 373C–376A.

[94] *CA* III. 20, 364C–365A.

[95] *NPNF* iv. 528.

[96] *NPNF* iv. 532. See also, e.g., *Letter* V. 2 (*NPNF* iv. 517–18); V. 5 (*NPNF* iv. 519).

[97] *CA* III. 45, 417C.

salvation which corresponds to the indwelling grace of the Holy
Spirit. In a long passage in *Letter* X. 4 , in terms that echo those of
Origen, he writes about the fact that the Word meets each
Christian believer at his individual level of need and spiritual
perfection. But he notes that though there are many rooms in the
Father's mansion 'in proportion to the advance in moral attain-
ment, yet all of us are within the same wall, and all of us enter
within the same fence'.[98] In our perfecting by the Son and the
Spirit, we become more and more like the Father and the Son and
collectively express this in the bonds of love. But we are all within
the wall.

Origen also had written of the place of moral endeavour in our
adoption as sons. He, like Athanasius, had said that we could lose
our sonship if we did evil things, though he also seemed to suggest
that we could reach a point in our ascent from which it was
impossible to fall out of sonship. But his sense that our status as
sons is contingent on our moment-by-moment moral choices is not
present in Athanasius; neither is his vivid sense of the polarity of
man's possibilities to be a son either of God or of the devil. The
devil plays no role in Athanasius' concept of fatherhood and
sonship by adoption. This is partly because Athanasius' attention
is so much given to the fatherhood of God on the one hand and the
objective reality and permanence of the victory of Christ over the
sinfulness of man on the other. Though we may fall away from the
Spirit, Athanasius has a strong sense that we none the less remain
within the wall of the church and God's grace. In Athanasius'
world, it would seem, we may be able to count a little more on the
constancy and efficacy of God's grace than in Origen's world.
Athanasius is aware that our relation with the Spirit and the
Christian pilgrimage is not an easy thing to maintain: because of
our wicked deeds we do fail to keep the Spirit within us. We may
also recover our participation in the Spirit through repentance, but
Athanasius is quite certain that this recovery is only possible
because of the granting of the Spirit by the Son and the consequent
gift of being in the Father. Because of the incarnation 'the grace

[98] *NPNF* iv. 528–9.

remains irrevocable for those who are willing'.[99] Jesus' words in John 17: 22, 'that they may be one even as we are one', are not a request for an identity of nature between us and God, but a request that 'such grace of the Spirit as is given to the disciples may be without failure or revocation'.[100]

From Athanasius' point of view, it is essential that the gift of the Holy Spirit, and the oneness with the Father and the Son and with each other that it brings, should be irrevocable, for only thus can it meet man's need. Man, according to him, is trapped in a perpetual inclination to sin and is unable to help himself. Only through the incarnation of the Son, prepared from eternity because of the Father and the Son's pity and love for mankind, and the giving of the Holy Spirit, is it possible for this pattern to be broken and for us to be given another way to live. Our redemption, established in the historical events of incarnation, death, and resurrection of the Son—events fitted to man's need and capacity to apprehend them, and made actual in the experience of the Christian life through the presence of the Spirit—is an objective reality that persists even in the face of the Christian's failure to desist from doing evil. We may fall away from the Spirit, but the enduring grace of the Father and the Son, made present to us by the Spirit, means that our participation in the divine life, and in the life of the community, is guaranteed, provided that we are willing to repent. Our dilemma is solved; our inability to remain faithful is anticipated and encompassed. By implication, we are then free from the fear of death and free to love one another.

It would be an exaggeration to say that Athanasius presents us with a systematic doctrine of the Christian life. His comments in *Contra Arianos* III. 17–25 give us a passing insight into his understanding of the complexity of the Christian life, an insight into his sense of compassion for those who fail, and an insight into his sense of the need for grace if we are to know the oneness of Father and Son in our love for one another. But the idea of the relation of Father and Son figures prominently in his statements in these sections about how we are to live as Christians. The idea of

---

[99] *CA* III. 25, 376C.
[100] 376B–C.

adoptive sonship is less prominent. Nevertheless, it is clear that
adoptive sonship is one of the ideas in terms of which he thinks
about the Christian life, along with the ideas of the life of virtue,
our perfecting, the unity in love of the Church, and divinization.
They signify the promise of a share in the eternal life of the divine
being, a promise that we are enabled to begin to realize now. As
with the life of virtue and unity, Athanasius believes that our entry
into adoption is made possible by the incarnation and the grace of
the Holy Spirit. Sonship is a status from which we may fall, and it is
a status which we may regain through repentance. It is a status that
is integrally connected with the oneness of the Father and the Son.
Towards the end of *Contra Arianos* III. 25 he writes, 'as we are
sons and gods because of the Word in us, so we shall be accounted
to have become one in the Son and in the Father, through the
Spirit being in us which is in the Word which is in the Father', and
then goes on to talk of our falling from the Spirit and the
irrevocability of grace.[101] Although he does not make a direct
connection between our being sons because of the Word in us and
our being in the Father and Son because of the Spirit in us, he
thinks of them in much the same way. He is not far from stating
that our sonship as sonship arises directly from the eternal sonship
of the Son and the Son's oneness with the Father.

[101] 376B–C.

Conclusion

BY way of a conclusion to the analysis of Athanasius' view of God as Father, it is interesting to compare what he has to say about the themes of our change from slaves to sons and the corresponding change in our relation with God with what Origen has to say. While these themes are important for both writers, Athanasius has comparatively little to say about them and Origen much. The reasons for this correspond to the differences in the structure of their theologies, and reflect both the differences in challenges each was attempting to meet—Arianism in the case of Athanasius, and Marcionism in the case of Origen—and, more generally, the differences in their relations to Greek philosophy and Christian tradition.

Writing under the pressure of the Arian challenge, Athanasius saw his primary task as securing the divine status of the Son as the basis of salvation. Consequently, he thought about the topic of fatherhood mainly in relation to the divine economy. The nature of our response to God's salvific act, the changes that it brings in our perception of God and the kind of life we lead, were not the issues that dominated his attention. Origen too was concerned with the relation of the Father and the Son, but his attention was given not so much to the divinity of the Son as to the establishment of the eternity of God's fatherhood over against the Marcionite distinction between the God of the Old Testament and the Father of the Son in the New Testament. While Athanasius was concerned with the question of how we come to *know* the Father, Origen was more concerned with the question of how we come to know that God *is* Father and the difference that makes to our relationship with him. Origen's concern reflects the fact that his reply to Marcionism largely depended on the answer to the epistemological question of what the revelation of the nature of God in the Scriptures actually amounted to. It might be said that Origen was orientated to analysing the significance of the fatherhood of God more for the human economy than for the divine. But such a statement would be anachronistic, since Origen did not posit a strict division in his cosmology between the divine and the created orders.

This epistemological orientation and the continuity Origen saw between God and the rational beings help account for his presentation of the process of salvation as the (ideally) continuous ascent of the soul in the knowledge of the divine aspects, which Origen distinguishes from each other, placing fatherhood at the top. We ascend from the knowledge of God as Creator and Lord to the knowledge of him as Father, and our relation to God is transformed from one based on fear to one based on love, as we ascend in our knowledge of the Logos.

Unlike Origen, Athanasius was disinclined to distinguish between the attributes of God, and he does not chart an ascent in stages to the full knowledge of God as Father. For him fatherhood is not so much the first attribute among many, as that which makes God what he is. It is not an object of progressive apprehension: God is known as what he is, namely Father of the Son, directly in the act of knowing him at all. Because for Athanasius, unlike Origen, the Son is divine in the same way that the Father is divine and he is so because he is *Son* of the Father, the Son's revelation of the Father is entire in the act of the incarnation and makes possible an immediate and entire apprehension of God who is Father. To receive the Spirit of the Word into one's heart is simultaneously to receive the Father. The fatherhood of God cannot be an object of perception over against the attributes of God, however superior it may be, because *as* Father and Son the divine being is the ground and source of those attributes and their expression. Accordingly, it is the ground of our existence and the ground of our being able to know God. Consequently, although Athanasius' theological and pastoral perceptions were deeply imbued with the belief that the phenomenon of the Christian life and its expression in community was directly dependent on the existence of God as Father and Son, unlike Origen he did not portray the Christian pilgrimage as an elaborate step-by-step ascent of the soul in parallel with an ascent in the knowledge of the Son and of God.

Origen's and Athanasius' respective interpretations of the Son's addressing God as Father in the Lord's Prayer well illustrate the

difference in their approach to our coming to know God as Father.
For Origen, while the Son's address is the revelation of the nature
of God as Father, he was especially interested in it because he was
inclined to see it as a new departure in the history of man's
knowledge of God, brought about through the revelation of the
Word in the incarnation.[1] Athanasius, by contrast, thought of the
Lord's Prayer (and the baptismal injunction) not in terms of its
place in revelation history, but as direct proof of the priority of
Father over unoriginate in the divine being, and he fitted them into
his argument for the eternal correlativity of the Son with the
Father. While he recognized that the Lord's prayer and the
baptismal formula are evidence of a change in our perception of
God, he was not obviously interested in their place in the *history* of
the perception of God. And whereas there is no evidence that
Origen was inclined to attribute the Son's addressing God as
Father to the Son's eternal knowledge of and relation with the
Father, it is apparent that Athanasius was so inclined,[2] though he
no more deliberately discussed this than Origen did. While Origen
pointed to the Son's addressing God as Father primarily as the
model for the *tenor* of the relation that adopted sons are to have
with God as Father, Athanasius points to it primarily as the model
for the practice of our piety which has been honoured by the
tradition of the church and which ensures that in our piety we will
acknowledge the most important thing to be known about God,
namely, that he is Father of the Son, and, in so doing, conclusively
affirm the salvific efficacy of the Son.

Athanasius' and Origen's attitudes to our adoption and relation
to God as Father were affected not only by their immediate
contexts of writing, but also more generally by their relation to
Greek philosophy and Christian tradition. Origen, intimately
familiar with the Platonist thought of his contemporaries, felt
strongly that the Christian conception of God and revelation

---

[1] As we have seen (above, pp. 110ff.), Origen's comments on the issue of
whether or not the incarnation plays a unique role in the revelation of the
fatherhood of God are ambiguous, though he is inclined to say that it does, and in
the *Commentary on Matthew* (above, pp. 113ff.) he says this without qualification.

[2] His discussion in *CA* I. 33–34, 80A–84A strongly suggests this.

marked a radical departure from the way in which the Greek philosophers and the Old Testament thought about God and our relation to him. The knowledge of God as Father, granted by the mediatorship of the Logos, was central to this revolutionary conception. Origen did not specifically contrast the Christian understanding of God as Father with the Greek idea of God, but such a contrast is implicit in his insistence on the superiority of the Christian's knowledge of God, and although he was cautious in his comments, he plainly drew a contrast between the Christian understanding of God as Father and the Old Testament idea of God.

Origen was the first theological writer to have his imagination struck by the wealth of the biblical references to God as Father, particularly by the Son's use of the term to address God, and by what this implied for our relation with God. The knowledge of God as Father meant that we could stand before God not in fear but in love. He was the first to attempt to establish systematically how this knowledge made the Christian faith distinctive from and superior to the contemporary philosophical and religious thought.

Subsequent Christian tradition was heir to Origen's exploration of this novel theme. Athanasius, in his references to the ideas of servanthood, sonship, and the confidence with which we come to address God as Father, may well have been assuming the Origenian background to them. The affirmation that we might know God as Father and that such a knowledge would transform our lives was not for him, as it had been for Origen, newly discovered good news. Athanasius wrote at a greater chronological, cultural, and emotional distance from the theological speculations of the Middle Platonists, and within a tradition of piety that had been deeply influenced by the writings of Origen. He could afford not to give his attention to the spiritual dimension of our coming to know God as Father because he could assume that this would already have been understood and accepted in the worship and piety of his Christian contemporaries. In any case, these were not the terms in which the Arian challenge was presented. Although the implications of Arian thought for the idea of the fatherhood of God were unacceptable to Athanasius, the Arian debate was not primarily about the belief that God was Father. The Arians accepted that proposition. The debate was about the way in which the Son is Son, and thus, from Athanasius' point of view, about the way in which the Father is Father. He attempted to establish systematically what it meant for the divine being to be conceived as a relation of mutual love between the Father and the Son. Father became with him not a name with which to address God but part of the definition of what God is. The life of the redeemed, which arises from that love and is sustained by it, is to be lived in imitation of that love through the presence of the Holy Spirit.

Postscript

THE concept of the fatherhood of God was central to the Alexandrian theological tradition, Arius excepted. For both Origen and Athanasius, the divine fatherhood was the given revelation of Scripture; for both, fatherhood identified the being of God as a relation of Father and Son in which love was mutually given and received. Athanasius went beyond Origen in making fatherhood the subject of systematic analysis. Taking his starting-point from the belief that descriptions of the Son as Son and of the Father as Father were essential to an adequate understanding of the Christian experience of salvation, Athanasius argued that the priority of the description of God as Father made sense both of the idea of God as the unoriginate first principle, an idea to which the Alexandrian tradition was deeply committed, and of the idea of God as directly involved in the process of salvation. God's nature as God, his perfection as God, the source and goal of all existence, turned for Athanasius on the conception of God as inherently generative, a conception entailed in the description of God as Father. It is because God is eternally and entirely Father and Son that there is anything else to be in relation with him; it is because God is eternally and entirely Father and Son that we may come to share in the love and unity of the divine nature. The idea that God is Father describes relations internal to the divine being, and it describes the relation he has with those whom by grace he calls to participate in the divine life.

Athanasius' outline of the relation between the Father and the Son, and of the place of the Holy Spirit in that relation, was filled out by his theological successors, especially the Cappadocian Fathers and Augustine. Following Athanasius, the Fathers in the Eastern and Western theological traditions alike understood the Father to be the 'fount of the godhead' and that it was this that distinguished his persona from that of the Son and the Holy Spirit.

In modern theology, however, this theology and the very description of God as Father has been called into question. It is a commonplace of much contemporary Christian thinking that the biblical description of God as Father is to be regarded simply as a reflection of the particular values of a patriarchal society[1] and has little or nothing to do with the nature of God. However the divine nature is to be described, it is not appropriate to describe it with words that are gender specific. It is, of course, anachronistic to pose the question of what the Fathers might have thought of such a view—it was not something they themselves asked. Nevertheless, there is value in asking how what we have seen of their thought relates to these modern concerns.

It is notable that Origen and Athanasius, and the other Fathers discussed in this study, did not support their picture of God as Father either by drawing on the biological or on the psychological and sociological dimensions of human fatherhood. Contemporary ideas about the family and about adoption play no role in their discussions of the divine being or of the Father's relation to us. In the second century, apologists such as Justin Martyr and Theophilus had sought to distinguish the Christian understanding of the generation of the Son from Greek theogonies. For Origen, the problem was more subtle and complex. He strove to distance himself from any suggestion that the fatherhood of God and the process of generation could be compared to the bodily and passionate nature of human fatherhood and generation. Such ideas arose from an incorrect notion of the terms within which discussion about the transcendent divine nature was to be conducted. Specifically, anthropomorphic assumptions and the materialist assumptions of Stoicism and of Gnostic emanationism were to be rejected in favour of a discourse about the first principle in which the ideas of incorporeality and eternity were part of the the basic grammar.

By the early fourth century Christian writers seem to have had little fear that a crudely anthropomorphic comparison of the generation of the Son with that of humankind might be made. But

---

[1] For instance, D. Hampson, *Theology and Feminism* (Signposts in Theology: Oxford, 1990), p. 84, writes that 'The Hebrew scriptures are bound up with the history of a particular society, and that society was patriarchal', and (p. 92) maintains that the 'prevalent masculinity' of the Hebrew scriptures 'does not change in the Christian scriptures'.

some at least continued to be wary of language of the Son's relation to the Father which they felt could be taken to attribute corporeality to God. Thus Arius seems to have rejected the term ὁμοούσιος to describe the Son's relation to the Father in part because he was concerned that it implied materiality. In the surviving documents, however, Arius gives no sign of having thought that the descriptions of God as Father and of the Son as generated from the Father had in any way themselves materialist connotations. Of course, as we have seen, Arius did not think the terms Father and Son told us about the essence of the divine being; compared with the description of the first principle as uniquely ingenerate and eternal, they would appear to have occupied a secondary place in his thinking about the divine being. Nevertheless, they were the terms used in the Bible and in Christian tradition. To the extent that God had chosen to reveal himself through the incarnation, he had revealed himself as Father of a Son and the two terms were not to be abandoned or avoided.

In company with his fourth-century contemporaries, Athanasius appears not to have been concerned that the idea of the generation of the Son from the Father might lead to a simplistic comparison of God with humankind. The making of such a comparison he clearly considered absurd and in his polemic happily charges the Arians with having fallen into the trap of having done just that. The charge is part of his rhetoric for showing that the Arians are not to be taken seriously and are utterly irreligious. Neither does he appear to have felt a need to defend either the description of God as Father, or the idea that the Son was generated from the being of the Father, against materialist interpretations. He took largely for granted that the attributes of incorporeality and eternity were the necessary presuppositions of the analysis of the divine being. The comparisons he made between the Son's generation and human generation were made for two reasons: the one, to establish that the Son's generation in contrast to that of humankind's is eternal and does not take place in time, and the other, to demonstrate that generative language conveys the idea of a relation of being and not simply a relation of willing and making. He did not use any particular characteristics of the human relation of father and son to make specific statements about the divine relation of Father and

Son. In Athanasius' theology, the term Father implied anything but sexuality and gender in the divine nature. The word Father is not to be used univocally of God and we can see in Athanasius' idea that the fatherhood of humankind reflects that of God the beginnings of an understanding of language as having its primary meaning with reference to God and because of that reference being applicable to human and finite things, a Barthian *analogia fidei* as opposed to an *analogia entis*.

It is possible certainly that the association of God as Father with the ideas of primacy and source reflects the influence of third- and fourth-century assumptions about fatherhood, generation, and authority. But if the association does reflect such an influence, it is in no way obvious. The language and approach of the Fathers do not give any indication that they even unwittingly drew on contemporary discussions of fatherhood in the larger Greek culture to help them in their thinking about the fatherhood of God. Discourse about the nature of God is to be undertaken within the correct context of reference, a context which begins with the biblical witness and which presupposes that the signification of God's fatherhood is to be interpreted in relation to the understanding that as first principle God is ingenerate, eternal, and incorporeal, a context which does not include facile references to, and explorations of, human experience.

The terms Father and Son for third- and fourth-century Christians were not arbitrary terms, reflective simply of the assumptions and values of a particular kind of culture. Their use of the word Father to refer to God was based on the example and teaching of Jesus himself and on the Bible's witness to the early church's practice. The Scriptures were regarded as inspired by God, and so their witness was authoritative. This was as true for Arius as it was for Origen before him and Athanasius after. It would not have occurred to Origen, Arius, or Athanasius that the proper method to approach the systematic reflection about the nature of God was to begin from the knowing human subject and her or his culturally conditioned experience of God. The terms Father and Son were for Origen and Athanasius the core terms of Scripture, in relation to which all others were to be considered; they were the terms given by God himself and by the Son; they were the terms of

Christian initiation in baptism and of Christ's prayers and ours. Appropriately interpreted, they truly do tell us about divine nature; they are not arbitrary ascriptions.

Two of the suggested approaches in modern theology—and there are many—to the perceived problem of the gender-specific nature of the language of fatherhood are that the description of God as Creator, Redeemer, and Sanctifier is a more satisfactory description than Father, Son, and Holy Spirit because it is gender neutral[2] and that the description of Jesus as Son of God indicates that parenthood rather than paternity is an attribute of God.[3] Both these approaches, however, would probably have been unacceptable to Athanasius. He would have thought about the description of God as creator in much the same way as he thought about the description of God as unoriginate, a description he regarded as sub-Christian. For him it was not adequate to speak only of the act or function of God, or even of the relation which he has with us; it was necessary also to speak of the being of the one who acts, the being who initiates the process of our redemption and enters into relation with us. The divine will is not to be regarded in abstraction from the divine nature. Our experience of salvation must begin and end in a relationship with one who loves because he *is* love.

Lash maintains that the description of Jesus as Son of God declares that the Son was 'lovingly produced' and 'effectively cherished with a love that transcends destruction in mortality'.[4] The metaphor Son of God signifies then that the faithfulness of the Father to his Son and to the whole of his creation, a faithfulness that is absolute and overcomes the power of death, is an expression of the divine being itself, whatever form it may take in our historical experience. With this Athanasius could have agreed. But with Lash's further point, that in the confession that Jesus is the

---

[2] Noted by Hampson, *Theology and Feminism*, p. 96, where she remarks that reference in Christian worship to God as 'Creator, Redeemer, and Sanctifier' may help feminists, but she goes on to observe that 'as long as one remains within a biblical and Christian tradition, the problem [of the conception of God as male] may be thought to be without solution'.

[3] N. Lash, '"Son of God": Reflections on a Metaphor', *Concilium* (March, 1982), p. 15.

[4] Ibid.

Son of God 'it is "parenthood", rather than either "paternity" or "maternity", which is declared to be a divine attribute',[5] he might well have had difficulties. While none of the content that Athanasius affirmed of the description of God as Father is specific to fatherhood in contrast to motherhood—motherhood, like fatherhood, presumably could have been understood to convey the idea of shared being, and it too could have identified the divine being as a relation of love—parenthood he might have found slightly too abstract, and, as with creator, too functional, if it was a concept he would have recognized at all. In the event, however, the Jesus that Christian tradition declared to be Son of God is seen in the Bible to address God not as mother or parent but as Father, and that testimony was decisive for both Origen and Athanasius and for subsequent orthodox tradition.

Only as reality is perceived to arise from eternally purposeful and loving subjects is it possible to attribute order and coherence to it; only so is it possible to conceive of the divine nature as not simply reflecting the chaos of human disorder; and only so is it possible for us to participate in that order and coherence through our being drawn into a share in the divine relation of love. For Athanasius the core meaning of the terms Father and Son was that they signified a relation of being between the Father and the Son. The mutuality of love between the Father and the Son, their mutuality as perfect and reciprocal subjects of the divine attributes, based on the generation of the Son from the being of the Father, meant that the divine being could be conceived as a relation existing only for its own sake and so free to exist for the sake of others; it could be conceived as both perfectly free and fruitful, as both transcendent of and involved in a creation which was other than, but reflective of, the divine being. Although they have no need of creation, the Father and the Son nevertheless take delight in bringing it into existence and in redeeming it. The freedom of God allows the freedom of creation. In the incarnation of the Son, human history is taken seriously by the Father.

It is the mutuality of the Father and the Son which allows God to draw near to creation and to be immanent in it. The revelation of

[5] Ibid.

the Son is truly the revelation of God; the redemptive activity of the Son is truly the activity of God. The fatherhood of God and the sonship of the Son are Athanasius' answer to Arius' apophaticism: we may truly know and describe God because in the incarnation of the Son we are dealing with God himself. In our adoption and divinization we share in the eternal knowledge and love of the Son for the Father and we may know and experience that as we live our lives as members of the redeemed community.

For Athanasius, the Cappadocians, and Augustine, reflection about the nature of God had its beginning and its end in the reflection about what it meant for the divine being to be defined as a relation of Father and Son. It was with reference to these two biblical images of Father and of Son that all other images were to find their true theological significance. The task of the theologian is to explore and order the truths about God in relation to the truth that God is Father and Son. It is in reference to the divine nature conceived as an eternal relation of mutual love and joy that Christian worship and life are to be experienced; for, according to Athanasius, it is as Father of the Son that God created us and makes himself known to us in the crucifixion of the Son. God's eternal purposes arise from and are given effect by the eternal nature of God as Father and Son.

Bibliography

I. TEXTS AND TRANSLATIONS

Acta Conciliorum Oecumenicorum, iii, ed. Eduard Schwartz (Berlin, 1940).

ALBINUS, *Épitomé,* ed. P. Louis (Collection Budé: Paris, 1945).

ALEXANDER OF APHRODISIAS, *In Aristotelis Metaphysica,* ed. M. Hayduck, in *Commentaria in Aristotelem Graeca,* i (Berlin, 1891).

Analecta Sacra, ed. Jean Baptiste Pitra, iv (Paris, 1883).

Arian Documents:

    Athanasius Werke, ed. H.-G. Opitz, iii. 1, *Urkunden zur Geschichte des Arianischen Streites* (Berlin, 1934).

    U. 1   Letter of Arius to Eusebius of Nicomedia.

    U. 2   Letter of Eusebius of Nicomedia to Arius.

    U. 3   Letter of Eusebius of Caesarea to Euphration of Balanea.

    U. 4a Letter of Alexander of Alexandria to his Clergy.

    U. 4b Letter of Alexander of Alexandria to all the Bishops.

    U. 6   Confession of Arius and his Companions to Alexander of Alexandria.

    U. 7   Letter of Eusebius of Caesarea to Alexander of Alexandria.

    U. 8   Letter of Eusebius of Nicomedia to Paulinus of Tyre.

    U. 9   Letter of Paulinus of Tyre.

    U. 11 Letter of Athanasius of Anazarbus to Alexander of Alexandria.

    U. 12 Letter of the Presbyter George to Alexander of Alexandria.

    U. 13 Letter of the Presbyter George to the Arians in Alexandria.

    U. 14 Letter of Alexander of Alexandria to Alexander of Thessalonica.

    U. 30 Letter of Presbyters Arius and Euzoius to Emperor Constantine.

ARISTOTLE, *Works* (Loeb Classical Library).

ATHANASIUS:

1. *Patrologia Graeca,* ed. J. P. Migne (Paris, 1857).

    PG 25   *Epistola Encyclica ad Episcopos Aegypti et Libyae.*

    PG 26   *Orationes contra Arianos* I–III.

             Epistolae ad Serapionem Episcopum.

Tomus ad Antiochenos.
Epistola ad Jovianum.
Epistola ad Afros.
Epistola ad Epictetum.
Epistola ad Adelphium.
Epistola ad Maximum.
Epistolae Festales.
2. *Athanasius Werke*, ed. H.-G. Opitz, ii. 1 (Berlin, 1935/40):
   Apologia de Fuga Sua.
   Epistola de Decretis Nicaenae Synodi.
   Epistola de Sententia Dionysii.
   Epistola de Synodis.
3. Others:
   Contra Gentes and De Incarnatione, ed. and trans. R. Thomson (Oxford Early Christian Texts: Oxford, 1971).
   Sur l'incarnation du Verbe, ed. and trans. Charles Kannengiesser (SC 199: Paris, 1973).
   Der Zehnte Osterfestbrief des Athanasius von Alexandrien, ed. and trans. Rudolf Lorenz (*ZNTW*, Beiheft 49: Berlin, 1986).
4. Translations:
   The Letters of Saint Athanasius Concerning the Holy Spirit, trans. C. R. B. Shapland, (London, 1951).
   Select Writings and Letters of Athanasius of Alexandria, various trans., ed. Archibald Robertson (NPNF 4: Grand Rapids, 1978).
CLEMENT OF ALEXANDRIA, *Stromata*, I–VI, ed. O. Stählin and L. Früchte; VII–VIII, ed. O. Stählin, L. Früchte, and U. Treu (GCS 15 and 17: Berlin, 1960 and 1970).
DIONYSIUS OF ALEXANDRIA, *The Letters and Other Remains of Dionysius of Alexandria*, ed. Charles Feltoe (Cambridge Patristic Texts: Cambridge, 1904).
—— *St. Dionysius of Alexandria: Letters and Treatises*, trans. Charles Feltoe (Translations of Christian Literature, Series 1: Greek Texts: London, 1918).
EUSEBIUS, *Praeparatio Evangelica*, in *Eusebius Werke*, viii. 1 and 2, ed. K. Mras (GCS 43: Berlin, 1982–3).
—— *Contra Marcellum*, in *Eusebius Werke*, iv, ed. E. Klostermann (GCS 14: Berlin, 1972).
HOMER, *The Iliad*, ed. M. Willcock (London, 1978).
JUSTIN, *Die ältesten Apologeten*, ed. E. J. Goodspeed (Göttingen, 1915).
—— *The Apologies of Justin Martyr*, ed. A. W. F. Blunt (Cambridge Patristic Texts: Cambridge, 1911).

—— *Dialogue avec Trypho*, ed. and trans. G. Archambault (Textes et Documents pour l'Étude Historique du Christianisme 8, vols. i and ii: Paris, 1909).

—— *The Apostolic Fathers with Justin Martyr and Irenaeus*, trans. A. Roberts and J. Donaldson (1867), ed. A. C. Cleveland Coxe (The Ante-Nicene Fathers 1: Grand Rapids, 1979).

METHODIUS, *Opera*, ed. D. G. Bonwetsch (GCS 27: Leipzig, 1917).

NUMENIUS, *Fragments*, ed. Édouard des Places (Collections des Universités de France: Paris, 1973).

ORIGEN:

1. GCS (Leipzig):

1	*De Martyrio*	P. Koetschau (GCS 2: 1899).
	Contra Celsum, I–IV	
2	*Contra Celsum*, V–VIII	P. Koetschau (GCS 3: 1899).
	De Oratione	
3	*Homiliae in Ieremiam*	E. Klostermann (GCS 6: 1901).
4	*Commentaria in Ioannem*	E. Preuschen (GCS 10: 1903).
5	*De Principiis*	P. Koetschau (GCS 22: 1913).
6	*Homiliae in Genesim*	W. Baehrens (GCS 29: 1920).
	Homiliae in Exodum	
	Homiliae in Leviticum	
7	*Homiliae in Josuem*	W. Baehrens (GCS 30: 1921).
8	*Homiliae in primum*	
	Regnorum Librum	W. Baehrens (GCS 33: 1925).
	Commentaria in	
	Canticum Canticorum	
9	*Homiliae in Lucam*	M. Rauer (2nd. edn., GCS 49: 1959).
10	*Commentaria in Matthaeum*	E. Klostermann (GCS 40: 1935).

2. *Patrologia Graeca*, ed. J. P. Migne (Paris, 1862):

12 *Commentaria in Genesim.*

14 *Commentaria in Epistulam ad Romanos.*

3. SC (Paris):

Homélies sur Jérémie, ed. P. Nautin and trans. P. Husson and P. Nautin (SC 232, 238: 1976–7).

Homélies sur Saint Luc, ed. and trans. H. Crouzel, F. Fournier, and P. Périchon (SC 87: 1962).

Commentaire sur Saint Jean, ed. and trans. Cécile Blanc (SC 120, 157, 222, 290: 1966–82).

Entretien d'Origène avec Héraclide, ed. and trans. Jean Scherer (SC 67: 1960).

Traité des principes, ed. and trans. Henri Crouzel and Manlio

Simonetti (SC 252, 253, 268, 269, and 312: 1978–84).
4. Others:
'The Commentary of Origen on the Epistle to the Romans', ed. A. Ramsbothan, *JTS* 13 (1911–12), 209–24 and 357–68.

Le Commentaire d'Origène sur Rom. III. 5–V. 7 d'après les extraits du papyrus No. 88748 du Musée du Caire et les fragments de la Philocalie et du Vaticanus Gr. 762, ed. J. Scherer (Institut Français d'Archéologie Orientale, Bibliothèque d'Études 27: Cairo, 1957).

'Origen on I Corinthians IV', ed. C. Jenkins, *JTS* 10 (1908–9), 29–51.

'The Commentary of Origen upon the Epistle to the Ephesians', ed. J. Gregg, *JTS* 3 (1901–2), 233–44, 398–420, and 554–76.

Opera Omnia, ed. C. H. E. Lommatzsch, vi and xxiv (Berlin, 1836 and 1846).

Der Scholien-Kommentar des Origenes zur Apokalypse Iohannis, ed. C. Diobouniotis and Adolph von Harnack (TU 38: Leipzig, 1911).

The Philocalia of Origen, ed. J. A. Robinson (Cambridge, 1893).

Vier Bücher von den Prinzipien, ed. and trans. H. Görgemanns and H. Karpp (Texte zur Forschung 24: Darmstadt, 1976).

5. Translations:
The Song of Songs: Commentary and Homilies, trans. R. Lawson (Ancient Christian Writers 26: London, 1957).

Commentary on Matthew I, II, and X–XIV, trans. John Patrick (The Ante-Nicene Fathers 10: 5th edn., Grand Rapids, 1978).

Commentary on John Books I–X, trans. Allan Menzies, ibid.

Dialogue of Origen with Heraclides and the Bishops with him concerning the Father and the Son and the Soul, in J. E. L. Oulton and H. Chadwick (trans.), *Alexandrian Christianity* (Library of Christian Classics 2: London, 1954).

Exhortation to Martyrdom, ibid.

On Prayer, ibid.

Origen on First Principles, trans. G. W. Butterworth (Gloucester, Mass., 1973).

Origen: Contra Celsum, trans. Henry Chadwick (Cambridge, 1953).

Traité des principes (Peri Archôn), trans. M. Harl, G. Dorval, and A. Le Boulluec (Paris, 1976).

PAMPHILUS, *Apologia pro Origene*, ed. J. P. Migne *(PG* 17: Paris, 1860).

PHOTIUS, *Bibliothèque,* i, trans. R. Henry (Collection Byzantine: Paris, 1959).

PLATO, *Works* (Oxford Classical Texts).

PLOTINUS, *Enneads,* ed. P. Henry and H.-K. Schwyzer, trans. A. H. Armstrong (Loeb Classical Library).

PORPHYRY, *In Aristotelis Categorias*, ed. A. Busse, *CAG* iv. 1 (Berlin, 1887).

PROCLUS, *In Platonis Timaeum*, ed. E. Diehl (Leipzig, 1903, 1904, 1906).

PSEUDO-JUSTIN, *Cohortatio ad Graecos* 22, ed. J. P. Migne *(PG* 6: Paris, 1857).

Reliquiae sacrae, ed. M. Routh, iii and iv (Oxford, 1846).

SIMPLICIUS, *In Aristotelis Categorias*, ed. C. Kalbfleisch, *CAG* viii. (Berlin, 1907).

THEOPHILUS, *Ad Autolycum*, ed. and trans. Robert M. Grant (Oxford Early Christian Texts: Oxford, 1970).

II. SECONDARY SOURCES

BALAS, DAVID L., 'The Idea of Participation in the Structure of Origen's thought: Christian Transposition of a Theme of the Platonic Tradition', in *Origeniana* (below), 257–75.

—— *ΜΕΤΟΥΣΙΑ ΘΕΟΥ: Man's Participation in God's Perfections According to Saint Gregory of Nyssa* (Studia Anselmiana 55: Rome, 1966).

BAMMEL, C. P. H., 'Philocalia IX, Jerome, Epistle 121, and Origen's Exposition of Romans VII', *JTS* NS 32 (1981), 50–81.

BARDY, GUSTAVE, 'Origène et la magie', in *Mélanges offerts au P. de Grandmaison, RSR* 18 (1928), 126–42.

—— *Recherches sur l'histoire du texte et des versions latines du 'De principiis' d'Origène* (Paris, 1923).

BARNES, TIMOTHY, *The New Empire of Diocletian and Constantine* (Cambridge, Mass., 1982).

BARR, JAMES, 'Abba Isn't "Daddy"', *JTS* NS 39 (1988), 28–47.

—— *The Semantics of Biblical Language* (Oxford, 1961).

BERCHMAN, R., *From Philo to Origen: Middle Platonism in Transition* (Brown Judaic Studies 69: Chico, Calif., 1984).

BIENERT, WOLFGANG, *Dionysius von Alexandrien: Zur Frage des Origenismus im dritten Jahrhundert* (Patristische Texte und Studien 21: Berlin, 1978).

—— 'Neue Fragmente des Dionysius und des Petrus von Alexandrien aus Cod. Vatop. 236', *Kleronomia* 5 (1973), 308–14.

BIGGS, CHARLES, *The Christian Platonists of Alexandria: The 1886 Bampton Lectures* (Oxford, 1913).

BLUME, H., and MANN, F. (eds.), *Platonismus und Christentum: Festschrift für Heinrich Dörrie (JAC.*E 10: Münster, 1983).

BOSTOCK, D., 'Quality and Corporeity in Origen', in *Origeniana Secunda* (below), 323–37.

BROWN, RAYMOND, *The Epistles of John* (The Anchor Bible 30: New York, 1982).

—— *The Gospel According to John* (The Anchor Bible 29A and B: New York, 1971).

CHADWICK, HENRY, *Early Christian Thought and the Classical Tradition: Studies in Justin, Clement, and Origen* (Oxford, 1966).

—— 'Origen, Celsus, and the Resurrection of the Body', *Harvard Theological Review* 41 (1948), 83–102.

—— 'Rufinus and the Tura Papyrus of Origen's Commentary on Romans', *JTS* NS 10 (1959), 10–42.

COX, PATRICIA, *Biography in Late Antiquity: A Quest for the Holy Man* (Transformation of the Classical Heritage 5: Berkeley, Calif., 1983).

—— '"In My Father's House are Many Dwelling Places": κτίσμα in Origen's *De principiis*', *Anglican Theological Review* 62 (1980), 322–37.

CRANFIELD, C., *A Critical and Exegetical Commentary on the Epistle to the Romans*, i. (The International Critical Commentary on the Holy Scriptures of the Old and New Testaments: Edinburgh, 1975).

CROUZEL, H., 'L'Apocatastase chez Origène', in *Origeniana Quarta* (below), 282–90.

—— 'Grégoire le Thaumaturge et la Dialogue avec Élien', *RSR* 51 (1963), 422–31.

—— *Origène et la 'Connaissance Mystique'* (Museum Lessianum, Section Théologique 56: Paris, 1961).

—— *Origène et la philosophie* (Paris, 1962).

—— 'Les personnes de la Trinité sont-elles de puissance inégale selon Origène, Peri Archon I. 3. 5–8?', *Gregorianum* 57 (1976), 109–25.

—— *Théologie de l'image de Dieu chez Origène* (Théologie 34: Paris, 1956).

CULPEPPER, R. A., 'The Pivot of John's Gospel', *NTS* 27 (1980–1), 17–31.

DIEKAMP, F., 'Ein neues Fragment aus den Hypotyposen des Alexandriners Theognostus', *Theologische Quartalschrift* 84 (1902), 481–98.

DILLON, JOHN, 'Logos and Trinity: Patterns of Platonist Influence on Early Christianity', in Godfrey Vesey (ed.), *The Philosophy in Christianity* (Cambridge, 1989), 1–13.

—— *The Middle Platonists: A Study of Platonism 80 BC to AD 220*, (London, 1977).

—— 'Origen's Doctrine of the Trinity and Son: Later Neo-Platonic Theories', in D. O'Meara (ed.), *Neoplatonism and Christian Thought* (Albany, 1982), 19–56.

—— 'Plotinus, Philo and Origen on the Grades of Virtue', in Blume and Mann (above), 92–105.

DODDS, E. R., 'The Parmenides of Plato and the Origin of the Neoplatonic "One"', *Classical Quarterly* 22 (1928), 129–42.

—— 'The Unknown God in Neoplatonism'. Appendix 1 of his *Proclus: The Elements of Theology* (2nd edn., Oxford, 1963).

DORIVAL, G., 'Origène et la résurrection de la chair', in *Origeniana Quarta* (below), 291–321.

—— 'Remarques sur la forme du Peri Archôn', in *Origeniana* (below), 33–45.

DÖRRIE, H., 'Emanation: Ein unphilosophischen Wort in spätantiken Denken', *Platonica Minora* (Munich, 1976), 70–86.

FESTUGIÈRE, A. J., *La Révélation d'Hermès Trismégiste* (Études Bibliques: Paris, 1944–54).

FLOROVSKY, GEORGES V., 'The Concept of Creation in Saint Athanasius', in F. L. Cross (ed.), *Studia Patristica* 6 = TU 81 (1962), 36–57.

FONTAINE, J., and KANNENGIESSER, C. (eds.), *Epektasis: Mélanges patristiques offerts au cardinal Jean Daniélou* (Paris, 1972).

GAGER, J., 'Marcion and Philosophy', *VC* 26 (1972), 53–9.

GRANT, ROBERT M., 'The Stromateis of Origen', in Fontaine and Kannengiesser (above), 285–92.

GREGG, ROBERT C., review of Rowan Williams, *Arius: Heresy and Tradition*, *JTS* NS 40 (1989), 247–54.

—— and GROH, DENNIS E., *Early Arianism: A View of Salvation* (London, 1981).

GUTHRIE, W., *A History of Greek Philosophy*, iv and v (Cambridge, 1975).

HALL, S., review of R. Gregg and D. Groh, *Early Arianism: A View of Salvation*, *King's Theological Review* 5 (1982), 28.

HÄLLSTRÖM, GUNNAR A. F., *Charismatic Succession: A Study of Origen's Concept of Prophecy* (Publications of the Finnish Exegetical Society 42: Helsinki, 1985).

HAMPSON, DAPHNE, *Theology and Feminism* (Signposts in Theology: Oxford, 1990).

HANSON, R. P. C., *Allegory and Event: A Study of the Sources and Significance of Origen's Interpretation of Scripture* (London, 1959).

—— 'The Arian Doctrine of the Incarnation', in Robert C. Gregg (ed.), *Arianism: Historical and Theological Reassessments* (Patristic Monograph Series 11: Philadelphia, 1985), 181–211.

—— 'Did Origen Apply the Word Homoousios to the Son?', in Fontaine and Kannengiesser (above), 293–303.

—— 'Did Origen Teach that the Son is *ek tes ousias* of the Father?', in *Origeniana Quarta* (below), 201–2.

—— *The Search for the Christian Doctrine of God: The Arian Controversy 318–381* (Edinburgh, 1988).

HARL, M., 'Citations et commentaires d'Exode 3, 13 chez les Pères Grecs des quatre premiers siècles', in *Dieu et l'être: Exégèses d'Exode 3, 14 et de Coran 20, 11–24* [no editor] (Paris, 1978), 87–108.

—— *Origène et la fonction révélatrice du Verbe incarné* (Patristica Sorbonensia 2: Paris, 1958).

—— 'Origène et l'interprétation de l'Épistle aux Romains: Étude du chapitre IX de la *Philocalie*', in Fontaine and Kannengiesser (above), 305–16.

—— 'La préexistence des âmes dans l'œuvre d'Origène', in *Origeniana Quarta* (below), 238–58.

—— 'Structure et cohérence du Peri Archôn', in *Origeniana* (below), 11–32.

HARNACK, ADOLPH VON, *History of Dogma*, iii and iv, trans. E. B. Speirs and J. Millar (London, 1897 and 1898).

HEINE, R. E., 'Can the Catena Fragments of Origen's Commentary on John be Trusted?', *VC* 40 (1986), 118–34.

JEREMIAS, JOACHIM, *The Prayers of Jesus* [various translators] (London, 1967).

JUNOD, E., 'L'Impossible et le possible: Étude de la déclaration préliminaire du *De Oratione*', in *Origeniana Secunda* (below), 81–93.

KANNENGIESSER, CHARLES, *Athanase d'Alexandrie évêque et écrivain: Une lecture des traités contre les Ariens* (Théologie Historique 70: Paris, 1983).

—— 'Les "Blasphèmes d'Arius" (Athanase d'Alexandrie, *De Synodis* 15): un écrit néo-Arien', in E. Lucchesi and H. Saffrey (eds.), *Mémorial André-Jean Festugière: Antiquité païenne et chrétienne* (Cahiers d'Orientalisme 10: Geneva, 1984), 143–51.

—— 'La Date de l'Apologie d'Athanase *Contre les païens* et *Sur l'incarnation du Verbe*', *RSR* 58 (1970), 383–428.

—— *Holy Scripture and Hellenistic Hermeneutics in Alexandrian Christology: The Arian Crisis* (Colloquy 41 of the Center for Hermeneutical Studies in Hellenistic and Modern Culture: Berkeley, Calif., 1982).

—— 'Où et quand Arius composa-t-il la Thalie?', in P. Granfield and J. A. Jungmann (eds.), *Kyriakon: Festschrift Johannes Quasten* (Münster, 1970), i. 346–51.

—— 'Le Témoignage des *Lettres festales* de Saint Athanase sur la date de

270   BIBLIOGRAPHY

l'Apologie *Contre les païens–Sur l'incarnation du Verbe'*, *RSR* 52 (1964), 91–100.

KELLY, J. N. D., *Early Christian Creeds* (5th edn., London, 1977).

KOCH, HAL, *Pronoia und Paideusis: Studien über Origenes und sein Verhältnis zum Platonismus* (Leipzig, 1932).

KOPECEK, THOMAS A., *A History of Neo-Arianism*, 2 vols. (Patristic Monographs Series 8: Cambridge, Mass., 1979).

—— 'Professor Charles Kannengiesser's View of the Arian Crisis: A Critique and Counter-Proposal', in *Holy Scripture and Hellenistic Hermeneutics in Alexandrian Christology: The Arian Crisis* (Colloquy 41 of the Center for Hermeneutical Studies in Hellenistic and Modern Culture: Berkeley, Calif. 1982), 51–68.

LASH, NICHOLAS, '"Son of God": Reflections on a Metaphor', *Concilium* (March, 1982), 11–16.

LILLA, S. R. C. *Clement of Alexandria: A Study in Christian Platonism and Gnosticism* (Oxford, 1971).

LOENEN, J. H., 'Albinus' Metaphysics: An Attempt at Rehabilitation', *Mnemosyne* 9 (1956), 296–319, and 10 (1957), 35–56.

LOGAN, ALISTAIR, 'Origen and the Development of Trinitarian Theology', in *Origeniana Quarta* (below), 424–9.

LORENZ, RUDOLF, *Arius judaizans? Untersuchungen zur dogmengeschichtlichen Einordnung des Arius* (Göttingen, 1980).

LOUTH, ANDREW, 'The Concept of the Soul in Athanasius' *Contra Gentes–De Incarnatione'*, in E. A. Livingstone (ed.), *Studia Patristica* 13 = TU 116 (1975), 227–31.

—— *The Origins of the Christian Mystical Tradition: From Plato to Denys* (Oxford, 1981).

—— 'The Use of the Term ἴδιος in Alexandrian Theology from Alexander to Cyril', in E. A. Livingstone (ed.), *Studia Patristica* 19 (Leuven, 1989), 198–202.

LOWRY, CHARLES W., 'Did Origen Style the Son a κτίσμα?', *JTS* 39 (1938), 39–42.

MCLELLAND, JOSEPH C., *God the Anonymous: A Study in Alexandrian Philosophical Theology* (Monograph Series 4: Philadelphia, 1976).

MACLEOD, C. W., *'ANAΛΥΣΙΣ*: A Study in Ancient Mysticism', *JTS* NS 21 (1970), 43–55.

—— 'Origen, Contra Celsum 7: 42', *JTS* NS 32 (1981), 447.

MARCHEL, W., *Abba, Père! La prière du Christ et des chrétiens* (Analecta Biblica 19: 2nd edn., Rome, 1971).

MEIJERING, E. P., 'Athanasius on the Father as the Origin of the Son', *NAKG* 55 (1974), 1–14; repr. in his *God, Being, History* (below).

—— 'The Doctrine of the Will and of the Trinity in the Orations of Gregory of Nazianzus', *NedThT* 27 (1973), 224–34; repr. in his *God, Being, History* (below).

—— *God, Being, History: Studies in Patristic Philosophy* (Oxford, 1975).

—— 'God, Cosmos and History: Christian and Neo-Platonic Views on Divine Revelation', *VC* 28 (1974), 248–76; repr. in his *God, Being, History:* (above).

—— *Orthodoxy and Platonism in Athanasius: Synthesis or Antithesis?* (Leiden, 1968).

MEREDITH, A., review of R. Berchman, *From Philo to Origen: Middle Platonism in Transition*, *JTS* NS 37 (1986), 557–9.

MORTLEY, R., *From Word to Silence* (Theophaneia: Beiträge zur Religions- und Kirchengeschichte des Altertums 30 and 31: Bonn, 1986).

NAUTIN, P., '"Je suis celui qui est" (Exode 3, 14) dans la théologie d'Origène', in *Dieu et l'être: Exégèses d'Exode 3, 14 et de Coran 20, 11–24* [no editor] (Paris, 1978), 109–19.

—— *Origène: Sa vie et son œuvre* (Christianisme Antique 1: Paris, 1977).

NEMESHEGYI, P., *La Paternité de Dieu chez Origène* (Bibliothèque de Théologie Série 4, Histoire de la Théologie 2: Tournai, 1960).

OPITZ, HANS-GEORG, 'Die Zeitfolge des arianischen Streites von den Anfängen bis zum Jahr 328', *ZNTW* 33 (1934), 131–59.

Origeniana, ed. H. Crouzel, G. Lomiento, and J. Ruis-Camps (Quaderni di 'Vetera Christianorum' 12: Bari, 1975).

—— *Secunda*, ed. H. Crouzel and A. Quacquarelli (Quaderni di 'Vetera Christianorum' 15: Rome, 1980).

—— *Quarta*, ed. L. Lies (Innsbrucker theologische Studien 19: Innsbruck, 1987).

OSBORN, ERIC, 'The Intermediate World in Origen's "On Prayer"', in *Origeniana Secunda* (above), 95–103.

OSBORNE, CATHERINE, *Rethinking Early Greek Philosophy: Hippolytus of Rome and the Presocratics* (London, 1987).

PATTERSON, LLOYD, 'Methodius, Origen, and the Arian Dispute', in E. A. Livingstone (ed.), *Studia Patristica* 17.2 (Oxford, 1982), 912–23.

PRESTIGE, G. L., *God in Patristic Thought* (2nd edn., London, 1952).

QUELL, G., πατήρ, B, in G. Kittel (ed.), *Theological Dictionary of the New Testament*, ed. and trans. G. Bromiley, v (Grand Rapids, 1967), 957–74.

RABINOWITZ, C., 'Personal and Cosmic Salvation in Origen', *VC* 38 (1984), 319–29.

RADFORD, L., *Three Teachers of Alexandria: Theognostus, Pierius and*

Peter: A Study in the Early History of Origenism and Anti-Origenism (Cambridge, 1908).

RIST, J. M., 'Beyond Stoic and Platonist: A Sample of Origen's Treatment of Philosophy (*Contra Celsum* IV. 62–70)', in Blume and Mann (above), 228–38.

—— 'The Greek and Latin Texts of the Discussion on Free Will in *De Principiis* Book III', in *Origeniana* (above), 97–111.

—— 'The Importance of Stoic logic in the Contra Celsum', in H. D. Blumenthal and R. A. Markus (eds.), *Neoplatonism and Early Christian Thought: Essays in Honour of A. H. Armstrong* (London, 1981), 64–78.

—— *Stoic Philosophy* (Cambridge, 1969).

ROBERTSON, A., Prolegomena to his edition, *Select Works and Letters of Athanasius Bishop of Alexandria* (NPNF 4: Grand Rapids, 1978), pp. xi–xc.

ROLDANUS, J., *Le Christ et l'homme dans la théologie d'Athanase d'Alexandrie: Étude de la conjonction de sa conception de l'homme avec sa christologie* (Studies in the History of Christian Thought 4: Leiden, 1968).

SCHRENK, G. πατήρ, A, C–D, in G. Kittel (ed.), *Theological Dictionary of the New Testament*, ed. and trans. G. Bromiley, v (Grand Rapids, 1967), 948–59 and 974–1014.

SIMONETTI, MANLIO, *Studi sull'arianesimo* (Rome, 1965).

SKARD, E. 'Zum Skolien-Kommentar des Origenes zur Apokalypse Johannis', *Symbolae Osloenses* 16 (1936), 204–8.

SORABJI, RICHARD, *Time, Creation and the Continuum: Theories in Antiquity and the Early Middle Ages* (London, 1983).

STEAD, CHRISTOPHER, 'Athanasius' Earliest Written Work', *JTS* NS 39 (1988), 76–91.

—— 'The Concept of Mind and the Concept of God in the Christian Fathers', in B. Hebblethwaite and S. Sutherland (eds.), *The Philosophical Frontiers of Christian Theology: Essays Presented to D. M. MacKinnon* (Cambridge, 1982), 39–54; repr. in his *Substance and Illusion* (below).

—— *Divine Substance* (Oxford, 1977).

—— 'The Freedom of the Will and the Arian Controversy', in Blume and Mann (above), 245–57; repr. in his *Substance and Illusion* (below).

—— 'Knowledge of God in Eusebius and Athanasius', in R. Van Den Broek, T. Baarda, and J. Mansfeld (eds.), *Knowledge of God in the Graeco-Roman World* (Études Préliminaires aux Religions Orientales dans l'Empire Romain 112: Leiden, 1988), 229–42.

—— 'The Platonism of Arius', *JTS* NS 15 (1964), 16–31; repr. in his *Substance and Illusion* (below).

—— review of Charles Kannengiesser, *Athanase d'Alexandrie évêque et écrivain: Une lecture des traités contre les Ariens*, *JTS* NS 36 (1985), 220–9.

—— 'Rhetorical Method in Athanasius', *VC* 30 (1976), 121–37; repr. in his *Substance and Illusion* (below).

—— *Substance and Illusion in the Christian Fathers* (London, 1985).

—— 'The *Thalia* of Arius and the Testimony of Athanasius', *JTS* NS 29 (1978), 20–52.

STROUMSA, G., 'The Incorporeality of God: Context and Implications of Origen's Position', *Religion* 13 (1983), 345–58.

TELFER, W., *The Forgiveness of Sins: An Essay in the History of Christian Doctrine and Practice* (London, 1959).

TORJESEN, K., *Hermeneutical Procedure and Theological Method in Origen's Exegesis* (Patristische Texte und Studien 28: Berlin, 1986).

—— 'Hermeneutics and Soteriology in Origen's *Peri Archôn*', in E. A. Livingstone (ed.), *Studia Patristica* 21 (Leuven, 1989), 333–48.

TRIGG, JOSEPH W., *Origen: The Bible and Philosophy in the Third-Century Church* (London, 1985).

WEST, M. L., 'The Metre of Arius' *Thalia*', *JTS* NS 33 (1982), 98–105.

WESTCOTT, B. F., 'The Fatherhood of God', in his *The Epistles of St. John* (4th edn., London, 1905), 27–34.

WHITTAKER, J., '*Ἄρρητος καὶ ἀκατονόμαστος*', in Blume and Mann (above), 303–6; repr. in his *Studies in Platonism* (below).

—— "*ΕΠΕΚΕΙΝΑ ΝΟΥ ΚΑΙ ΟΥΣΙΑΣ*", *VC* 23 (1969), 91–104; repr. in his *Studies in Platonism* (below).

—— 'Moses Atticizing', *Phoenix* 21 (1967), 196–201; repr. in his *Studies in Platonism* (below).

—— *Studies in Platonism and Patristic Thought* (London, 1984).

WILES, M., *The Divine Apostle: The Interpretation of St Paul's Epistles in the Early Church* (Cambridge, 1967).

—— 'Eternal Generation'. *JTS* NS 12 (1961), 284–91.

—— 'Eunomius: Hair Splitting Dialectician or Defender of the Accessibility of Salvation?', in Rowan Williams (ed.), *The Making of Orthodoxy: Essays in Honour of Henry Chadwick* (Cambridge, 1989), 157–72.

—— 'The Philosophy of Christianity: Arius and Athanasius', in Godfrey Vesey (ed.), *The Philosophy in Christianity* (Cambridge, 1989), 41–52.

WILLIAMS, ROWAN, *Arius: Heresy and Tradition* (London, 1987).

—— 'The Logic of Arianism', *JTS* NS 34 (1983), 56–81.

—— 'The Quest of the Historical *Thalia*', in Robert C. Gregg (ed.), *Arianism: Historical and Theological Reassessments* (Patristic Monograph Series 11: Philadelphia, 1985), 1–35.

—— 'The Son's Knowledge of the Father in Origen', in *Origeniana Quarta* (above), 146–53.

—— *The Wound of Knowledge: Christian Spirituality from the New Testament to St John of the Cross* (London, 1979).

WITT, R. E., *Albinus and the History of Middle Platonism* (Cambridge, 1937).

WOLFSON, H. A., *The Philosophy of the Church Fathers*, i (3rd edn., Cambridge, Mass., 1970).

YOUNG, FRANCES, *From Nicaea to Chalcedon: A Guide to the Literature and its Background* (London, 1983).

—— 'The God of the Greeks and the Nature of Religious Language', in W. Schoedel and R. Wilken (eds.), *Early Christian Literature and the Classical Intellectual Tradition: In Honorem Robert M. Grant* (Théologie Historique 54: Paris, 1979), 45–74.

Index of Scriptural References

Index of Ancient Authors

General Index

adoption as sons:
  baptism 170, 237
  creature 237–40
  moral endeavour 97–8, 101–5, 136
  by nature 92, 99, 136–7, 189, 194, 197
  New Testament 228–9
  Old Testament 231–5
  the Son 97–8, 137–8, 221–2
  soteriology 227–41
  true 240–1
  see also Holy Spirit; soteriology
Aetius 129 n.
Albinus 9, 10 n., 48
Alexander of Alexandria 28, 129–38, 151, 157, 161, 162, 194–5, 197, 233 n.
Alexander of Aphrodisias 9, 10 n., 83 n., 131, 142, 143
anthropology 223–4
anthropomorphism 13, 16, 256
Apollinarius 147 n.
apophaticism 133–4, 139, 261
Aristotle 23, 58–9, 69 n., 88 n., 131, 143, 164, 196
Arius, Arianism 128–9, 138–44, 163–71, 172–80, 184–6, 189–91, 195–6, 201, 210–12, 222, 241–2, 245, 253–4, 255, 257
Asterius 166
Athanasius 145–9, 153–4, 163–4, 250–4

Barnes, Timothy 147 n.
Barr, James 1 n.
Barthian 258
Basil of Ancyra 33 n.
Basilides 77, 115 n.
begetting of the Son:
  being and will 155, 180–1
  making 210–12, 213–17, 218–20
  Scripture 210, 238
  see also generation of the Son

Berchman, R. 10 n., 13 n., 23 n., 25 n.
Bienert, Wolfgang 125 n.
Bostock, D. 20 n.

Chadwick, Henry 14 n.
Clement of Alexandria 49
correlativity 69, 70–6, 91, 122, 123–4, 125, 130–2, 135, 138, 143
Creation 89–90
  divine goodness 27–8, 71–3, 183–4
  eternal 72–5, 179, 183–4, 207, 260
  ex nihilo 127, 149, 152, 155, 167, 180, 187
  Father–Son relation 75, 187, 207–8
  pre–existent souls 72–5, 122, 125, 126, 127, 128, 179
Christian life 226, 242–8
Chrysostom 216 n.
Colluthus 129
Cranfield, C. 194 n.
Crouzel, H. 12, 20 n., 57 n., 83, 87 n., 89 n.
Culpepper, R. A. 1 n.

death 224, 237, 248
Diekamp, F. 125 n.
Dillon, John 27 n., 35 n.
Dionysius of Alexandria 121, 122–4, 125, 140, 149, 194, 210
Dionysius of Rome 122
divinization 226, 231, 235–6, 239, 244, 249
Dodds, E. R. 23 n.
Dorival, G. 10 n., 20 n.

Epicurius 59, 77 n.
ἐπίνοια 80, 81, 82, 83–5
Epiphanius 33 n., 59 n.
Eunomius 33 n.
Eusebius of Caesarea 135, 141, 173
Eusebius of Nicomedia 128, 133, 139, 141, 190, 211–12, 213, 217, 220, 222